Radical
KNOWING

"One of the most readable books of philosophy I have ever encountered, from a philosopher equally at home with mystics, shamans, and scientists. Christian de Quincey is one of those rare visionaries who blends scientific rigor and deep metaphysical insights for transforming consciousness. Immensely inspiring as well as informative, *Radical Knowing* offers a surprising, yet solid, foundation for exploring the alchemy of relationships. This may be the first book to focus the power of philosophy on the joy and challenges of being in relationship."

STEPHEN SIMON, Academy-Award-winning
producer/director of *What Dreams May Come, Somewhere in
Time,* and *Indigo*

"The most mysterious question confronting us is consciousness—its nature, origin, and destiny. *Radical Knowing* reveals dimensions that are crucial for anyone in our third millennium. Highly recommended!"

LARRY DOSSEY, M.D., author of *Healing Beyond the Body,
Reinventing Medicine* and *Healing Words*

"A ground-breaking book. Christian de Quincey brings a lifetime of studying consciousness to a little-explored aspect of the subject—its essential role in all our relationships. More than just philosophy simply explained, *Radical Knowing* offers valuable guidance on how to put spirituality into practice in our lives."

PETER RUSSELL, author of *From Science to God* and
Waking Up in Time

"Animals naturally do what Christian de Quincey recommends we humans do: forge an unobstructed dialogue between the mind and the heart, and 'feel our thinking.' We are not alone; we are part of an infinite web of relationships. In cultivating the art of relationship, we reunite mind and heart, becoming conscious collaborators with the mysteries that stir within us, around us, and beyond us. In *Radical Knowing*, de Quincey shows us how it is ultimately through conscious, consensual relationships that we mine the depths of what it means to be a human tuner and receiver for a much vaster intelligence, ultimately fulfilling our destiny: that of 'giving voice to the cosmos.'"

LINDA KOHANOV, author of *The Tao of Equus* and
*Riding between the Worlds: Expanding Our Potential
through the Way of the Horse*

"When it comes to the subject of consciousness, Christian de Quincey is like a dragon on fire. His evocative, lively, and remarkably engaging prose is a bracing antidote to the glum academicism of most philosophical writing. With new and penetrating insights into ever-topical and pesky questions, de Quincey invites us to feel our way into consciousness in ways that transform the reader. The split between inner and outer knowing is healed, and we are awakened to the sky-high possibilities of enlightenment as a manifestation of universal mind. This book alters energy patterns and installs new microchips into the philosopher's stone."

SUZI GABLIK, author of *Has Modernism Failed?* and
Living the Magical Life

"If interconnectivity is an inherent feature of life, as both ancient wisdom and postmodern science suggest, then relationships are primary to the human experience, not secondary additions to 'our lives.' Starting here, *Radical Knowing* takes the reader on a provocative journey beyond the boundaries of traditional philosophy. Expect reversals of perspective, innovative formulations, and, most importantly, opportunities to experience anew the integral fabric of consciousness."

CHRIS M. BACHE, PH.D., author of
Dark Night, Early Dawn

"In this wonderful new book Christian de Quincey shares personal experiences to reveal the central importance of consciousness in our relationships. Consciousness isn't simply a lonely, isolating subjectivity. In all its multi-faceted majesty, consciousness is shared, like the precious air we breath. Relationships naturally begin and exist within our shared consciousness—and de Quincey teaches us to use our relationships for exploration and understanding of consciousness itself."

OBADIAH HARRIS, president of the University of
Philosophical Research and Philosophical Research Society

"*Radical Knowing* deals with one of the most important, and neglected, subjects: how we know what we know. Christian de Quincey writes in joyfully simple language and thinks through complicated questions with great clarity. As soon as I heard about this book it went straight to the top of my must-read pile."

JEREMY NARBY, PH.D., anthropologist and author of
The Cosmic Serpent and *Intelligence in Nature*

R a d i c a l
KNOWING

Understanding Consciousness
through Relationship

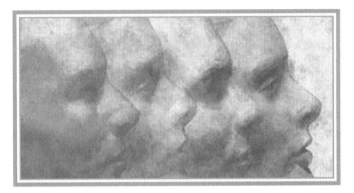

Christian de Quincey, Ph.D.

Park Street Press
Rochester, Vermont

Park Street Press
One Park Street
Rochester, Vermont 05767
www.InnerTraditions.com

Park Street Press is a division of Inner Traditions International

Library of Congress Cataloging-in-Publication Data
de Quincey, Christian.
  Radical knowing : understanding consciousness through relationship / Christian
de Quincey.
      p. cm. — (Radical consciousness trilogy ; v. 2)
  Summary: "An exploration into the nature and origins of different styles of
consciousness and the way they affect how we know what we know"—Provided
by publisher.
  Includes bibliographical references (p.   ) and index.
  ISBN 1-59477-079-4 (pbk.)
  1. Consciousness. 2. Interpersonal relations. 3. Intersubjectivity. 4. Knowledge,
Theory of. I. Title.
  B808.9.D4 2005
  126—dc22
                                                            2005012426

Printed and bound in Canada by Transcontinental Printing

10 9 8 7 6 5 4 3 2 1

Text design and layout by Rachel Goldenberg
This book was typeset in Sabon, with Agenda as a display typeface

To Rita, Mamie, and Jack, with love.

Strange is our situation here on Earth. Each of us comes for a short visit, not knowing why, yet sometimes seeming to divine a purpose. From the standpoint of daily life, however, there is one thing we do know: that we are here for the sake of each other, above all, for those upon whose smile and well-being our own happiness depends, and also for the countless unknown souls with whose fate we connect with a bond of sympathy. Many times a day I realize how much my own outer and inner life is built upon the labors of others, both living and dead, and how earnestly I must exert myself in order to give in return as much as I have received and am receiving.

ALBERT EINSTEIN

And since you know you cannot see yourself,
so well as by reflection, I, your glass,
will modestly discover to yourself
that of yourself which you yet know not of.

WILLIAM SHAKESPEARE

In formal logic, a contradiction is the signal of a defeat,
but in the evolution of real knowledge it marks the first
step in progress towards a victory.

ALFRED NORTH WHITEHEAD

It's all just a likely story . . .

PLATO

Contents

Appendices

Acknowledgments

"Write what you need to know." I remember hearing this sage advice a long time ago, and throughout my career, both as a journalist and as an academic, that is what I have done. Writing is notoriously a solitary profession, and although I always enjoy the exquisite "retreat" and silence of capturing ideas and feelings in words, I am also deeply aware that everything I write is, nevertheless, a collaborative process. Yes, words sometimes pour out of my fingers as though giving voice to a soul on fire; but souls are fluid creatures with shadowy boundaries, and, as I hope to show in this book, our souls (our sense of vital individual identities) flow into and through each other, always dynamic, always in a mutual in-forming dance.

Relationship is at the core of who we are, and I want to take a moment here to celebrate key relationships and contributions that made this book possible. I'll begin with my partner Reba Vanderpool, who has provided a living crucible for exploring the alchemy of relationship over the many years it took to create this book. As I discuss in chapter 2, my professional training as a philosopher has sharpened my intellectual tools for dissecting ideas and language—tools, I admit, that at times I may have used to excess. In my early days with Reba, I soon realized that I was living with someone who *knew* and negotiated the world using a very different set of tools. Usually called "intuition," or spiritual experience, her preferred way of knowing often short-circuited my attempts to understand her rationally. We experienced frequent clashes, not just of ways of knowing, but also of worldviews. I wanted to find a way into her world, and in time I saw that I needed to begin by acknowledging and honoring, and then cultivating, a sensitivity for *feeling*—which leads me to the second great influence in this book.

Stanford University anthropologist E. Richard Sorenson opened my eyes to the drastic consequences that follow encounters between feeling-based and reason-based ways of knowing. He used the dramatic and evocative terms "preconquest" and "postconquest" consciousness to describe these two radically different modes of awareness. As I discuss in chapter 2, I realized that the clash of worldviews between indigenous people and modern Westerners that he described echoed my own experience of the interpersonal dynamics in my relationship with Reba (and with others). Along with the events and experiences I write about later, recognizing the fundamental importance of feeling and relationship has radically altered my approach to philosophy.

Radical Knowing is just that: It is both a tribute to and a defense of the need to reconnect with the wisdom of embodied feeling typical of indigenous cultures—as crucial, I believe, for the future of philosophy of mind as it is for our interpersonal relationships. Amateur anthropologist and author Jean Liedloff, both in her writings and in conversations with me (as I write in chapter 3), helped me see the deep evolutionary roots of this tug-o'-war between our ancient, innate *embodied* knowing and the relatively new arrival: reason. This feeling/reason tension has profound implications for how we relate to our children, for how we design our educational systems, for how we understand mental and physical addictions, and for how we relate to the natural world.

The threads of contribution to this book span continents and ages. As obvious (or even as trite) as it may seem, I wish to include the often unacknowledged background of all our ancestors reaching back to the beginnings of life on this planet, and beyond to the infinite immensities of the cosmos itself—the vast evolutionary heritage that has brought us all to this point in history.

Besides these innumerable and nameless evolutionary progenitors, I am indebted to a long list of intellectual ancestors and scholars, some of whom are named in the pages that follow. Too many to list here, I will mention just two: philosopher-theologian Martin Buber, who first named the "between" as the fundamental essence in every "I-Thou" relationship; and process philosopher A. N. Whitehead, who, more than anyone else, provided a rigorous intellectual foundation for understanding how *feeling* is at the root of all forms of knowing, and, indeed, at the core of how the universe both creates and knows itself.

Among contemporaries that I can name, I give heartfelt thanks to my friend and colleague Dr. Eric Weiss for the many dialogues we've had over the years on the metaphysics of Whitehead, and for his feedback on chapters 7 and 8 on the topic of synchronicity and causality. Similarly, I thank Dr. Martin Schwartz from the University of Virginia for his tenacious questioning of my ideas on the nature of science and spirituality. His comments helped me reshape and refine the contents of chapters 9, 10, and 11. Friend and colleague Dr. Chris Bache, at Youngstown University, one of the most articulate and insightful scholars on the implications of altered states of consciousness, helped me to clarify important issues on different ways of knowing in the concluding chapter dealing with interspecies consciousness and communication. And for our always-delightful conversations (often late into the night on his houseboat), and for inviting me to swim with dolphins off Hawaii, I am especially grateful to my good friend, physicist, author, and Renaissance-man, Peter Russell.

Peter and I, together with Dr. Kaisa Puhakka, her husband and Silicon Valley businessman Michael Miller, Eric Weiss, and Reba Vanderpool, often met in Half Moon Bay as the "Apollo Group" for deep dialogues that embodied mutual respect, authenticity, and courage. These meetings with "no agenda yet serious intent" frequently took us to the edge of knowing, and beyond into the paradoxical "no-knowledge" of sacred silence. (Always present, and always reminding me to reconnect with non-verbal intelligence, our dogs Oblio and Ubu, and cats Noel, Mesa, Tatchi, and Pecos undoubtedly contributed, too.) Experiences from those dialogues infuse and inform the pages of this book.

Still on the topic of "dialogue," I also acknowledge and thank quantum physicist David Bohm for devising what, in my experience, is the most effective method for exploring collective consciousness—Bohmian Dialogue (described in chapter 13). I also give thanks to my many students at John F. Kennedy University, California, as well as at the University of Philosophical Research, California; The Graduate Institute, Connecticut; and Schumacher College, Devon, both for engaging with many of the ideas now expressed in this book and for participating with me in numerous transformative Bohmian Dialogue sessions over the years. One JFKU student in particular, Matthew Purdon, deserves special recognition for contributing new insights (and diagrams) into the "Four Gifts of Knowing" described in chapter 18.

In the interest of space, I will simply name other friends and colleagues who have supported and encouraged me and my work in one form or another: Dr. Ervin Laszlo, Dr. Larry Dossey, Dr. Jeremy Narby, Michael Toms, Dr. David Lorimer, Suzi Gablik, Dr. Amit Goswami, Dr. Rupert Sheldrake, Shawne Mitchell, Gay Hendricks, Stephen Simon, Dr. Harris ("Bud") Stone, and Dr. Obadiah Harris.

Of course, I am honored and delighted to thank Harville Hendrix, co-founder of Imago Relationships International, and Linda Kohanov, founder of Epona Equestrian Services, for contributing, respectively, the Foreword and Afterword to this book. Besides gratitude for their generous endorsements of my work, I greatly value their insights and commitment to transforming some of my philosophical ideas into real-world *applications* that can make positive differences in people's lives.

Finally, without the commitment and support of my publisher, Inner Traditions • Bear & Company, this book would not be in your hands. In particular, I am grateful to Jon Graham for seeing the potential of this book and for taking it on board; to my excellent editor, Anne Dillon, for her many suggestions that helped and inspired me to rewrite some key sections and even whole chapters; and to Jeanie Levitan, managing editor, for shepherding this book through the publication and distribution process.

All of these individuals, and many more I have not named, have contributed to the chorus, and I am honored to sing my part. If at any time the "song" falls out of tune or skips a beat, I take full responsibility. If, on the other hand, you wish to join in the symphony I welcome your participation with open arms . . . I hope to hear from you one day.

Foreword

By Harville Hendrix

I could not put this book down. I read it at one sitting. Each page spoke to the "unlanguaged" in me—those feelings and intuitions that some part of me *knows,* but for which I didn't have the words to express satisfactorily. And it opened me to new vistas I had not contemplated. *Radical Knowing* is a courageous and cutting-edge project, which I think reflects the emergence of a new paradigm from the Cosmos itself—I call it the archetype or "paradigm of relationship."

It is appearing everywhere these days: in couples, in organizations, in the eco-movement, in feminism, in the new spiritualities, in biology and physics, and in philosophy (as Christian de Quincey reveals to us in this book). The new paradigm sounds the death-knell of the old archetype in which things are separate—a system of belief reflected today in the desperation of all conservative movements (particularly in religion and politics) to maintain the status quo. We need a new vision of *relationship* to correct the fragmentation and confrontation so prevalent in today's world, and I think this book gives us that vision in often surprising, creative, and profound ways.

However, I would like to make a disclaimer. I am really not qualified to write a Foreword to this brilliant book because I am not a technical expert in philosophy, theology, or psychology, although I have training in all three disciplines. I am a clinical pastoral counselor specializing in marital therapy and writing about intimate partnerships.

My passion, for the last thirty years, has been trying to understand intimate relationships, the phenomenon of falling in love and, more profoundly, the process of learning to love. This passion led to a theory and therapy I developed with my wife and partner, Helen, called Imago Relationship Therapy (IRT).

The bottom line of IRT is that *romantic* love is fusion with another driven by needs unmet in childhood; but to truly love another person one has to differentiate, discover, engage, know, accept, and value *Otherness*—without judgment. In my view, romantic love and its successor, *real* love, is the universe trying to heal its most wounded part—us.

While I had discovered the difference between "interpersonal" and "intersubjective" relationships in writers such as Stephen Mitchell from the relational school of psychoanalysis, until I read *Radical Knowing*, I wasn't aware that the relationship therapy we had developed was really based on *epistemology*—that is, it works by transforming my clients' *ways of knowing*. Having read this book, I now see that I had inadvertently stumbled onto what Christian de Quincey refers to as "radical knowing"—knowing by participation or what he also calls "engaged presence."

That realization (and an invitation from the author) is the reason I am writing this Foreword. I am using this opportunity to share my personal odyssey as an endorsement of the author's brilliance and courage in tackling a topic that has hardly yet been addressed in the emerging field of "consciousness studies."

THE POWER OF KNOWING

Before I became a marital therapist, I was a spiritually oriented, psychodynamically trained psychotherapist. My methods were analysis and interpretation of the transference between client and therapist (learned from psychoanalysts), along with empathy (learned from Carl Rogers), and support and guidance (learned from pastoral care). As "therapist," I believed that I was the expert and source of healing. But I was in for a surprise.

Like Christian de Quincey, I am particularly interested in *dialogue*—in my case because that is the core intervention in IRT. Long before I had read theologian Martin Buber or quantum physicist-turned-philosopher

David Bohm, I had been taught about the value of dialogue by a client couple: George and Mary. I remember them well. They were what we would call "neurotic," not a "couple from hell," but they were in deep trouble, and Mary was considering divorce. That is how she got George into my office. She was very feminine, expressive, and exasperated. He was kind, warm, very rational, and cooperative, and he wanted his marriage.

Although it was clear that he wanted to understand her, he did not have a clue about what she wanted. Nor did she, until I asked her; and it turned out that what she wanted most was to be heard. She felt invisible in his presence, especially when she talked about her feelings of invisibility. She did not want her problems solved, which is what he wanted to do. So, I asked him if he would listen again, not thinking about how to solve her problems, but just listen.

He tried again, and when she was finished, I asked her if that was what she wanted.

She said: "I want to know if he heard what I said." Then, turning to George, she added: "Tell it back to me."

He tried, but failed, so I helped him. Finally, he "got it right." Before he could relax, however, she said, "But do you see what I mean? Do you see my point of view?"

Then I got it. She wanted more than accurate listening; she wanted to know if he could see how she was thinking, if he could appreciate the reasons behind her thoughts and feelings of invisibility. *She wanted to know if he knew* how *she knew.*

Later, I called this "validation." So, I asked him if he could see the sense she was making.

He said, "No, she does not make sense to me. She is not invisible; I love her and respect her."

"But can you see how her thoughts make sense to her?" I asked.

She interrupted: "Yes, it is not about you, it is about me. Can you see me?"

So I coached him to experiment by saying to her: "You make sense, Mary. I understand that when I listen to your problems I give you a solution rather than just listening and sympathizing, and that's why you feel invisible. I can see that now."

Her body softened, and after she finished crying, she said: "That is the first time in my life I have felt visible. Thank you."

In the next session, they reported they had resumed making love, and after many more sessions, in which she also listened to him, validated his point of view, and expressed empathy, they ended therapy feeling deeply connected.

WHERE HEALING HAPPENS

I began my career in therapy with the assumption that my job was to help couples solve problems. Eventually, I came to the conclusion that *what all couples basically want is to feel connection,* and that all their problems are rooted in disconnection.

But I was in for another surprise. At that time, I had not yet discovered the term "intersubjectivity" or the idea of "second-person knowing"—the "I–I" de Quincey espouses. The notion of *relationship as foundational* was far from my mind. I still thought of couples as two individuals creating relationship, and that in a successful relationship they felt connected. I was looking for a new way of *being,* not for a new way of *knowing.* Isn't that what therapy is: becoming who you are, developing your potential, being at peace with others?

My thinking shifted when my wife Helen told me that my work with couples reminded her of Martin Buber's "I-Thou" distinction. I disagreed, saying I did not understand him. Nor did I appreciate a comment by renowned psychotherapist Harry Stack Sullivan that "what happens inside persons is not as important as what happens between them." Helen insisted that I read Buber again, and reconsider Sullivan, which I did.

After rereading Buber, I learned that his focus was not so much on the "I" and the "Thou" as on the hyphen—the *"between,"* which is where he located Love and God. I then began to connect the dots and realized: *It is the relationship that heals.* Therapists do not heal; couples do not heal their relationship—rather, it heals them.

And so, I concluded, *relationship* is foundational. It gives birth to the infant in conception, to the self in parenting, and to transformation in conscious partnership. But what constitutes "relationship?" That became the new mystery, and, as usual, I began by assuming that relationship is a way of *being*. Not until I read de Quincey did I discern that dialogue is actually a new way of *knowing*, and so is therapy.

Through dialogue and deep engagement, couples differentiate from each other and come to know each other in a new way that transforms the sense of self within each of them. A new way of knowing creates a new way of being.

CONSCIOUS PARTNERSHIP

And that leads to yet another mystery. Helen and I began referring to a healing marriage as a "conscious partnership." But we had not given much thought to the meaning of "conscious." It was an adjective that distinguished the "conscious" marriage from the "unconscious" marriage. In retrospect, we unconsciously used "conscious" to refer to a change in the *contents* of consciousness—a change brought about by dialogue.

Some years ago, I began to muse about the nature of the universe —what the universe has to be in order for couples to be able to have a "conscious" marriage. So, I set out to discover the meaning of "consciousness." Delving into the literature, I learned that, basically, in Western science consciousness is considered an epiphenomenon or by-product of the brain, whereas in Eastern meditative traditions consciousness is understood to be the foundation of all that exists.

In the West, it is assumed that the brain (believed to be made up of non-conscious matter) has evolved to the point where it can become self-reflective. At first, that made sense to me, but little did I know that I was an unconscious materialist. Discovering this was shock because, as a theologian, I assumed, also unconsciously, that "non-material" activities such as prayer, inspiration, love, values, hope, and faith were both real and potent. In short, I was living with contradictory metaphysical beliefs, and the confrontation with this split in me was sobering and healing.

Without going into the details of my emotional, spiritual, and intellectual transformation, I will share only that intuitively I arrived at the conclusion that "Consciousness" (with a capital "C") is "what is."

Consciousness, I came to accept, is Being, and therefore *all* "beings" are conscious. They do not possess consciousness as something added on.

I finally adopted the position that all things, organic and inorganic, are conscious because they are made of Consciousness, but not all things are alive. The universe, including us, is conscious, not as a quality but as *essence*—and that part of the universe that is us (biological beings) is conscious *and* alive. Thus rocks, which clearly are not alive, are nevertheless conscious—echoing de Quincey's position that consciousness goes all the way down.

Consciousness creatively self-organizes into a diversity and multiplicity of forms, all of which innately "know" how to be that form, and how to function as that form. The human brain, existing in a network of Consciousness, has evolved to the point where it can receive and meditate on the information streaming in from the Cosmos. We are that aspect of the Cosmos that can reflect upon itself and know itself. Thus, the answer to my question—What would the universe need to be in order for couples to have a conscious partnership?—is: "It would have to be Consciousness itself." Couples can be conscious because they are "made" of consciousness.

Over the years, then, I learned something new and powerful: that when couples achieve and maintain connection with each other they began to feel connected to something "larger"—variously referred to as the "Cosmos" or the "Divine." I intuited that some form of "ruptured connection" is behind all couples' problems, and that "restoring connection" is the "cure." And I now theorize that this may be true of everyone in all our relationships—with ourselves, with other people and animals, with the planet, with the Cosmos, and with the Divine.

I believe that this perspective is needed more than ever in our times, and I sense that it is emerging all around us as a new relational archetype.

Christian de Quincey appears to be in the grips of this archetype and has been assigned a role in giving it birth. He has distinguished *intersubjectivity* from the objectivity and subjectivity that have dominated debates on consciousness for a long time, and in this book he weaves all three into a new form of knowing and being. In doing so, I believe, he is a conscious agent aiding the evolutionary process.

Radical Knowing is a monumental undertaking: giving voice to the changing forms of the Cosmos—a project, of course, that is never complete. This intelligent author and his provocative book spearhead a future that is coming toward us whether we are ready for it or not—a future in which all forms of knowing and being will be unified, thus reflecting the grand unity of a Conscious Cosmos.

I encourage the reader to enter here with an open mind, and to be open to being grasped by this archetypal energy. Be prepared to be surprised.

HARVILLE HENDRIX, PH.D.,
AUTHOR OF *GETTING THE LOVE YOU WANT*
NEW JERSEY, APRIL, 2005

Introduction

I wrote this book to help liberate people from deeply held beliefs, well-worn grooves of thought about who we are, about the nature of consciousness, and what it means to be in relationship.

We are now living through a time of great uncertainty about so much that previous generations took for granted. Based on philosophical explorations and personal experiences beyond the borders of academic learning, I offer a radically different view of what it means to be human, of how we *know* anything about ourselves, about body and soul, and about sharing a world with others.

In the pages that follow, I will try to direct attention away from the usual distracting beliefs and "facts" that fill our minds. Instead, I encourage and invite you to engage in a novel approach to using your mind by *feeling your thinking*, by paying attention to the experience of consciousness itself—to what I call "experience beyond belief."

This is the second volume in my "radical consciousness" trilogy.[1] The first book *Radical Nature*, explored the nature of reality and the "mind-body problem."*

This volume, *Radical Knowing*, explores the nature of consciousness and *knowing how we know*, using different lenses that will help bring this elusive aspect of our lives into sharper focus:

The four gifts. In order to explore consciousness we need to cultivate other ways of knowing beyond reason and the senses. In short, we need to balance our "four gifts": the Philosopher's Gift of *reason*; the

---

*The third volume, *Radical Science*, will explore the "final frontier" and ask, "Can we have a science of consciousness?"

Scientist's Gift of the *senses* (and methodology); the Shaman's Gift of participatory knowing through *feeling*; and the Mystic's Gift of sacred silence or *direct spiritual experience*. In this book, I focus on two of these gifts in particular, the Philosopher's Gift of reason and the Shaman's Gift of participatory knowing. I show that in order to know *who* we are, and to find deep meaning in our lives, we need to engage in "radical knowing"—by that I mean we need to learn to *feel our thinking* (not merely *think* our *thoughts*). When we are able to do this, we discover that we exist in a web of interconnection. In a very literal sense we *are* our relationships. Philosophers call this "intersubjectivity."

   The three perspectives. I then go on to explore this idea of intersubjectivity more fully by identifying three complementary ways to integrate the science and spirit of consciousness. These are: *subjectivity* (first-person meditation and contemplation), *intersubjectivity* (for example, second-person dialogue), and *objectivity* (third-person study of the brain and nervous system). I pay special attention to intersubjectivity (abbreviated "I–I" and pronounced "I-to-I"). Intersubjectivity is "knowing through relationship"—a form of non-sensory, non-linguistic connection through *presence* and *meaning*, rather than through mechanism or exchanges of energy. Whereas *Radical Nature* made a case for panpsychism ("consciousness all the way down"), *Radical Knowing* goes further by making a case for intersubjectivity ("consciousness as communion") as the foundation for all other modes of knowing.

   The two modes. Throughout this book, I use the power of personal narrative to show how two very different ways of relating to the world and to each other have profound effects on human relationships and our connection with nature. I discuss the distinction between *"preconquest"* (feeling-based) consciousness typical of indigenous peoples and *"postconquest"* (reason-based) consciousness typical of modern "civilized" cultures. Many of us may recognize the tension between feeling and reason as a source of misunderstanding and conflict in our personal and business relationships. In this book, we will explore why people who rely more on *feeling* as a guide for decision making often seem at odds with people who rely more on *intellect* and *reason*. Understanding these tensions will go a long way to resolving them. We will learn about a new way to balance thinking and feeling, head and heart, in ways that can restore power and even "magic" to our personal and professional relationships.

The unity of communion. Finally, we go right to the heart of consciousness by following the example of great sages and mystics. Here, we learn to experience the value and potency of *silence* by simply *being present*. Naturally, I have less to say about this. In a short chapter on a special form of dialogue developed by quantum physicist David Bohm, I describe an effective way to explore consciousness and relationship communally using the intersubjectivity of sacred silence. Knowing our own consciousness involves "feeling our thinking" rather than habitually "thinking our thoughts." When we learn to feel our thinking in this way, we allow the wisdom of silence to find its unforced natural expression in appropriate and evocative language. I call this process "giving voice to the cosmos."

Radical Knowing aims to open up a different kind of philosophy— one very much needed in our confused and troubled times. Here, I resume my attempts begun in *Radical Nature* to return philosophy to its original meaning: "love of wisdom." I use the power of narrative to tell the story of my own transformation from being a logic-chopping academic, trained to be "right" and to win at any cost, to becoming a more openhearted and compassionate lover of shared wisdom. *Radical Knowing* invites you to feel the power of true philosophy as an antidote to the sense of separation and conflict so prevalent in the world today.

Part 1
Personal Transformation

1

Relationship

How Are You Connected?

What is most important in your life? Put this question to a wide range of people and, sure enough, you'll get a wide range of answers . . . everything from "money," "sex," "career," to "good health," "family," "love." And if you were to ask some deeper questions about why such things are so important my guess is that underneath all the answers you would find some common ground. What you and I really want most of all are meaningful, satisfying relationships.

Relationships? Everybody has them. In fact you can't avoid them. Even if you decided to live alone in a log cabin on a remote island, you'd still be in relationship—at the very least with your memories of other people, and with the animals and insects and plants that surround you, and on which you rely for companionship and nourishment. Yes, we are always embedded in relationships, and the mark of a good life is the quality of our interconnectedness.

This may come as a surprise to some people: You cannot *not* be in relationship. It is a fact of life. Yet so many of us spend a lot of our precious time and money trying to find relationships, or *the* perfect one. But after some reflection and clear thinking we come to recognize a basic, simple fact: *We are always in relationship . . .* of some kind. It's part of the welcome package we get on arrival into this world. Every one of us— no exceptions—gets the basic package: a *body*, a *mind*, and *relationships*.

At home and in school we are trained to take care of and develop our bodies and minds. For the body, we go to the gym, play sports, eat healthy food; for the mind, we learn how to count, to spell, to read.

Our culture spends untold billions of dollars each year to help us take care of our bodies and minds—from medical and healthcare institutions, parks and recreation services, to colleges and universities and other institutions of higher learning. Yes, we are trained and encouraged to care for our bodies and to develop our minds.

But when was the last time you entered an "institute for relationship"? The phrase even *sounds* peculiar. It is an alien idea in our culture. It's as if we have been led to believe that our relationships will take care of themselves. Just put two or more individuals together, and, if they have sound bodies and minds, chances are they will develop good relationships. Oh, if only it were that simple! Check out the divorce statistics and you'll soon see that, as a society, we're not very good at relationships at all.

Of course, there are all kinds of relationships besides love and marriage. Relationships with our family of origin (and her/his family of origin!). Relationships at work and in our careers. Relationships with our neighbors and community. Relationships with our pets, and with all the other animals and plants we rely on for companionship and nourishment. Relationships with bacteria and other microbes that influence our health and vitality. Relationships with our homes, and cars, and boats, and all our other worldly possessions. Relationships with our environment. Relationships with our church, synagogue, mosque, temple, or stupa. Relationships with our God or gods, whatever we conceive him, her, it, or them to be.

You get the picture. Relationships are pervasive. Take a few minutes to write out your own list of all the kinds of relationships you have. You will think of many not listed here. It's a useful exercise that will help you become more aware of just how embedded you are (like the rest of us) in a rich tapestry of relationship. Yes, just as the new sciences keep telling us: We are all interconnected. The question, then, is: What is the *quality* of our connections?

HOW ARE WE CONNECTED?

We can begin to answer this question by exploring the nature of our relationships. In today's world, one way we are all related is through fibers and filaments of physical connection—through, for example, the local and global networks of telephones, computers, and the Internet, using the media of voice and images to keep each other informed about the things that matter to us. The common factor in all these modes of connection is that they are physical—involving exchanges of energy and information.

However, we are also deeply interconnected in other important ways—through *non-physical* connections. These are much less obvious and less easy to identify and define, though not because they are less real or have less impact on our lives. In fact, I believe our non-physical connections have a *much deeper* influence on the quality of our lives and relationships than the more visible and tangible physical links and networks.

What are these "non-physical" connections? I'm not talking about some esoteric, "far out" metaphysical lines of force running through our lives and world, shaping our destinies (for example, the kinds of connections astrologers say link us to the positions of the planets and stars). No, I mean something much more mundane and closer to home—something common to all of us, something we all share, something so familiar and intimate that many of us rarely pay much attention to it. I'm talking about *consciousness*.

Yes, consciousness.

But, I hear you say, isn't my consciousness my own private affair, my own private world? My consciousness, my mind, exists inside my head, and nowhere else. No one else has access to my thoughts, feelings, and desires unless I express them. Right? So how can I be connected to other people through consciousness? How can consciousness be one of the fibers of relationship?

Actually, I hope to show you that not only is consciousness a key ingredient in all relationships—I will emphatically state that it is not just a fiber but the very *fabric* of all our relationships. And that without cultivating our consciousness we will not be very successful in cultivating *any* of our relationships. Look at the list of relationships you have created, and now ask yourself: "How is the quality of my consciousness reflected in the quality of those relationships?" If you meditate on this question for some time, I think you will discover, as I have, that consciousness and relationship are so deeply and intimately related that we could confidently say: "The quality of my consciousness *is* the quality of my relationships," and vice versa.

Relationship is all about consciousness. And consciousness is all about relationship.

This last claim may need a little unpacking.

Let's go back to our "welcome package," the one we all received at birth: body, mind, relationships. I said above that our society, our civilization, trains us to take care of body and mind, through healthcare, diet, exercise, and education. Now I'm going to take back what I just said. Or at least modify it a little.

Yes, it is true enough to say that we have developed social institutions for taking care of body and mind—but only to a degree. And in many ways to a very small degree when it comes to "mind." In Western cultures, we are trained to develop a certain kind, or part, of our mind. We are trained to think rationally and logically. Our entire educational system is designed to foster skills for working with the *contents* of our minds. We are fed "facts." Passing exams is all about getting the right answers, about getting our facts right. Getting a job is all about being able to apply the facts in a commercial environment in a way that adds value to our employer's bottom line.

FACTS WRAPPED IN FEELING

In Western cultures, we are trained to work with facts, we are *not* trained to work with feelings and intuition. Picture it this way: Every fact comes wrapped in a tissue of feelings. There is no such thing as a stand alone, pure objective fact. Every so-called fact—*every* fact—every item of knowledge only *becomes* a fact when someone's consciousness becomes aware of it. All facts, all the thoughts and ideas that fill up our minds, exist only because they have found a place in someone's consciousness. And everyone's consciousness is notoriously *subjective.*

The key distinguishing mark of consciousness *is* its subjectivity. Consciousness does not exist in physical space. You cannot see it, cannot touch it, cannot measure it. Subjectivity means this: It *feels* like something from the inside. When you have a toothache, it is subjective; you feel it from inside your own consciousness. Nobody else can feel or experience your toothache for you. And this is just as true for so-called objective facts—whether it's this month's financial statement, the flat tire on your car, the rain beating on the window, your computer crashing, or the book in your hands. Every "objective" known fact always shows up in someone's subjective mind. That's the *only* way it can be known. *Facts come wrapped in feeling.*

I know, you're already saying, "Hey, this is getting pretty deep. Heavy-duty philosophy." But it's "deep" only because it may be unfamiliar to you. And that's my point. Our educational system—our entire culture—has missed this crucial part of the "human welcome package." In other traditions, for example in Buddhist societies, this kind of thinking is not at all deep. It is part of their everyday exploration of what it means to be a human being.

Rather than fall off the "deep" end into bottomless philosophizing, I want you to simply, and easily, just *pay attention* to your own experience, to the feelings coursing through your body right now, at this very moment, as you read these words. What are you feeling? Where in your body do you feel it? What does it feel like? Is it moving? Is the feeling stuck?

Now, if you are an educated Westerner, you have probably already begun *thinking* about what I've just said. But don't try to analyze my words, trying to figure out what they mean—even though that's what you've been trained to do (and I'm sure you do it very well). This book is about stepping outside your training and the usual way you use your mind. So don't think. Just *feel.* Later on, we will explore what it means to *feel your thinking.*

In our culture, we are trained to use our minds to figure out what's best for our bodies. What I would like you to open up to now is the idea of the *body* being in service to the *mind.* Or, more accurately, learning to use the feelings in our bodies in ways that will help improve the quality of our consciousness. I want us to learn to pay attention, not just to the contents of our minds, but also to the *quality* or "context" of our minds—to consciousness itself.

YOU ARE NOT AN INDIVIDUAL

And (letting the secret out right at the start) I suspect that when you engage in this exploration, when you pay attention to your own mind, to your consciousness—to your *feeling of subjectivity*—you will discover, as I have, something quite unfamiliar, perhaps even startling: The deepest nature of consciousness is communion, or *relationship*. Subjectivity is actually *inter-subjectivity*. (Don't worry about that word for now. It will become much clearer soon enough.).

Here's a different way of looking at this "startling discovery": Of the three items in our "welcome package" (body, mind, and relationships), our culture has got at least two of them very, very wrong. We've been given very inaccurate information about the nature of consciousness and the nature of relationship.

Let's look at consciousness first: It is not isolated within our private brains. It is shared, communal. (Yes, *contents* of consciousness may be, for the most part, private. I don't have access to your memory of what you had for breakfast, for example. But the *context* of consciousness, the source from which all thoughts arise, is shared. It's like we have a time-share for our thoughts. We get to keep them private if we choose, but the consciousness that houses our thoughts—the "building"—does not belong solely to us.)

And then there's relationship. Contrary to what we've been trained to believe, relationship does not happen when two or more people come together. This is the "rugged individual" view of relationship. Typically, we believe that each individual is kind of like an "atom," and when two atom-individuals bump into each other, they form a relationship.

We even talk about the "chemistry" of relationship. Think of your own first love affair, perhaps in high school. You went to the dance, or the mall, or wherever, no doubt with some friends, a group of "atoms" out for a good time. And then your eyes met. You encountered your partner-to-be, two "soul atoms" coming together, and forming a relationship. First you were individuals. Then you entered into a relationship. Seems kind of obvious, right?

Well, I'm proposing that *that* view of relationship is wrong and, in so doing, I'm turning the usual view of things on its head. I'm saying that relationship comes first, and *then* our individuality grows out of our relationships—not the other way around. The illusion of individualism is the "box" we will be thinking and feeling outside of as our journey through radical knowing unfolds.

At John F. Kennedy University, in California, where I teach, I begin many of my classes by advising students *not* to believe anything I am about to tell them. And I'm now extending the same advice to you. Don't believe a word I say. I don't want you to believe *anything*. Not what I say, or what anybody else says. I want you to learn a new way of using your mind that liberates you from "facts" and "beliefs" by focusing on your own direct, moment-to-moment experience. This is where your real power resides; this is the way to wisdom.

PHILOSOPHY, STORIES, AND HEALING

I will begin with a personal story, a narrative about how I came to realize the limitations of mainstream academic philosophy, and how I opened to a different kind of philosophy—one more aligned with its original intent and meaning (*philosophia*, love of wisdom). In the next chapter, I will tell this story of my own awakening, and how I came to understand two different kinds of awareness: reason-based consciousness and feeling-based consciousness.

While developing the ideas for this book, I gave many public talks to test the material with different kinds of audiences. Almost invariably after each presentation, women would come up to thank me for putting into words an issue they had difficulty articulating. As these women explained it to me, they felt most comfortable relating to the world through their *feelings*, whereas the men in their lives typically used *reason* as a basis for communication. Many of these women had spent years in relationships where they felt that their husband, boss, teacher, father, or brother had used the power of intellect to invalidate their feelings and in so doing, dominated them; these men and women were experiencing a clash of worldviews.

For the women, feelings were the best guide to speaking their truth; for the men getting at truth involved a process of probing and questioning. Frequently, communication would break down, with each accusing the other: "You're stuck in your head. You have no heart." Or, from the other side, "You're too emotional. You don't think clearly enough." After hearing about the two modes of consciousness discussed in this book, the women told me that they now had a new perspective that gave them insight into the dynamics of their relationships.

It's not that one way of knowing is right or better than the other—we need both reason *and* feeling for getting on with the complicated business of living. However, if we can develop an awareness and sensitivity first of all to the fact that these differences exist, and then achieve some comprehension of their underlying dynamics, we can begin to exercise more choice in how we understand and relate to the "other."

GENDER AND CONSCIOUSNESS

We should be careful not to generalize or to stereotype genders. Not all women use feeling as their primary mode of consciousness or communication. And, of course, women can be just as rational and intellectual as men. Similarly, not all men are unskilled in the "arts" of feeling, either. Furthermore, feeling-based consciousness is not always so gentle or nurturing.

For example, I remember teaching a class on the evolution of consciousness where the women in the class (the majority), ganged up on a couple of the men. The women accused the men of being "too intellectual." This was at a university, and of course the men were entitled to use their knowledge and powers of reasoning to explore the topic; it was entirely appropriate. But the women let rip, and the force of their emotions clamped down on the two men, effectively silencing them for the rest of the class.

Fortunately, I had designed the course to include, the following week, some Bohmian dialogue (a form of communication that encourages and facilitates truthful and authentic self-expression, as we will see in a later chapter), and this turned out to be a fruitful learning opportunity for all involved.

Employing the technique of Bohmian dialogue, the women came to recognize that even while *talking* about the value of feeling the previous week, they had actually been using forceful, rational arguments that were driven by charged emotions. By attacking the men, the women had effectively demonstrated that strong feelings can dominate reason—especially when expressions of the feelings are distorted by emotions such as fear or aggression. This interaction served as a dramatic real-life example of what can happen when thinking and feeling get tangled up without sufficient discernment between them.

From my perspective as a class instructor on dialogue, I saw the irony: women using reason distorted by emotions to express their feelings against men who were speaking clearly and rationally, guided by their own felt sense of what was true. In this case, the women "conquered" the men, switching the usual gender roles of feeling and thinking.

INTELLECTUAL VS. INTUITIVE KNOWING?

We can learn to discern which life situations call for intellect or *instrumental* knowing, and which call for feeling or *intuitive* knowing. For example, in balancing your checkbook or finding your way through the streets of an unfamiliar city it probably works best to rely on reason and intellect (though, of course, even in these situations we would not want to block off all access to our intuitive faculties, either).

But developing a relationship is not at all like balancing a checkbook. And it is here that people often get into difficulty. Trying to "figure out" relationships by relying predominantly on our rational instrumental mind is likely to result in breakdown. It's simply the wrong tool for the job. As we will see, relationships form and develop through participation in *shared meaning* and cannot be figured out the way we would analyze parts of a machine.

Even though some people may find the ideas in this book to be "therapeutic" (in the style of "philosophical counseling"), that is not my central intent. Yes, certainly, I am passionately interested in what I called "epistemotherapy" in *Radical Nature*—healing the split between our different ways of knowing, between intuition and intellect, between feeling and thinking, between body and mind. But I don't believe *ideas* can do it, certainly not on their own. The best I can hope for is that the words on these pages may loosen up some deeply held beliefs and create openings for meaningful insights and experiences to arise. I am not a psychotherapist; I am a philosopher committed to exploring the nature of consciousness. Nevertheless, paradoxically, it seems that a willingness to openly explore consciousness without having any therapeutic agenda can lead to a kind of healing—especially when we successfully integrate thinking and feeling.

But this is not your typical philosophy, either.

I have deliberately chosen to weave personal narrative into this book because I am urging us to honor different ways of knowing when exploring consciousness. Including a "first-person" narrative, I feel, helps balance the more objective and academic "third-person" approaches typical in most philosophy and science. Further, as you will see, one of the key themes in my story is the crucial importance of acknowledging and including the "*second-person*" perspective ("I-you" or "I-to-I" relationships).

As a result, readers familiar with the first volume in this trilogy will notice a shift from a predominantly philosophical writing style to (in this book) a style that is more "user-friendly"—more an *anthropology of consciousness*. (I promise there will be no mathematical equations or complex formulas. Even though we will be moving into some deep philosophical territory, my aim is to keep the message simple.) I believe a user-friendly approach is appropriate given the subject matter of this book: exploring different ways of knowing consciousness and who we are in the world. As in my previous book, I believe the role of story is fundamental both to how we understand our place in the greater cosmic scheme and to how nature itself has produced beings who thrive by sharing meaning.

We are such beings—*storytellers.*

CONSCIOUSNESS KNOWING CONSCIOUSNESS

In recent years, consciousness has been described as the "final frontier" for science. It is also the hardest problem in philosophy, and the great mystery in spirituality. All three disciplines offer ways to study consciousness—it is the one reality common to all of them, and *essential* to all of them. Each discipline relies on its own particular way of knowing: for science, it's the senses; for philosophy, it's reason; for spirituality, it's direct experience.

But what is the best way to know the mind? How do we know what we know? We will attempt to unravel this mystery by asking three crucial questions:

1. How far back in evolution does consciousness go?
2. Are philosophical truth and spiritual wisdom compatible?
3. What is the essential nature of consciousness?

As you will see, these questions reflect my own evolving struggles as a philosopher who, while rigorously investigating "mind," honors the very different perspectives of science and spirituality. I am particularly interested in what happens when philosophy and spirituality engage in dialogue about consciousness: Can *reason* enlighten our steps on the *spiritual* path? Can mystical *experience* guide *philosophy*?

In exploring the relationship between reason and nonrational ways of knowing, our first clues will come from the science of anthropology, and the discovery of two radically different forms of consciousness found in different cultures. One, typical of indigenous peoples, is rooted in *feeling* and focuses on communal well-being. The other, typical of modern culture, is rooted in dialectical *reason* and uses confrontation to dispel ignorance and get at truth. In the chapters ahead, we will see that unless the rational mind reconnects with its own deep roots in feeling, and opens to transcendental intuition, it will continue to conquer and suppress other ways of knowing.

When reason *is* rooted in feeling, however, philosophy can attain wisdom beyond mere truth. In a nutshell, the central theme of my work in philosophy is this: In exploring consciousness are we searching for *truth* or for *wisdom*? Are we looking for decisive *facts* or for enlightening *experience*? Do we want more *theory* or do we want deeper *insights* into how we might better live our lives?

In short: Are we looking for consciousness through *words* or through *silence*?

On the one hand, we may study mind because we want to *understand* it—to talk or write about it coherently. On the other hand, we may study consciousness because we want to *experience* it—to know it from *within* in a way that illuminates our lives. The first approach gives us philosophical truth; the second can lead to spiritual wisdom. This book honors and integrates both.

2

Consciousness

Truth or Wisdom?

My earliest relatives were bacteria! The revelation truly amazed me as I sat, one rainy winter's afternoon, daydreaming out the window, imagining the vast panorama of evolution: From humblest beginnings, life had grown and had produced all *this*—including me sitting there thinking about it all!

I first became fascinated with consciousness as a seven- or eight-year-old kid in Ireland. With nothing else to do that rainy afternoon, I took down my father's old and tattered encyclopedia from the bookshelf and stopped at an entry on "Evolution." A line drawing of a dinosaur had caught my attention, then I lost myself in the text, understanding what little I could at such a young age. But I did grasp enough that day to set in motion the direction that my life's work would take.

I discovered that not only was I descended from my parents, grandparents, great grandparents, and so on all the way back to the beginnings of humanity, but that the entire human race had evolved from some apelike ancestors, who came from even more primitive mammals, who came from reptiles, who came from amphibians, who came from fish, who came from jellyfish, who came from clumps of cells, all the way down to single-celled creatures identified, in that old book, as "infusoria" (today, we'd call them "protozoa" or "bacteria").

So this was evolution! I spoke the word aloud, enjoying the onomatopoeia: "e-v-o-l-u-t-i-o-n." It sounded like a great unfolding, a rolling out of hidden forms, now mimicked in the way my tongue uncurled from the roof of my mouth.

But something else even more astounding grabbed me. Not only was I mesmerized by images of descending species, somehow that stupendous unfolding managed to produce the ability to *look back and contemplate the process of evolution itself.*

Somehow, somewhere along the line, evolution had become aware of itself.

At that time, I don't think I knew the word "consciousness," but probably I was familiar with words such as "mind" or "thinking" or "knowing." How could those ancient "infusoria" have ever produced mind or thoughts? And just *where* did mind first appear?

I could very easily believe that our dog and cat had something like a mind. The same was true of our pet bird and, as I looked closely at the eyes of my pet goldfish, I was convinced I could include it, too. But what about the worms in the back garden? What about the starfish and jellyfish washed up on the sand at the beach? I was less sure. I couldn't decide one way or the other.

So I came to believe that this remarkable ability we call "consciousness" came into existence somewhere between worms and fish. But *where* exactly? *Where, in the great unfolding of evolution, did mind or consciousness first appear?*

I had no answers. The encyclopedia gave no clues, and my parents and teachers, it seemed, could hardly understand my question. They spoke to me of "souls" and "God's mysterious ways," and I was left wondering and unsatisfied because, as far as I could make out, they were telling me only humans had souls. But such religious "explanations" did not fit what I had learned from the encyclopedia, or what I experienced for myself. No, whatever "consciousness" or "soul" was, it was not unique to humans—but how far back did it go?

I grew up puzzled. Not that such questions burned in my thoughts every day; but from time to time I would think back on those dinosaurs and infusoria, and wonder about evolution and about the feelings pulsing through me and other creatures.

I wondered, too, why the stories I was learning from science and religion didn't match. As I reached my teens and began to deal with the first blushes of adolescent emotions—girls and sexual attraction—the old questions returned with a new force. Fears of unrequited love triggered bouts of existential anguish. What was it all about? Trying to figure things out didn't help a whittle. Emotions were so powerful they swamped cool reason? Why the conflict?

In my later teens and early twenties, the cauldron of questions boiled over and I was driven to find answers. But again, no account satisfied the deepest and most troubling questions about the origin of consciousness, about the clash between reason and emotion, or the gap between science and religion.

By then, I had lost faith in the traditional priestly stories and had turned to science as the most reliable source of truth. I began to study psychology, but those textbooks talked only about nervous systems, conditioned reflexes, stimulus, and response. Nothing in the words I read came anywhere close to connecting with what I was actually *feeling*. The disconnect between academic attempts to *explain* the mind and my youthful highly-charged *lived-experience* was dramatic.

Disappointed with both science and religion, I eventually turned to philosophy. At first, the philosophical writings on mind were even more incomprehensible than the scientific treatises on neurons and brains. I learned, then, that there are two English languages: one, the common speech of everyday folk; the other, the jargon used by philosophers. Yes, I could read and even understand their words, but the *meaning* seemed to evaporate off the page before I reached the end of their highly nuanced and complex sentences. I couldn't crack the code. So I turned to the ancient teachings of the East. Here, in the traditions of Taoism, Buddhism, and Hinduism, I discovered language, imagery, and ideas that indeed resonated with my own experiences.

But beyond telling me that consciousness or spirit was the source of everything, including matter, in the end I found little in Eastern philosophies to quench a growing and burning desire to know about the relationship between body and mind, or how consciousness could have evolved from matter. By then, this had become the driving question for me.

Years later, I returned to the philosophical texts of the West, particularly those focused on the precise questions that troubled me. I went back to college and, through perseverance and determination, cracked the code of Western philosophical jargon—I began to understand what they were saying about "the mind-body problem."

I came to appreciate, and then love, the rigor and precision that philosophers applied to language; to hone and dissect distinctions that lay buried beneath superficial assumptions. I learned to use the surgical skills of logic and analysis to cut through linguistic and conceptual confusions surrounding the "great questions." I learned to use and value the philosopher's gift of reason.

In debates, discussions, and arguments, I wielded saber and scalpel to slash away at incautious and sloppy thinking about the nature of consciousness and its emergence from matter. I enjoyed diving into the academic fray, pursuing a "no mercy" approach to the search for truth. If others were bemused, cornered, or offended by the sharpness of my philosopher's tongue, well, that was an acceptable— even necessary—price to pay for truth. I made short work of the conceptual knots befuddling the philosophical worldviews of dualism, materialism, and idealism and, in the process, found serious flaws in all of them.

I was still looking for "the answer" when, shortly after my fortieth birthday, the "eureka" arrived like a thunderbolt the day I rediscovered the work of Alfred North Whitehead—one of the twentieth century's greatest philosophers, a thinker who recognized the profound importance of *feeling* at all levels of reality.

After all this time, the answer to my life-long question "Where in the great unfolding of evolution did consciousness first appear?" was simple—*nowhere!* Consciousness had *always* been there, no matter how far back along the path of evolution one went. Back beyond the fish and jellyfish, back beyond even the bacteria and "infusoria"— further still, back beyond the organic chemicals of life, DNA and proteins, back beyond the molecules and their constituent atoms, back to the elementary particles, and back to the quarks, quanta, or superstrings, or whatever the fundamental constituents of the entire cosmos of matter and energy might be.

I had discovered panpsychism—the philosophical worldview that *all* matter possesses some form of mind. Consciousness, I now could see, must go *all the way down.*

COMPETING WORLDVIEWS

Of all the worldviews attempting to account for the mind-body relation, panpsychism was the most controversial, and the least academically respectable. Few philosophical books or articles gave even passing notice to its ideas. And those that did mention it tended to dismiss it as unworthy of serious consideration. Throwaway comments such as "panpsychism asks us to believe that rocks and trees have thoughts" implied we were being asked to accept that lowly clumps of matter could think like humans: "How absurd to believe rocks could spin out sonnets like Shakespeare's, or equations like Einstein's." But such criticisms completely misrepresented panpsychism—and consciousness. Its critics rarely, if ever, took the trouble to find out first-hand just what Whitehead and other panpsychist philosophers were actually *saying*.

I did take the trouble, and I found what seemed to me to be the most coherent and sensible philosophical position on the mind-body problem. And because panpsychism was so controversial and misunderstood, I took extra trouble to make sure I could offer a respectable defense against inevitable attacks.*

My academic training had taught me that the best line of defense is to be rigorous and ruthless in attack. So I spent years mastering and dissecting the opposing views of dualism, materialism, and idealism, and I discovered along the way that the bottom-line failure of each of these worldviews could be expressed simply: They all required a "supernatural" intervention; none could offer a *natural* account of the relationship between mind and body. (The accompanying sidebar gives a thumbnail of the major views on the "hard problem"—how mind and body, consciousness and the physical world, are related. See also appendix 4 "Integrating Worldviews.")

The more I investigated the various worldviews, the more I became convinced that the only rational explanation for the relationship between mind and matter is some form of panpsychism, or what I came to call "radical naturalism." Nature is "radical," I say, because it is

---

*See the first volume in this trilogy, Christian de Quincey, *Radical Nature: Rediscovering the Soul of Matter* (Montpelier, VT: Invisible Cities Press, 2002).

Major Worldviews on the Mind/Body Problem

Dualism—*The problem of interaction.* Dualism requires a miracle to "explain" how the two utterly different and separate substances of mind and body could ever interact. Yet, plainly, mind and body interact moment by moment in our own experience.

Dualism makes no sense if we cannot explain how the "ghost enters the machine"—it asks us to accept that supernatural soul or spirit "somehow" interacts with the natural world of matter. Dualism defends the position that half of reality is supernatural.

Materialism—*The problem of emergence.* Materialism, likewise, requires a miracle to "explain" how sentient, subjective minds could ever evolve or emerge out of matter that was *wholly* insentient and objective to begin with.

Materialism also asks us to accept not only that mind is wholly natural, but that it is also wholly physical and objective, which completely leaves the undeniable subjectivity of consciousness wholly unaccounted for. For mind to emerge from matter, for consciousness to appear in the natural world, would require some kind of miraculous intervention. Materialism defends the paradoxical position that everything real is natural, physical, and objective—including mind, which is undeniably subjective. But in a world made up *wholly* of objective physical stuff the appearance of subjective mind could *not* happen naturally. Such emergence would require an inexplicable ontological jump—a miracle. *In a purely physical world, the appearance of mind would be a supernatural event.*

Idealism—*The problem of realism.* Idealism, too, requires a miracle of one kind or another: either the unreality of physical reality, or the creation of real matter from pure spirit. Idealism asks us to believe that either all matter is ultimately illusion *(maya),* or that matter emanates from pure mind or spirit. The first option leaves unresolved the pragmatic problem of living in the world if we do not treat matter as real. Matter forces us to acknowledge its reality, despite the claims of idealists. The second option is merely the flip side of materialism: It asks us to believe physical matter could evolve or emerge or emanate from *wholly* non-physical mind or spirit.

Idealism asks us to reject the natural world as having any substantial reality in its own right. According to this position, *everything* is ultimately supernatural—all physical manifestation, the entire panorama of nature, derives *all* its reality from the mind that creates it. What we call the natural world is merely appearance or illusion generated by pure mind. In idealism, nature is merely an epiphenomenon of mind.

Panpsychism, on the other hand, requires no such miracles or supernaturalism. It takes the position that: 1) Both mind and matter are real and natural (neither one has ontological priority over the other); and 2) it is inconceivable that subjectivity and sentience could ever evolve or emerge from wholly objective and insentient matter-energy (likewise, objectivity and physicality could never emerge from wholly nonobjective and nonphysical mind).

made of real objective matter-energy that is subjective and sentient through and through. Nature itself is sentient *all the way down,* it literally has a mind of its own—and that explains the commonsense experience we all have of a world where both consciousness and matter-energy are obviously real. In short, matter tingles with the spark of spirit.

"NO MIRACLES"

I delighted in responding to critics of panpsychism by pointing out flaws in all the other positions. I felt like a warrior for truth, the defender of a philosophical underdog, and an outcast. I crusaded for rational coherence in any attempt to solve the mind-body problem—and, very simply, that meant: "no miracles allowed."

"Miracles" are a measure or indication of our ignorance. When we don't understand how something could happen, but want to insist that it did happen nonetheless, we invoke the non-explanation of "miracle."

This is not to say real miracles can never occur. It just means that if they do, they are beyond our ken.

By definition, miracles lie beyond the pale of knowledge. As far as epistemology is concerned, the great problem with miracles is this: By what criteria do we decide when to invoke their occurrence? What are the rules of evidence by which we decide when and where to insert a "miracle" into our explanations, thereby revealing a breakdown in our sequence of reasoning? If we allow miracles to pepper our explanations, then what's to stop any of us from resorting to "and then a miracle occurred" every time we fail to understand anything? Why bother with seeking any explanations at all? Why not just say "it's all a miracle" and leave it at that?

I wasn't just a philosopher seeking rational answers to difficult questions, I was also, first and foremost, a *human being*. And I knew very well from personal experience that the road to truth was not exclusively via reason. It was perfectly possible that, despite the best efforts of the intellect, the deep nature of reality would forever elude rational understanding.

Given that, I knew I had at least three options: 1) Reason *could* penetrate the mind-body mystery (the rationalist position); 2) Reason could *not* comprehend that mystery (the position of so-called mysterians); or 3) Reason *alone* would be insufficient to solve the mind-body problem, but supported by other ways of knowing, human consciousness could indeed penetrate the mystery (the noetic position).

Nevertheless, *as a philosopher,* I believed I had a duty to honor the gift of reason and pursue it as far as it could take me. Anyone, philosopher or not, attempting to discuss the mind-body relation or the nature of consciousness is automatically in the territory of philosophy—and therefore should be subject to the strictures of reason and logic. I had developed the attitude: "If you do not respect the rules of logic and rational coherence—and take the trouble and effort to discover what others have said about this topic—you have no business talking about philosophical issues such as consciousness and the mind-body problem." And if you did, I would show little mercy in pointing out inconsistencies in your reasoning, try to convince you of the errors in your thinking, and get you to give up your fractured and incoherent beliefs.

If accused of being unnecessarily harsh in my arguments, I would remind my challengers and myself that what mattered most was the search for truth. If, along the way, we had to let go of cherished beliefs, and if this meant feeling upset, anxious, or diminished, so be it. Such bruising experiences should be welcomed as valuable stages in the learning process. "No pain, no gain"—is as true in philosophy as anywhere else. And although this attitude may have been justified within its own limited context, it often felt flat and one-dimensional. It left out something precious about human relationship.

TRUTH AT ANY COST?

This realization came home to me with full force a few years ago during one of the early conferences on consciousness, hosted by the University of Arizona at Tucson. At one of the sessions, a young materialist philosopher enthusiastically presented his own defense of the emergence of mind from matter. He handled his material well, spoke eloquently, and beamed in delight as he passionately guided the audience through his insights. I could barely restrain myself as he spoke because it was so clear to me he was completely missing the point. Whatever he was talking about, it couldn't have been *consciousness*.

As soon as he invited questions I rose to my feet and proceeded to harangue him with a merciless critique. Since consciousness is nothing if not subjective, how on Earth could his model account for the emergence of subjectivity from wholly objective matter? "Your whole thesis is built on shifting sands, mere castles in the air, and doesn't even begin to tell us anything about consciousness. It is nothing more than tightly argued materialist supernaturalism—that is, utter hogwash."

These were not my exact words, but they capture the essence of the tone and content of my response to his lecture. He sat off to the side, visibly shaken, as the next speaker took the podium. All the fire and enthusiasm had drained from his face. Just a few short minutes ago, this young man was vital and vibrant, excited by his ideas, putting forth something he passionately believed in. Now he looked shattered. "Oh my God, *I did that,*" I said to myself, burning with shame and guilt. If this was the price of truth, at that moment it became clear to me that it wasn't worth it.

This was a turning point for me. There must be another way to do philosophy.

And of course there is. Not all philosophers are so insensitive, though many are trained to be. For the rest of the day, and throughout the night, the image of that shaken young philosopher haunted me. I resolved to no longer search for truth "at all costs." If the pursuit of truth leads to a bifurcation, separating it from wisdom and compassion, then something must be wrong. At best, such philosophizing could lead only to eviscerated abstractions and could tell us nothing much of value about the *lived* world, the world as we actually experience it. If philosophy of mind produces fine, detailed, meticulous arguments but fails to embrace the fact that *feeling* is central to the very nature of consciousness—the "what-it-feels-like from within"—then, I was beginning to realize, the discipline is moribund.

The study of consciousness cannot rely exclusively on rational coherence—on connections between concepts and ideas. It must also involve the ineffable, preverbal, pre-rational process I can best describe right now as "feeling our way into feeling," of *experiencing* experience. And the more I pay attention to this, the more I come to realize that first-person exploration of experience sooner or later comes with a message: *"We are not alone."* We are not isolated, solipsist bubbles of consciousness, experience, or subjectivity; we exist in a world of relationships. We are—consciousness is—*intersubjective.* Any comprehensive investigation of consciousness must include the second-person perspective of *engaged presence,* of being-in-relationship.

The next day I looked around for the young materialist and, when I found him, the light had come back into his eyes. I apologized for my earlier behavior, but he looked at me with surprise. He hardly remembered the previous day's incident, and he expected no apology (the philosopher's training!). Maybe my verbal attack had not fazed him after all. Perhaps I had just imagined it or had projected my own reactions onto him. Real or imagined, the encounter served up an important lesson to me nonetheless.

CONSCIOUSNESS AND CONQUEST

The lesson deepened that afternoon. Between lectures, I strolled around the conference poster sessions (where students and scholars presented their ideas on display boards in a large hall) and was struck by one presentation in particular—"Preconquest Consciousness" by a Stanford University anthropologist, E. Richard Sorenson. I didn't have time to read the entire piece, but what I did see caught my attention. Sorenson distinguished between two very different forms of consciousness: "preconquest," characteristic of the minds of indigenous peoples, and "postconquest," typified by modern rationalism. "Conquest" refers to what happened to indigenous consciousness and ways of life when Spanish *conquistadors* invaded the New World.

His presentation was also a chapter in a then-recently published book *Tribal Epistemologies,*[1] and I picked up a copy to read on my flight back to San Francisco. Sorenson's thesis, based on many years of field study with numerous "isolates" or indigenous cultures, shocked me. Preconquest consciousness is rooted in *feeling*, he said, a form of liminal awareness hardly recognized in modern scholarship.

Shaped by a "lush sensuality"—where from infancy primal peoples grow up accustomed to a great deal of body-to-body contact—preconquest consciousness aims not for abstract truth but for *what feels good*. Individuals in such societies are highly sensitive to changes in muscle tension in others, indicating shifts in mood. If others feel good, they feel good; if others feel bad, they feel bad—Sorenson calls this "sociosensual" awareness. In other words, the entire thrust and motivation of this form of consciousness is to optimize feelings of well-being in the community. In such cultures, the "right" or the "true" or the "real" is a question of *value,* not a correspondence between some pattern of abstract concepts and empirical fact.

Significantly, postconquest consciousness is radically different. Based on dialectical reasoning, it intrinsically involves domination or conquest: A thesis is confronted and "conquered" by its antithesis, which in turn is obliterated by a new synthesis. By its very nature, then, dialectic, rational, postconquest consciousness is *confrontational*. This insight alone stopped me in my tracks—particularly following my experience with the young materialist philosopher.

But what I learned next shook me to my core. Given the different dynamics and intrinsic motivations underlying both forms of consciousness, when postconquest rationalism meets preconquest feeling the result is outright suppression and conquest of feeling by reason—*inevitably.*

In its search for truth, reason operates via conquistadorial dialectic: One idea, or one person's "truth," is confronted and overcome by an opposite idea or someone else's "truth." The clash or struggle between them produces the new synthesis—perceived as a creative advance in knowledge.

By contrast, liminal or preconquest consciousness, in striving for what feels right for the collective, *seeks to accommodate differences.* When confronted by reason, it naturally wants to please the other, and so invariably yields. Reason strives to conquer, feeling strives to please, and the result: obliteration or suppression of liminal consciousness by reason.

Even more disturbing to me was the realization that none of this implies malicious intent on the part of reason. Simply encountering an epistemology of feeling, reason will automatically overshadow it—*even if its intent is honorable.*

As I looked back on my own career and personal relationships, I found plenty of confirming instances of this. In my work, I have had many opportunities to engage people from other disciplines—mysticism, shamanism, aesthetics, for example—in dialogues about consciousness. More often than not—*even if I was trying to be considerate* of their different ways of knowing—these people left the encounter feeling abused or squashed by having to match accounts of their experiences against the rigorous and probing logic of my rational analysis. When a search for truth pits dialectic reason against dialogic experience, the "feeling" component of the other's knowledge can rarely withstand the encounter. Feeling feels invalidated. Wisdom is blocked by "truth."

Sorenson's thesis allowed me to understand this dynamic in a way I hadn't before. His paper didn't leave me with merely an intellectual appreciation of the preconquest-postconquest dynamic. He backed his thesis with a truly moving and shocking firsthand account of the disintegration of an entire way of life of a New Guinea tribe when their remote island was discovered by Western tourists after World War II.

Before the "invasion," the Neolithic hunter-gatherer tribe lived with a "heart-felt rapprochement based on integrated trust"—a sensual "intuitive rapport" between the people. Their communication was spontaneous, open, and honest. For them, "truth-talk" was "affect-talk" because it worked only when "personal feelings were above board and accurately expressed, which required transparency in aspirations, interests, and desires."[2] "What mattered was the magnitude of collective joy produced."[3] Sorenson had written:

> In the real life of these preconquest people, feeling and awareness are focused on at-the-moment, point-blank sensory experience—as if the nub of life lay within that complex flux of collective sentient immediacy. Into that flux, individuals thrust their inner thoughts and aspirations for all to see, appreciate, and relate to. This unabashed, open honesty is the foundation on which their highly honed integrative empathy and rapport become possible. When that openness gives way, empathy and rapport shrivel. Where deceit becomes a common practice, they disintegrate.[4]

All of this happened without malice or intent on the part of the "invading" tourists. The Westerners, families of returning WWII GIs, simply arrived on the remote island hoping to meet some "Stone Age" people, and to ask questions about their way of life. But within a week of the tourists' arrival—and merely by asking questions rooted in Western rational, dialectical thinking—the preconquest tribal way of life and a form of consciousness that had lasted for hundreds, if not thousands, of years had collapsed—irreversibly. Sorenson describes a "grand cultural amnesia" where the whole population of this New Guinea tribe forgot even recent past events and made "gross factual errors in reporting them. . . . In some cases, they even forgot what type and style of garment they had worn a few years earlier or that they had been using stone axes and eating their dead close relatives a few years back. . . . The selfless unity that seemed so firm and self-repairing in their isolated enclaves vanished like a summer breeze as a truth-based type of consciousness gave way to one that lied to live."[5]

Thirty thousand feet up in the sky, on that airplane back to San

Francisco, Sorenson's account of the crisis point in this people's cultural collapse brought tears to my eyes:

> In a single crucial week a spirit that all the world would want, not just for themselves but for all others, was lost, one that had taken millennia to create. It was suddenly gone. Epidemic sleeplessness, frenzied dance throughout the night, reddening burned-out eyes getting narrower and more vacant as the days and nights wore on, dysphasias of various sorts, sudden mini-epidemics of spontaneous estrangement, lacunae in perception, hyperkinesis, loss of sensuality, collapse of love, impotence, bewildered frantic looks like those on buffalo in India just as they're clubbed to death; 14-year-olds (and others) collapsing on the beach. . . . Such was the general scene that week, a week that no imagination could have forewarned, the week in which the subtle sociosensual glue of the island's traditional way-of-life became unstuck.[6]

I had gone to that Tucson conference to make a case for the second-person perspective in the study of consciousness. I had written a detailed paper and had presented a talk calling for the inclusion of intersubjectivity, for a relational-based approach to understanding the nature and dynamics of consciousness. Few participants there grasped the significance of dialogic consciousness.

I was moved to include the second-person perspective because for years I felt something important was being left out in the debate between first-person (subjective/experiential) and third-person (objective/abstract) investigations of consciousness. Since most of our day-to-day experiences involve relationships of one sort or another, it seemed to me that overlooking this common aspect of consciousness remained a conspicuous gap in philosophy of mind and consciousness studies in general.

The paradox or irony of the situation did not escape me. I was there to champion the primacy of relationship in consciousness—implying a mutuality of shared feeling—yet the contrast between my intellectual analysis of intersubjectivity and my lack of *experienced relational consciousness* was stark. Not only in my relationships with others, but within myself, I had been using reason to the virtual exclusion of any real depth of feeling. My own professional life was a microcosm of the encounter between postconquest and preconquest consciousness—between the modern, rational mind and the traditional, intuitive mind. I was accumulating philosophical knowledge *about* consciousness, but losing touch with the living roots of wisdom.

DIFFERENT WAYS OF KNOWING

If Sorenson's analysis of the fateful clash between postconquest and pre-conquest consciousness is correct, the prospect for nonrational ways of knowing seems bleak—but only if we accept the (rather unlikely) prem-ise that rationality is the epistemological endgame. Clearly, we have abun-dant evidence from the perennial philosophy and from modern spiritual teachers and practitioners that mystical experience transcends reason. We can evolve beyond reason, and when we do so we do not obliterate the benefits we've gained from reason over the past few thousand years.

Put another way: Even though historically—as Sorenson's work documents—when primal feeling-based knowing (let's call it the "Shaman's Gift") meets modern reason-based knowing (call it the "Philosopher's Gift") or sense + reason-based knowing (the "Scientist's Gift"), the encounter invariably decimates the former, *this need not be the end of the story.* Beyond reason, we all have the potential to develop transmodern spiritual or mystical intuition (the "Mystic's Gift")—and this way of knowing includes and integrates all the other epistemologi-cal "gifts."

From below, reason is grounded in the body's preverbal feelings; above, reason projects imagination toward transverbal and transra-tional experiences and intuitions. Pre-rational feelings and altered states of consciousness appear to reason as mystery or magic—the indefinable domain of the shaman. Beyond reason, unities and communions of experiences and higher states of consciousness appear to reason as inef-fable and noetic—the infinite domain of the mystic.

Whereas reason dominates feeling, mystical knowing does not "conquer" reason—it envelops it, embraces it, *transcends* it. Thus, mys-tical or spiritual intuition is integrative: It includes, while transcending, both reason and somatic feeling.

Nothing is ever quite so neat, however, that it fits comfortably into such models (which, after all, are mostly the product of rational thought). For example, it is not accurate to say that in every case where postconquest reason encounters preconquest liminal consciousness the result is obliteration of the indigenous mind. This may well be true *culturally*—at least I'm not aware of any meeting between groups bearing modern reason and groups using primal knowing where the modern mind was consumed by the indigenous mind. But it is not true *personally*, at the level of the individual.

For example, we know from the literature (anthropological and psychological), and from copious anecdotal reports, that when a modern, reason-dominated individual ingests powerful psychoactive plant-derived substances such as South American *ayahuasca* or synthetic compounds such as LSD, the overwhelming effect is that reason takes a back seat. It is swamped by non-rational feelings and other ways of knowing—and according to many of the participants in these "experiments" or "rituals" the states and contents of such "altered" consciousness are highly meaningful, informative, and veridical. In these instances, primal, shamanic knowing *does* overshadow rational knowing.

More importantly, reason doesn't *have to* decimate feeling—it does so only when unplugged from its roots in the deep wisdom of the body. Reason is optimally effective when it retains or regains contact with its preverbal, somatic roots. Reason works very differently when we *feel* our thinking.

In *Radical Nature*, I pointed out that "*Bodies in nature spoke to each other* long before the development of grammatical speech. Semantics preceded syntax."[7] In other words, meaning came before logic.

We have lost touch with these deep meaningful roots. Our only hope is "to reinvigorate the language of the body, learn to let our muscles, sinews, blood, and bones sing again in harmony with the wild chorus of the land, sea, and air—to *feel* again the pulse of natural kinship. We need to open the vital channels between our words—even our written words—our bodies, and the articulate flesh of the world."[8]

Humans are creatures of language, yet language cannot capture who we are. We use language to connect, but words also separate us from each other and from feeling at home in the natural world.[9]*

Many scientists and philosophers point to language as the key that makes humans unique among the animals. They are talking, of course, about a specifically human form of language—*rational* language. Possessing reason, and the ability to express it through words, is considered to be the essence of what it is to be human. Reason is supposed to be our shared essence, our unique identity as a species.

And it is true that much of human life is embedded in language. However, words and ideas, the currency of human communication, are double-edged: They help us with *instrumental* knowing but remove us from *intuitive* knowing. When we speak our thoughts, we lose touch with the feeling of nature. Words enclose us in a kind of abstract bubble, a film of language separating us from the forces, flows, and patterns of the natural world around us.

And it's not just spoken language. We are even more removed from nature and its sacred patterns when language is written down. The alphabet has erected a barrier between our embodied intuition, between the natural wisdom of our flesh and the flowing web of feelings coursing through the world.[10]

THE DILEMMA OF REASON

In the modern world, we have developed an *over*-reliance on reason, and this has shifted modern cultures out of balance with the rest of nature. But we fail to see that such overreliance on reason is not at all rational; such overreliance on reason is a *distortion* of reason. And that's a major part of the problem.

This is not a new insight. Some of our best philosophers have recognized the imbalance between what we may call "clear reason" and "distorted reason"—or, as I prefer to call it, between "grounded" or "embodied" reason—and "abstract" reason. At the dawn of Western

---

*Recently, I went swimming with dolphins in the warm ocean off Hawaii. As we cavorted with a pod of about two hundred spinners, surrounded by their complex vocalizations, a colleague remarked that unlike the dolphins we humans let our language get in the way of communication. Her observation hit home. I will return to this in more detail in the Epilogue, "Cosmos and Communion."

philosophy, Socrates and Plato knew that reason was limited, and that before anyone could know what those limits were, they had to master reason to get there. Only then, could they move on to the next stage. In the eighteenth century, Immanuel Kant took on this challenge as his life's major project, and in his great work *Critique of Pure Reason* he demonstrated both its power and its limits. Alfred North Whitehead, too, was a master of reason, perhaps the best, because he moved far enough along to know that clear reason is rooted in feeling.[11]

Clear, embodied reason knows that the limits of reason are not the limits of *knowledge*—and certainly not the limits of reality. And failing to recognize this is a major part of the problem—not just *my* problem, but a dilemma for the modern world in general. My story, I came to see, is itself a microcosm of what is happening not only in modern philosophy, but throughout modernity.

Here's the dilemma: On the one hand, we have lost touch with the deep foundation of reason in the feelings of the body, and the network of feelings in nature. On the other hand, we have not made full use of the gift of reason we already have. This second problem is rooted in the first. But both must be worked on together. Our problem, then, is not really too much, but not enough, reason—not enough of the right kind: *clear reason* rooted in the feelings of the body and open to transcendental shafts of wisdom.

In honoring feeling and intuition as ways of knowing, we may be tempted to reject or ignore reason. But we would do so at our peril. We cannot think or talk or write coherently without reason; so much of our culture's knowledge is communicated through thoughts and ideas—especially philosophy.

TRUTH OR WISDOM?

For a long time, psychology was a misnamed science because it no longer studied *psyche* (consciousness or soul). In a similar way, modern academic philosophy is no longer an accurate description of this discipline as it is actually practiced. Having disconnected from feeling, philosophy has lost touch with *sophia* (wisdom).

These days, in exploring consciousness, science and philosophy seek *truth*, spirituality seeks *wisdom*. By "truth" I mean: i) *propositional truth* where language is rigorously self-consistent and non-contradictory; and ii) *correspondence truth* where propositional truth (expressed in ideas/words) is confirmed by empirical evidence.

By "wisdom" I mean an often ineffable knowing born of direct experience, a kind of *intuitive pragmatism* that works to the extent that it takes account of the whole. It is inclusive and integrative, and invariably involves empathy and compassion.

Important questions about the relationship between truth and wisdom arise from this: Is the incompatibility between truth and wisdom contingent or necessary? And if rational truth and spiritual wisdom are mutually exclusive, so that both cannot be operating at the same time, are they—can they—also be complementary? We have already seen that truth grounded in "clear reason"—that is, rational truth informed by the natural intelligence of the body, and open to transrational shafts of wisdom—can indeed be compatible with spiritual knowledge. Disembodied, abstract rational truth, however, is not only incompatible with spiritual wisdom, it is inimical to it. It blocks it, suppresses it, or, at best, distorts it.

But in no case can reason—either "grounded" or "abstract"—fully comprehend or express the enlightened knowing we call wisdom. The deepest core and highest reaches of spiritual wisdom forever remain beyond the reach of reason and language.

Though limited, the complementarity between philosophy and spirituality may be summarized as follows: On the one hand, philosophic knowledge of consciousness requires insights that come with the compassion and serenity of spirituality in order to expand from mere truth to wisdom. While on the other hand, mystical experience, invariably ineffable, requires the assistance of conceptual and linguistic rigor (as well as poetry) to express, as best it can, the wisdom of spiritual insight.

Unfortunately, this complementarity is hardly recognized in modern Western philosophy as it searches for truth about consciousness. So much of academic philosophy of mind is about finding flaws in the other guy's logic, and taking no prisoners. It operates from the assumption that progress is built on discovering what is wrong and putting it right. (We might even call it a "via negativa"—except that would distort the meaning of that phrase in spiritual practice.)

But philosophy need not be built on conflict, on clashing world-views, as John Stuart Mill noted when he said (paraphrase): "Philosophers tend to be right in what they affirm, and tend to be wrong in what they deny." Perceptive and wise insights like this show that philosophy can live up to its name.

Imagine practicing philosophy by looking for what is *right* about the other guy's position. That kind of attitudinal shift begins to pull philosophy and spirituality closer to one another, and truth begins to approach wisdom. My own variation on this insight is:

> Every worldview expresses some deep truth—and is in error only if it claims possession of the *whole* truth. . . . That is, there is probably some deep kernel of uncommon truth in every worldview—whether scientific materialism, spiritual idealism, mind-body dualism, or panpsychism—and the task of honest philosophers is to uncover such truths. The task of great philosophers is to find how these uncommon truths cohere in a common reality.[12]

If anything, wisdom is integrative, whereas much philosophical truth is fragmentary—that is, it is either confrontational or it tries to separate and compartmentalize different subdisciplines. But philosophy doesn't have to be this way. We can have "integrative philosophy."

In the next chapter, we will continue our exploration into the adventure of evolution and consciousness by focusing on a revolutionary theory of human development—one that starkly reveals the crucial importance of regaining contact with the preconquest, embodied, indigenous mind. This evolutionary perspective will expose the deep somatic causes for the greatest crisis of our time—the profound and widespread malaise in consciousness that alienates us from our true selves, from each other, from our human potential, and from the greater self and body of nature and cosmos.

{

Up in Arms about Being Put Down

There is a shocking secret, a deep shameful terror, that every one of us carries like a millstone every step of our lives. Few of us recognize it because it is so pervasive. Yet we are all aware of it at some level, but most of us don't know what to call it. Fewer still know what to do about it once we peel back the Medusa mask and see the demon for what it is. And even those of us who have confronted it, sometimes deny it because the soggy mess of anger, hurt, fear, guilt, and confusion is so painful it is easier to turn away and pretend. The pain, the fear, the guilt are all the more terrible because they came to us from our parents—and we are doing the same to our children.

The shocking truth is that modern Westernized parents have been seduced by a system of education that trains all of us to neglect and deny our deepest instincts toward ourselves and toward our children. Cut off from the flow of evolutionary instinct, we are all victims, suffering the severe shock of amputation from the natural relationship between mother and child. The price we pay is high: stunted emotional and spiritual growth of our children—and as adults, we carry the scars.

In the previous chapter we saw that human consciousness is split into two radically different modes that Stanford University anthropologist E. Richard Sorenson called "preconquest" and "postconquest." The first refers to a kind of consciousness rooted deeply in the feelings and wisdom of the body and is the wellspring of instinct and intuition. For millennia, it has been the dominant mode of consciousness for tribal, indigenous peoples throughout the world. The second mode of consciousness refers to a way of thinking that has become disconnected from the body's feelings and tends to restrict itself to circuits of abstractions—often short-circuiting the vital connection between feeling and reason, cutting knowledge and truth off from wisdom.

In this chapter, we will now focus on another aspect of this split between feeling and reason, between instinct and intellect. We will see how modern civilization, by developing an overreliance on the type of consciousness that exalts abstract reasoning—at the expense of instinctual feeling-based consciousness—has severely distorted human relations, alienating us from a quality of life and innate wisdom still common among indigenous cultures. The split shows up as a chronic dysfunction in our relationships with ourselves, with other people, and with the natural world, creating a massive rupture in the human psyche that robs us of our deep evolutionary birthright.

Like many epiphanies, this one arrived for me during a time of crisis in my life, shaking me out of deep-worn grooves of thought and beliefs. The experience opened me up to a greater appreciation of feeling and a trust in my own instincts when my intellectual faculties no longer provided the kind of life-guidance I was seeking. Ironically, the "ah-ha!" came from reading a book. But the words rose off the pages, touching my heart and soul because I was already ripened from the emotional heat caused by a prolonged traumatic relationship.

SPEAKING TO MY SOUL

Some years ago when I was going through the upheaval of a divorce, one of the things I learned was that so much of the emotional force consuming me was welling up from long forgotten childhood pain. In some ways, I had become a child again, emotionally, in my marriage, separation, and divorce. More than anything, I knew I had to deal with that. I had to find a way to make peace with my fearful, angry, and grief-stricken child, to hold and comfort him and let him know it was all right to grow into a man.

By serendipity, I came across a slim volume called *The Continuum Concept* by Jean Liedloff.[1] This remarkable book describes how civilization has lost touch with our innate instinct for taking care of our infants and shows the drastic and far-reaching consequences this mistake has had on generations of civilized people.

You probably know the feeling: From time to time you pick up a book that speaks to your soul. I couldn't put this one down. Every page broke open a capsule of such clear commonsense that I came away amazed nobody had seen or revealed such truths before, and I was stunned at the implications of what we need to do, as a culture, to put things right.

Discovering Liedloff's book was one of those landmark events that influenced the direction my life was to take. Every time I turned a page I found another piece of the puzzle—a confirming insight into how I (and you, and everyone of us) is scarred by a jigsaw wound from our earliest infancy. I was so moved by what I read that when I got home I wanted to run down the street and grab people—especially journalists, government officials, psychologists, psychotherapists, educators, and pediatricians—and tell them about this book! I wanted all my friends to read it. I wanted to buy everyone a copy. *The world needs to know about this*, I thought. *This is too important to go unacknowledged by our society.*

The Continuum Concept had such an impact on me because I was emotionally primed for its message. I was ready to make contact with the deeper levels of my past: with the early childhood trauma that continued to live on in my body and in my deep unconscious beliefs about myself and the world—a trauma that erupted during moments of crisis, manifesting as dysfunctional ways of thinking that shaped how my life was unfolding. I was able to journey deeper through my layers of primal wounding as Liedloff unfolded her thesis. Through meditation, insight, writing, and conversations with other interested and informed people (including Liedloff herself), I worked at applying these insights to a deeper understanding of what I called "The Aftershock Effect"—those powerful emotional currents that reverberate through our mind-body systems long after the traumatic event itself has passed.[2]

THE CONTINUUM CONCEPT

The idea for Liedloff's Continuum Concept grew out of her observations while living with a Stone Age tribe deep in the Venezuelan rainforest. Jean Liedloff had been a *Vogue* fashion model who gave up the life of Parisian glamour for the adventure of ideas explored through an odyssey into humanity's deep past. Her repeated visits to a remote tribal culture allowed Liedloff to participate in a way of life that had hardly changed for thousands of years. By 1985, she had made five expeditions to the Venezuelan rainforest, to observe and participate in the tribal life of the Yequana. She based her controversial theory of human development on firsthand experience living with these Stone-Age tribal people.

Her thesis in a nutshell: For millions of years, our ancestors evolved with the expectation that as babies they would be held and carried by their mothers for the first year or so of life. She called this the "innate expectation" of "in-arms experience." Our prehuman ancestors lived this way for hundreds of thousands—millions—of years and, for most of our time on the planet, so have *Homo sapiens*. Only in the last thousand years or so, since the rise of intellect and reason (or perhaps much more recently than that, with the advent of the European Enlightenment and the dawn of the scientific worldview), have we dethroned instinct and turned to intellect, reason, and logic as our guides.

In recent generations, civilized society has established the norm of separating the baby from constant physical contact with its primary caretaker (usually its mother). Consequently, by the middle of the twentieth century, instinct had been so marginalized that we began to believe it was "natural" to turn to "experts"—like Dr. Spock—to tell us how to bring up baby. Meanwhile, the innate expectation for in-arms experience (the "continuum") continued to burn in the human baby's nervous system—unfulfilled. As a result, generations of humans have grown up with a deep sense of something missing, of something wrong.

PROGRESS AT A PRICE

Western culture has clearly moved light-years ahead of tribal societies in its mastery of nature, and in its ability to develop the impressive technologies of mass production and consumerism as well as the social and economic structures that support them. We have mushrooming cities of concrete and steel, vast systems of communications and transport, and institutions and industrial complexes for health, education, and entertainment that our culture considers the hallmarks of being civilized.

But the cost of all this progress weighs heavily on us as a profound and widespread psychological, social, and environmental malaise. How did this happen? How—compared to "primitive" indigenous cultures—did our apparently successful, progressive, Western values and behaviors become *pathological?*

Liedloff, now a counselor in Sausalito, California, maintains that the deep disconnect between mother and offspring in Western cultures is a colossal and catastrophic error at the heart of modern "civilized" societies. Paradoxically, it's an error that may be responsible for both our greatest glories and our deepest shame. This is the cornerstone of her theory and may well hold an explanation for many of the ills of modern socialized life.

As a theory, the Continuum Concept may explain such wide-ranging phenomena as the rampant failure of our relationships and marriages, our culture's need for progress and novelty, the effectiveness of advertising, the sources of criminality and addiction, the drive to adventure, the need for sexual conquest, our need to be noticed and to have heroes or to be martyrs.

Trust in the instinctive ability of people to do what benefits themselves and the common good is almost completely lacking in Western culture. Yet it forms a natural part of Native American and other tribal experiences. For countless generations, our species existed successfully as hunter-gathers, learning, along the way, a highly evolved sense of how to survive in a wide range of circumstances. Like our animal ancestors, we had an innate sense of what behaviors best served us. Mostly, we probably just did what we needed to do, without much thinking.

The turning point, according to continuum theory, came when we replaced our trust in instinct with dependence on our more recently acquired intellect. We handed over to reason many of the functions that had been honed and refined by instinct for hundreds of millennia. And this overdependence on rationality has created a lopsided civilization, weighed down by massive institutions, organizations, and structures that often crush the human spirit.

On the evolutionary continuum, intellect is a relative newcomer;

instinct has a far older ancestry and a much deeper base of experience and contact with reality. Yet we have trained ourselves to be suspicious of instinct, to regard it as somehow subhuman, a relic of our animal forebears. We have banished a great natural ally and have removed ourselves even more from the valuable feedback that results from direct interaction between instinct and environment. We are now so heavily under the spell of intellect that our inherent sense of "correct action," of what is good for us, is barely accessible. Most of the time, for most of us, we cannot distinguish an innate impulse from one that's distorted.

EXPERIENCE AND EXPECTATIONS

But what is "correct" behavior? Liedloff defines her terms: *"What is meant here by 'correct' is that which is appropriate to the ancient continuum of our species inasmuch as it is suited to the tendencies and expectations with which we have evolved. Expectation, in this sense, is founded as deeply in man as his very design."*[3]

How did these "expectations" evolve and come to be incorporated? What was the feedback mechanism between environment and organism that branded these lessons into our biological being? The answer, according to Liedloff, is *experience.*

For hundreds of millions of years, as simple living forms experienced environmental changes and adapted to them, they grew more complex and diversified. Gradually, they became more stable and survived to reproduce and pass on the benefits of their experience. They equipped their descendants with increasingly more effective and efficient means for dealing with a range of environmental conditions. Each individual, then, *embodied the experiences it expected to encounter*—literally encoding them in every cell. So today, every organism carries within its design the expectations of its entire ancestry, stretching back to the beginnings of life—and, conceivably, beyond to the natural selection of molecular and even subatomic interactions. That is the awesome pedigree of the continuum principle and the source of its explanatory power.

We come into the world with a ready-made set of expectations—our "continuum"—programmed by our long evolutionary heritage. For millions of years, our ancestors were carried about by their mothers, feeling secure and protected, while our species encountered the multitude of sights, sounds, and sensations impinging on mother and infant. As newborns, we expect certain things like nourishment and nurturing protection, and to hear and feel our mother's heartbeat, to hear her voice and the voices of other people laughing and crying, singing and shouting, coughing and snoring; we expect to feel our mother's body jiggling as she walks or runs or stoops or jumps, all the while secure in her arms. *We evolved to expect this and none of it disturbs or shocks us because the adaptations of our ancestors have taken it all into account over millions of years.*

Our continuum has conditioned us to expect to be in close physical contact with our mother from the moment of birth, to have ready access to her breast and to be held in her arms, to feel the warmth and security of her skin against ours *for as long as we feel we need it,* usually for most of our first year or two of life. When the continuum is fulfilled, the child grows up with a natural sense of "rightness." He or she is okay, the world is okay, and the child will behave accordingly.

These children are then, as Liedloff says, "continuum babies," developing naturally—as our long lineage of ancestors has always done—and growing into healthy, fully adapted, and adjusted "continuum children" and "continuum adults."

THE NEED TO BE HELD

An evolved expectation like this lives in us as a *certainty*—until it is betrayed. When it is not fulfilled we experience a break in our continuum and lose touch with our sense of essential rightness. Our behavior deviates from our evolved, innate ability to react correctly, wasting the benefit of millions of years of evolution. We attempt then to fill the void with *learned* expectations and behaviors, for instance, wailing if our caregiver is not available. But learned expectations, to the extent they deviate from our continuum, are tainted with disillusionment, doubt, suspicion, and fear. When the infant is abandoned, taken from its continuum of correct experience, no substitute experience is acceptable. All that remains is a feeling of want, a burning desire for the unfulfilled expectation to be satisfied.

"Every nerve ending under his newly exposed skin craves the expected embrace, all his being, the character of all he is, leads to his being held in arms," Liedloff writes.[4] Since this expectation is not fulfilled in our society, we grow up incomplete, with a deep sense of something missing, and we spend a great deal of the rest of our lives trying to fill that void with substitute experiences: successions of mother figures, lovers, status symbols, religions, professions, drugs, the drive for something new, something better—for *progress*. Our institutions are built on such unstable foundations. Ironically, as attempts to restore the lost sense of continuum, they succeed only in pushing us farther from our roots.

LIFE AS A CONTINUUM BABY

What would life be like if we were raised as continuum babies? Liedloff spent many years studying this question. On her earlier visits to the Venezuelan rainforest she noticed that the Yequana mothers always carried their babies with them as they went about their day's work, whether they were building fires, cooking, cleaning their huts, fetching water from a stream down the side of a steep slope, or sleeping with their husbands. Liedloff also noticed that Yequana children showed none of the symptoms of distress so common—now even expected—of civilized youngsters (for instance, fighting, competing, rebelliousness, temper tantrums, being accident-prone).

Without books, videos, classes, or web pages on baby care, Yequana mothers (as well as fathers, siblings, and other children) know instinctively what is correct for the infant. As the infant grows into a child, its caregivers expect and trust it to know what is best for itself—*and the infants and children fulfill these expectations.* Continuum theory tells us that, for its part, the infant *expects to be trusted* to behave according to its own initiative, to know what is correct.

From her observations of the Yequana, Liedloff suggested human children evolved to strive not only to fulfill their own expectations but, once they were aware of the expectations of their caregivers, to fulfill those expectations as well. As instinctively social beings, children want to please and to fit in. So, in the Yequanas' case, when adults treat their children as responsible enough not to endanger themselves, and are given free reign to roam and do as they please, they rarely injure themselves. The Yequana do not protect their crawling babies and young children from fires, sharp machetes, and knives or from mud pits or rivers, and the youngsters instinctively do what is in their own—and others'—best interests. Liedloff described how young babies would pick up razor sharp knives, *by the blades,* and not cut themselves; they would play with flaming sticks from the fire without burning themselves or others, and without torching the thatch on their huts.

By contrast, in Western civilized societies where the expectations of parents are that children need to be "socialized" and to learn what is good for them, youngsters fulfill the expectations—that they don't know what is correct—and behave accordingly. They are often "difficult," cantankerous, and tantrum-prone and, in fact, frequently do injure themselves if unsupervised.

Liedloff recounts a sad, but telling, example of this. A California family, nervous that their small child might fall into the swimming pool, built a fence around it and kept the gate locked. They explained to the child that the pool was dangerous and that if he went near it he could fall in and drown. The expectation they created was that he could not be trusted to take care of himself and, sure enough, the one day they left him alone for a few minutes with the pool gate unlocked, he did fall in and drown.

PUTTING IT INTO PRACTICE

Should we, then, simply throw caution to the wind and let our children do whatever they want? We cannot easily and suddenly revert to the ways of our ancestors or the contemporary Yequana. We have generations of learned expectations to deal with and it would be foolhardy to turn a blind eye on these. But that shouldn't mean turning a blind eye to the obvious, either—to the high price we pay for having lost touch with our instinctual ability to do what is right.

Liedloff comments: "For anyone trying to apply continuum principles in civilized life, this changeover to trust in children's self-protecting ability will be one of the most difficult problems. . . . We have no choice but to find our way back to that knowledge common to the Yequana and our own ancestors, *through* the use of the intellect. . . . *To make the intellect a competent servant instead of an incompetent master must be a major goal of continuum philosophy.*"[5]

The continuum concept is so crucial, it seems to me, that we cannot afford to have it languish as a minor backwater in the literature of psychology and psychotherapy. If, as the theory suggests, we are committing a grave error in the way we handle our children, leaving most, if not all of us, deeply emotionally retarded, we should make every effort to put it right. The problems of civilized life must be approached with the knowledge that we have been deprived of almost all the in-arms experience that was our birthright, and that we live our lives vainly striving to fulfill our stunted expectations. Since our evolved expectations must be fulfilled in their expected order, we are, then, left starving for the missing experiences, and parts of us as adults remain infantile and unable to contribute positively to our development and to the community. The extent of the social loss is unthinkable.

"The search for in-arms experience, as the years pass and we grow up, takes on a great many forms," Liedloff writes. "Loss of the essential condition of well-being that should have grown out of one's time in arms leads to searches and substitutions for it. *Happiness ceases to be a normal condition of being alive, and becomes a goal.*"[6]

ATTEMPTS TO FILL THE VOID

We have become a society of "if onlies." "If only . . . then I'd be okay." Fill in the blank with any of a million-and-one desirables, (winning the lottery, finding the perfect mate, getting the right job or education, buying new clothes), but none will succeed in filling the void. There will always be that unsatisfiable longing, a craving for that special something missing from long ago.

The list of "if onlies" is as endless as our consumer society's ability to create new products and services to fulfill our unquenchable need. Our culture is built on the persistent pursuit of novelty and labor-saving gadgets that will comfort us or make our lives easier (as our mothers were expected to have done). Therein lies the source of the motive force behind our culture's incessant, obsessive drive to progress.

Advertisers have mastered the art of capitalizing on the longings of an in-arms deprived market. Their slogans resonate in that empty place inside us where our birthright experience should have been. Buy their product and you will recover that feeling of rightness: "It's the real thing." "A diamond is forever." "Oh, what a feeling!" "The power to be your best." "Just do it." "Be all that you can be."

In stark contrast, because the Yequanas' in-arms experience is fully satisfied, they don't feel a need to compete for attention. In fact, since their emotional life doesn't require it, there is no competition in their culture. In our society, on the other hand, the dual drives for novelty and progress have turned us into "efficiency machines" and "productivity pawns," and the pace of life gets increasingly faster and full of things to do and things to have. This headlong rush into the rat-race maze has itself become yet another learned expectation in our culture. And advertisers prey on these secondary expectations, too: "The best never rest," shouts a TV ad from a well-known motor company.

We cannot obliterate the past. On the one hand, our multi-million-year-old continuum of expectations, with its age-old instinctual wisdom, is born again every day with every new baby. At the same time, our society has by now spent many generations ignoring this innate knowledge and has overlaid it with new sets of learned experiences. We have to deal with both; we have to find a way to retrain our culture to trust in our instinct, to honor the ancient expectations of babes in arms, while attempting to progressively narrow the gap between our evolved and our learned expectations.

CONFRONTING THE CHALLENGE

The social implications of resolving this dilemma are enormous. For instance, we would need to reorganize our workplaces so that mothers (and fathers) could carry their infants to work and keep them with them as they took care of business. To deal with the immense ramifications of such sweeping societal change, we would have to call on some of the best and creative powers of our intellect *in the service of this fundamental, instinctual human need.*

Governments would have to plan and pass the necessary legislation to foster the change, and that is likely to happen only when there is sufficient grass-roots pressure from their constituents. Businesses would need to be persuaded of the dubious economic benefits of allowing millions of infants into offices and factories. Massive disruption would be almost inevitable because, for at least the first few generations, both the parents and the infants in the workplace would still be reacting to many of the maladaptive learned expectations built into our culture.

There would be less obvious challenges to confront. Would capitalist governments and businesses be willing to risk unhinging the drive for progress that has built our fortunes and our cities, that has driven scientific and technological achievements to almost miraculous heights? As we have seen, the completely fulfilled continuum person does not have a longing for novelty and gadgets, is not competitive, and would be poor fodder for a consumer society driven by the advertising business and mass media. Realistically, it is highly unlikely we would, or could, ever return to the simplicity of the Yequana lifestyle (unless we obliterate our civilization through nuclear war or rampant global pollution and have to start all over again).

But with a proper balance between instinct and intellect, perhaps we can retrain ourselves to live in a radically altered culture, where the paranoia of competition is replaced by a more humane spirit of cooperation; where obsession with progress at any cost is replaced by a realistic respect for conservation; where aggression is replaced by tolerance; where dogma takes a back seat to dialogue; where power and greed are less attractive than service and contribution; where science is no longer at odds with the sacred.

It all begins with a willingness to respect an awesome fact: Our babies arrive in the world already primed with the unconscious wisdom of hundreds of millions of years of evolution. *They know what they need to survive.* It all begins with the miracle that happens when we honor our babies by fulfilling their instinctive expectations to be nourished and cared for according to *their* needs. It all begins by picking our babies up and holding them in our arms *until they decide it is time to move on.*

In chapter two, we learned from E. Richard Sorenson how the fragile relationship between feeling-based consciousness (typical of indigenous peoples) and reason (so dominant in our culture) can wipe out the ways of life of an ancient civilization in a matter of days. And now in this chapter we have learned from Jean Liedloff the critical need to find ways to integrate intellect and instinct—to honor our body's innate evolutionary intelligence laid down over many millions of years. In different ways, both of these researchers have shown us the limitations and dangers of overreliance on reason, thought, and belief at the expense of feeling and the silent wisdom of direct experience.

In the next two chapters, we will look more closely at the role of beliefs in shaping our consciousness, our lives, and the world around us. First, we will look at the currently popular idea that beliefs shape—or even create—our reality, and how beliefs function as lenses through which we come to know the world and our place in it.

4

Paradigms

Intention Creating Reality

The story goes that when Darwin anchored the *Beagle* in a bay off the coast of Tierra del Fuego, clearly within sight of land, he and his crew rowed a small boat up to the beach where a troupe of wide-eyed natives, spears quaking in their nervous hands, waited. To the aborigines, Darwin and his men were gods. They had appeared suddenly and miraculously out of nowhere, out of the sea. The great naturalist tried to explain to his hosts that he and his men had arrived in that big sailing ship, and he gestured to the majestic *Beagle* riding the tidal surge just offshore. The natives were now convinced these visitors must be *crazy* gods—there was *nothing* out in the bay but waves and sparkling foam. The islanders couldn't see the ship. They couldn't see it *because they didn't believe it*. A "canoe" of such enormous proportions was beyond their experience, expectations, and wildest imagination.*

This story of Darwin's invisible *Beagle*—apocryphal or not—illustrates an important psychological phenomenon. We can only perceive what we can conceive. The cliché used to run: "I'll believe it when I see

---

*Research indicates that this story of a perceptual anomaly is indeed fictitious. Nevertheless, like any potent myth, it seems to have taken on a life of its own as a cultural meme (an idea that spreads like a virus within a population). In a recent popular movie *What the Bleep Do We Know?* the myth pops up again, this time attributed to a report by Captain Cook when he first sailed to the Caribbean islands. The movie dramatizes the event as though it actually happened, and that is unfortunate because it perpetuates a historical fallacy. Nevertheless, I have decided to use the story because—even though it's just a myth—it illustrates the point about "believing is seeing."[1]

it"; now the twist is: "I'll see it when I believe it." The first version expresses a point of view embedded in conventional empirical science. It says, in effect, "If I can perceive and measure it with my senses, then it is worthy of my belief. Otherwise, I have to put it down to fancy, fantasy, illusion, hallucination, or superstition." It is a radically pragmatic, practical, and apparently commonsensical approach to knowing the world.

It is also out of date.

Discoveries in the frontier sciences of quantum physics, as well as in certain areas of psychology, neurology, evolutionary biology, and consciousness studies are ushering in a different worldview—a new *paradigm*. In this new approach, the fundamental "stuff" of the world is not solid, substantial material things—like particles, atoms, and molecules—it is something much more like fields of vibrating energy, or vortices in dynamic warps of space-time. In short, the world is made of *processes*, events rather than "things." *Reality is a "world processor."*

But just what is it that is undergoing the processing? According to the current state of knowledge in physics, the answer is still one big question mark. For convenience, we call it "energy"—or, more esoterically, "zero point energy"—but really we just don't know. And here's the interesting point: To a growing number of scientists and philosophers it is beginning to look suspiciously as if the ultimate nature of the universe is much more akin to what we call "consciousness" than matter—at least a form of energy that tingles with sentience all the way down. A great physicist, Sir James Jeans, anticipated this topsy-turvy worldview nearly a century ago when he proclaimed "The universe begins to look more and more like a great thought than a great machine."

Of course, this is what the mystics and sages of many cultures have been telling us for thousands of years. They—like the Tierra del Fuegans—have always lived in a universe where spirit, not "dead" matter, has been the primary shaping force of reality. As more researchers in emerging fields such as transpersonal psychology explore the storehouse of knowledge from "primal" religions and cultures, they are discovering a set of common beliefs—collectively known as "perennial wisdom." Central to this almost universal worldview is the insight that mind and spirit are co-creators of reality.

Similarly, many transformational psychotherapeutic systems—often confusingly labeled "New Age"—also affirm the primacy of intention and consciousness as creative forces directing the unfolding of phenomenal reality. Matter and mind, it is becoming clear, are far more deeply intertwined than classical science and philosophy have led us to believe. In fact, belief itself—or, rather, the intentional power of the mind—seems to be able to reach into the heart of matter and play with the physical world in ways that rattle the old paradigm of materialism.

According to the new or emerging paradigm, reality is not a given—not an already preexisting conglomeration of external "things" that we must perceive and adapt to if we want to survive. Reality, in the new view, is as much, if not more, "in here," inside consciousness, *and we create it from moment to moment.* Of course, since everybody is engaged in the same godlike act of creation, we don't live in a lone and isolated private universe (where only our own consciousness is real, and everything else is just a creation of our individual mind). No, in this maddeningly non-linear, non-commonsensical point of view, everybody is creating everybody else. I am creating you as, simultaneously, you are creating me. We live in a mutually self-sustaining universe. We all contribute to the dynamics of a vast web of interconnected and interdependent nested systems; so although we are creators, we are also participators and, therefore, we still have to adapt to survive.

To say "You are what you believe" is almost a tautology in new-paradigm thinking. And although the thrust of research and theory on the frontiers of physics, psychology, and consciousness studies seems to support this view, as a slogan for the "New Age" it is dangerously simplistic. We need to pay careful attention to what we mean by "belief." As a prescription for life, the slogan "You create your own reality" by what you believe can set unthinking, uncritical, and innocent minds up for some bloody-nosed confrontations with what philosopher A. N. Whitehead called the "stubborn facts" of experience. (And more than two-hundred years ago, U.S. president John Adams declared in a similar vein: "Facts are stubborn things; and whatever may be our wishes, our inclinations, or the dictates of our passions, they cannot alter the state of facts and evidence.")

Clearly, life is not so simple that all it takes is to choose to believe this or that and lo! so it turns out.

A WAVE MODEL OF REALITY

It could be, of course, that our beliefs behave something like energy waves that ripple out from us and meet up in a world brimful of other people's beliefs. We may be embedded in a global network of interference patterns of beliefs, like ripples and wavelets on a pond after handfuls of pebbles have splashed through the surface. When beliefs coincide and slip into phase, they may amplify each other; when they conflict and contradict each other, they may cancel each other out. Yet, I can't bring myself to believe it works quite that way.

For one thing, it is linguistically and philosophically problematic. As I pointed out in *Radical Nature*, spatial analogies and metaphors, borrowed from physics, for how mind works are likely to mislead us about the nature and operations of consciousness—particularly if we forget they are metaphors and begin to use them literally. Our language is steeped in metaphors derived from the senses of vision and touch, and these dominate much of the push-pull descriptions of causality in mechanistic physics.

I think it will serve us far better if we move away from the physics envy of "energy talk" and instead develop appropriate "mind talk" when exploring consciousness. When talking about the mind or consciousness, we should use words and ideas that refer to connections through *meaning*, not connections through mechanism. Energy talk about mind fails to account for the most fundamental characteristic of consciousness: its *subjectivity*. The *feeling* of consciousness has no objective, measurable, position in space. It is not even "nonlocal," as some so-called new paradigm theorists often proclaim; it is, rather, *nonlocated*—it is not located in space in any way whatsoever, either as "fields," "vibrations," or "waves."

But I question the "wave model" of mind for another, *evolutionary*, reason. If we claim that beliefs create reality through some wavelike set of interference patterns, then we need to be able to answer the following: What interference pattern of beliefs created reality before the first

Homo sapiens walked the Earth and wondered at the mystery of the stars? Do we accept that other non-human animals have beliefs? Do plants? And what created reality before the first living colony of "infusoria" slithered out of the primordial ooze?

And this brings us to the nub of the matter. I mentioned earlier that we must be careful about what we mean by "belief." Even if we understand beliefs, in some metaphorical sense, to interact in something like the "wave-interference" model just described—we should keep in mind there are beliefs and then there are *beliefs*. Let's look at this more closely.

We should distinguish first between wishes and beliefs, and between conscious and unconscious beliefs. Most of the time we don't even know what we believe. We think we believe this or that, but under closer examination these conscious beliefs are usually riddled with doubt and even contradictory counterbeliefs. For instance, on a few occasions I was sure *"This week* I will win Lotto," but when my numbers didn't come up I could hear the echo of my counterbelief "Who am I kidding? I'll never win a million dollars." Deeper, unconscious beliefs such as this may be closer to the truth of who I believe or fear myself to be. On the "wave model," the first type of belief is a kind of "wishful thinking" low in potency and is easily washed out by the force of stronger, more potent—and at times, self-defeating—beliefs. It is these deeper, unconscious beliefs that mostly create our reality.

HOW DO BELIEFS CREATE REALITY?

Another important distinction is the difference between beliefs about the world—externally directed beliefs—and beliefs about ourselves. The first set concerns our assumptions about the environment in which we are embedded. According to the new paradigm, our beliefs can and do shape the alignment of circumstances we find ourselves in. If I *really* believe I'll find a parking space on a crowded street, then somehow, miraculously or magically, it will be there when I turn the corner.

I choose this example, because it is a nagging exception in my own experience. I have tried it in the past and was sure it worked against chance odds (hard to prove, but *I believed that my belief made a difference*). Mostly, however, I doubt my power to effect such results. I think that even if my beliefs have causal potency to directly affect the physical world, they would be canceled out or reduced to practical insignificance by the potency of the laws of nature, not to mention the staggeringly complex and huge number of competing influences from other people's beliefs. It is not simply a case of "believe it and I'll see it." Many, many other factors are at work.

On the other hand, as stated above, the second class of beliefs—those deep-seated assumptions about myself—*do* have immense impact on how my life turns out. In this case, the potency of beliefs is focused internally, within the system that I consider to be my "self." Within this semi-permeable bubble universe, my deep beliefs can (and I'm sure at times do) dominate the behavior of my system. Here, my beliefs are not competing to nearly the same degree with the bombardment of contradictory and interfering external beliefs from millions, or billions, of other minds. That's what my "boundary" is for (my "skin-encapsulated ego," as the Taoist mystic Alan Watts poetically expressed it). It protects me, to a certain extent, from the pressure of the external web of "non-self," from that infinite nested set of systems I call my environment.

Metaphorically, by a network of internal feedback loops between my thoughts, emotions, and behaviors, my beliefs set up a "signature vibration" within my self-system, and it is this "vibration" that ripples out through my boundary, connecting me to the world outside. Only to the extent that these "vibrations"—call them my behavior or communication, if you like—trigger responses and feedback from the external web of environmental systems do my beliefs influence the reality beyond my skin.

Specifically, for example, if my "vibration" is fear, then I will act in a way that communicates, "I am afraid" to the world around me. People will respond, consciously or unconsciously, to these subliminal messages. And, for whatever reason, it seems that for the most part, people, like strange dogs, are programmed to react negatively at times to the vulnerability of fear. Fear provokes fear or its defense, aggression.

Similarly, my fear will determine how I might behave—and the consequences of that behavior—even in non-interpersonal circumstances. Let's say I'm walking across a bridge that is nothing more than a tree-trunk spanning a deep ravine. My fear may well fulfill my belief that if I step onto that moss-covered log I will slip and crash onto the rocks hundreds of feet below. I may simply choose a different behavior, of course, and stay put in safety (not noticing the boulder about to come unstuck just above my head!).

Beyond the simplistic "You create what you believe," I suspect that there is, after all, an indirect relationship between what I believe and the reality I find myself embedded in. However, it is *indirect*. It is unpredictable and uncertain, and probably non-causal. I cannot know that a specific belief will necessarily determine a specific outcome in the world of external events.

There does seem to be a kind of synchronicity—sometimes—between processes inside my consciousness and events in the world outside (see chapter 7 "Synchronicity-1: Beyond Energy"). But this is not a relationship I have been able to use to any advantage (such as winning Lotto). The best I can do, it seems, is to *engage in letting go*, slip into an alpha brainwave state, and flow with the processes that synchronize internal and external reality. Action through non-action—*wu-wei,* as Taoists sages advised.

LOCATING THE DIAMOND TRUTH

This same process of letting go seems to be necessary for tuning into the deeper levels of beliefs that shape our lives. Beneath the conscious and near-the-surface unconscious wishes and fears, other strata of beliefs run our lives. It takes work—a special kind of work that requires honesty and courage, integrity and authenticity—to excavate the core beliefs that shape our destiny.

For many of us, unfortunately, too many of these core beliefs are negative, and often self-defeating—primal wells of emotional stress, rooted in the existential void created by the rupture in our evolutionary continuum, from the lack of in-arms experience, explored in the previous chapter. These primal stresses erupt from time to time throughout our lives as "aftershocks." We have to uncover these core beliefs if we are ever to liberate ourselves from their destructive power. Only when that work is done are we ready to move even deeper.

At this deeper level, our living organism is a system tingling with purpose and "evolved expectations," a system designed for self-preservation, for reproduction, and, ultimately, for self-transcendence.[2] Beyond our conscious beliefs, beyond even our deepest self-defeating primal beliefs, are what I call our "diamond truths," our *cellular commitments.* These are our innate beliefs, the deep organic programming that underlies our sense of what is "right" for us—what German philosopher Martin Heidegger called our "thrownness," and Jean Liedloff calls our "innate expectations."

And just as each of us is a unique expression of our genetic code, inherited from the ancient flow of evolution, we are each, similarly, a unique expression of our cellular commitments—our "noetic code"— of our innate expectations (Carl Jung's "archetypes," and Aristotle's "entelechy.") These cellular commitments are the burning fuse of purpose that snakes through our lives, always focused on the explosive realization of our full human potential and eventual self-transcendence. Certainly, we all share a great deal of our evolved expectations in common; but we are also shaped by unique twists to our personal psycho-spiritual templates.

Successful psychotherapy, I suspect, is effective when it focuses attention on this aspect of our core nature. This is where the life-affirming aspect of self resides, the self that connects us with the deeper evolutionary continuum of our entire species—and beyond, with all natural systems. Here is where our self connects with Jung's collective unconscious and, ultimately, with the ineffable transpersonal, noetic experience of Self.

However, to call our core cellular commitments "beliefs" robs them of their power. A "belief" seems too static, too rigid, too passive, too cerebral, too self-righteous, and dogmatic. A belief is vulnerable to refutation, and so tends to build up a structure of defenses. I prefer the word "intention." When I intend something I summon up my whole being; it is a creative act. I engage with the world through my intention by creatively projecting something of myself into the ongoing stream of events in which I participate. My intention commits and contributes who I am to the world through my action. And although at times intention may be blocked and frustrated, it cannot be refuted or denied *as long as we continue to recreate it.*

Intention is sourced from the self, and directed outward. It derives its authority and validation from its own creative stance. In contrast, *belief* is validated (or not) by information from the world. Belief tends to freeze the ego that identifies with what it believes. Intention, on the other hand, is an expression of who we are *into* the world. It expresses our purpose and is more open to feedback than any belief we may hold. In my experience, the interaction between intention and feedback results in learning—the intending self adapts.

On the other hand, interaction between belief and the world typically leads to rationalizations and other psychological defense mechanisms to protect the presumed integrity of the ego that holds the belief. Think of how you sometimes feel threatened, as though your life or soul depended on it, when some cherished belief is challenged. Do you believe in God, in life after death, in the righteousness of your nation, in the laws of science, in the sanctity of marriage, in abortion, in the right to life, in the death penalty. . . ? What happens to your sense of self if someone rigorously challenges such a belief? Is your first instinct to openly accept the challenge with a willingness to adapt your belief, or is it more likely to be an almost-reflexive defensive search for an even stronger argument to support your cherished belief?

Like choice, intention is a free existential creative act, a pouring out of the self into the world, contributing to the unfolding of reality. Belief is a fixed way of holding reality.

I also prefer "intention" rather than "belief" because it allows us to extend the metaphorical wave-model of creation back beyond the emergence of human beings. As concepts derived from language and reason, beliefs did not exist before there were human minds to concoct them. But this is not the case with intention. As I argued in *Radical Nature,* there is an ordering principle, a kind of mind, at play in nature at every level of existence—a co-creating complement to the chaos-inducing principle of entropy. This proto-psychism is consciousness in its most basic state—what philosopher Alfred North Whitehead called "prehension," an elementary awareness that directs the motions of subatomic particles and atoms in their interactions.[3]

Intention, then, some degree of directional awareness, is active throughout the entire span of evolution, from the simplest quantum entities to the largest superclusters of galaxies and the most complex nervous systems and brains. This view allows for the existence and evolution of the world long before the arrival of thinking beings who could believe in it or believe in anything about it. It also allows us to trace the long lineage or continuum of intentions, of innate expectations, way back to the origins of the universe.

We are, therefore, embedded in infinite layers of intentions that have shaped the long cosmic journey of our ancestral forms that led to us. We carry these purposes in our psychic templates as well as in our genes, and they spell out for us—through that mysterious system of feedback loops between evolved expectations and learned experiences—the unique phenomenon we call our "self." These purposes are our embedded truths, our cellular (and our pre-organic) commitments that pull us through life—our "noetic code"—that connect us with the grand play of evolution here on our planet for four billion years, with the universe for around fourteen billion years, and with the cosmos for eternity and, perhaps, beyond. Intention is our creative contribution to the unforced, natural expression of these deep, embedded innate purposes common to all life, planet, universe, and cosmos. And in this sense, both our purposes and intentions transcend, while including, individual egoic identities.

As long as I'm aware that when I use the word "belief" (as in "core belief") to include this sense of intentionality, then I can use "belief" as a first-cousin synonym for intention. I mean it as a statement of commitment and action directed at transforming my relationship with the world, and not as a statement *about the world as it is*. For example, I could translate the phrases "cellular commitments" or "innate expectations" to mean *personal credo*—the evolutionary fuel that fires all individuals, giving us our sense of uniqueness, and the source of who we ultimately believe ourselves to be.

But there is a transpersonal credo, too—an archetypal vision that transcends any single individual purpose. For me, the most evocative expression of this transpersonal credo is captured in lines from a poem popular in the late Sixties and early Seventies: *Desiderata*. They sound a little dated now, even a little embarrassing to quote, but they are the closest I have seen to a philosopher's prayer:

> *You are a child of the universe;*
> *no less than the trees and the stars,*
> *you have a right to be here.*
> *And whether or not it is clear to you,*
> *no doubt the universe is unfolding as it should.*
> *Therefore be at peace with God,*
> *whatever you conceive [him/her/it] to be.*
> *And whatever your labors and aspirations,*
> *in the noisy confusion of life*
> *keep peace with your soul.*[4]
>
> —MAX EHRMANN

In this chapter, we have explored the potency of intention as a way to get a handle on how our "core beliefs," or "personal paradigms," contribute not only to understanding reality, but to seeing deeper into how reality actually unfolds. You will have noticed that the roots of these deep beliefs or "cellular commitments" reach back far beyond the evolutionary emergence in humans of reason or intellect. Without downplaying the importance or value of reason, we will continue in the next chapter to look more closely at the relationship between belief and experience, and see how we may begin, as individuals and as a culture, to move beyond an overreliance on intellect, reason, and belief systems. We will open to a wider, richer spectrum of knowing—paying particular attention to the innate wisdom of feelings in the body.

5

Transformation

Experience Beyond Belief

"I believe in God, the Father Almighty, Creator of Heaven and Earth. . . ." I grew up repeating the Apostles' Creed, over and over during prayer time at school and at home. Perhaps part of the purpose of prayer, like a mantra, is to induce an altered state of consciousness, for prayer certainly seems to have a hypnotic quality to it. In any case, as a youngster I found myself saying these words, without thinking, and without really having a clue about the meaning of my declaration. I was saying, "I believe" when in fact what I really should have said was "*They* believe in God, etc. . ."—"they" meaning the Church, the Apostles, my teachers, my parents, whomever. But not me; it was not my belief. When I first started uttering such phrases, I was far too young to know what belief was or whether I even had any worth proclaiming.

After many years hearing myself repeat the Apostles' Creed, *I came to believe that this is what I believed.* That distinction is important. It points to some very significant and fundamental aspects of what we mean by "belief." First and foremost, it reveals what I call the *"layering of belief"*—the fact that when we examine our beliefs closely we find that they are not atomistic units we can switch on or off independently at will. They are nested, interconnected systems of ideas, forming conceptual structures—our personal and collective paradigms.

These cognitive constructs shape our experience of the world and, therefore, hold our reality in place. This is why beliefs are often so difficult to dislodge, no matter how inaccurate, inappropriate, or even damaging they may be.

Notice, also, that this type of belief *was based on what others believed*. I came to believe as I did because authority figures told me I should, because *they* wanted me to believe it. Belief, then, was a function of *trust* and, as such, indistinguishable from what I later came to recognize as *faith*. People in authority had a vested interest in propagating their belief system. The more people shared their worldview, the more secure they felt, and the more stable their cognitive edifice became. Of course, within that structure, the "authorities" held positions of power and influence they wanted to preserve. By getting new recruits like me at such an early age they were bolstering up their positions in the hierarchy.

Now, all of this was invisible to me. I was born into it, steeped in my culture's belief system as deeply as any fish caught in invisible ocean currents. My beliefs were not my own; I had inherited them. Like everyone else, I was instantly a pawn in the paradigm. The "authorities" were not just parents, teachers, and church clergy; they included also more remote institutions such as political and economic ideologies, and the scientific establishment. What they all had in common, and what became part of the air that I breathed, was a Greco-Judeo-Christian philosophical heritage. Behind it all was the overarching notion of "The Creator" who started it all.

Later, as I became aware of the conflicts between the teachings of the Church and of science, inconsistencies in the fabric of the cultural belief system appeared. As these scratches and cracks accumulated, they brought the grain of the "transparent" cultural belief system into sharper relief. For the first time, I *noticed* I was swimming in a sea of beliefs, and I began to ask questions.

I wanted to find out which of the two competing belief systems—religion or science—was right. Even though my high school, Terenure College, was run by Carmelite priests, as I moved through the educational system I soon realized that the spoils and honors of the battle were going to science. Religion might still be a force to reckon with in Catholic Ireland, but the nation itself was steeped in the wider currents of Western culture, where science ruled.

For roughly three hundred years, science has been the primary shaper of the Western worldview. Through its technological applications, science has permeated every aspect of our society, and its successes have gained it the status of final arbiter of what is true, workable, and real. Science tells us what we ought to know—even if it doesn't tell us how we ought to live.

By the time I was sixteen or seventeen, I no longer took my cues from religion, I no longer believed in "God, the Father Almighty, Creator of Heaven and Earth." I had switched allegiances, my new authorities were the high priests of science—people like Newton, Darwin, Freud, and Einstein. Evolution, as noted, particularly caught my attention and swept me along in its grand flow.

I was awed at the intellectual spectacle of an evolutionary panorama connecting humans and animals, stretching all the way back beyond bacteria and the protists to some primordial bubbling brew of prebiotic molecules. And it didn't end there. These chemicals themselves were the result of an even greater evolutionary journey among the stars. In fiery plasma laboratories at the heart of every sun, gravity (and god-knows-what other forces) contrived to cook the simpler elements of hydrogen and helium and produced more complex atoms, such as carbon and nitrogen, which form the backbone of living matter.

It was truly an awesome and captivating picture. And nowhere did it speak of gods or holy ghosts. Matter, blind and random, following a mind-boggling series of purposeless interactions, pulled itself up by its chemical shoelaces over unimaginable eons of time and, through sheer trial and error and a great deal of chance, managed to produce living things that one day would turn around and contemplate this vast evolutionary spectacle. As soon as the primordial cosmic dust had climbed the spiral of matter to reach the bright lights of consciousness, the universe looked back and beheld itself: "Oh my! Did I really do *that?*"

Yes, I was captivated by this story, much more so than by the myth of Genesis that I quickly outgrew. The universe was now populated with new gods, such as Newton's laws of motion, the laws of thermodynamics and electromagnetism, relativity and quantum theories, and the principle of natural selection. I was a convert at the altar of science.

But in the back of my mind, whenever I stopped to listen, there was an insistent buzzing. I noticed that as I tried to connect my beliefs in science into a coherent picture of the world, there would often be a sort of crackling, as if oppositely charged beliefs were short-circuiting. It was irritating. I couldn't get it out of my mind and I began to grow suspicious of the narrative of science whenever this electric flash sparked between incompatible beliefs. Something smelled funny. Something didn't fit.

As I pushed farther back along the evolutionary track, back beyond the primordial cosmic gases, the big question always came bouncing up: Where did all this "stuff" come from in the first place? The stories of modern cosmology varied, but the most popular took its cue from Einstein's general theory of relativity. The Hubble red shift indicated that the universe is expanding, and this implied that, at one time, somewhere around fourteen billion years ago, the whole cosmos was squeezed into a particle the size of a proton. This cosmic egg exploded due to internal instabilities and the universe began with a big bang.

Without a doubt, this was a fascinating story to a young mind hot on the trail of origins. But it inevitably led to the question "What caused the Big Bang?" or "Where did the primordial particle or singularity come from?" Here, of course, we meet science at the end of its tether. Science, by its own definition, can say nothing about unique events and, besides, inside that putative cosmic particle, space and time are shredded beyond meaning, the laws of physics break down, and there is nothing scientific left to be said. Once again, science and religion meet head on. Science can no longer ignore the question of creation and, therefore, of a creator. As Whitehead so aptly put it: "Science suggested a cosmology; and whatever suggests a cosmology suggests a religion."

At that cosmic singularity, I was back where I started, with a new twist to my credo: "I believe in the Big Bang, the almighty explosion, creator of Heaven and Earth." In truth, I didn't know what to believe anymore, and I stopped saying prayers and offering intellectual allegiance to any form of creator—physical or divine. I ceased reciting my mantras and credos and was left dangling in an enigma.

LIVING INSIDE A QUESTION

And that was my first clue. I had followed this thread of belief as far back as it would take me, and what I found at the end of the line, at the ultimate edge of evolution, was a mystery. Belief had run aground and left me with a question. This was a shift for me. Instead of reciting my credo-mantra, instead of turning to authorities for the final word, I found myself living in the belly of a question. With no solution, all I could do was *live* the question, *be* the question. And here a new crack in my epistemology opened up. Here was an invitation to a different way of knowing. Here I glimpsed for the first time a whole new vista of knowledge—based not on authority, not on belief, but on *experience*.

This was another turning point.

I was in my early twenties, and I asked: What is this "experience" that is leading me in a new direction? Since, by then, science had become my touchstone to reality, I turned to physics, biology, and psychology to look for clues to the phenomena of experience and consciousness. Of these three, the most natural place to look, I assumed, would be psychology, and as implied earlier, I was soon relieved of that illusion. Until relatively recently, psychology was about behavior and, for the most part, the behavior of rats and pigeons. Mind or consciousness, this science was telling me, was not a proper subject for research because it was too subjective. Science, on the other hand, was nothing if not *objective*. . . . Right.

In other words, the science of psychology (the very science that means the study of the mind or soul) was telling me that, at best, my inner experience didn't count—and, at worst, it was just an illusion. This was deeply unsatisfactory.

So I turned to neuroscience to see what light *it* could throw on the question of consciousness. Neurophysiology was pretty much an ally of behaviorism, and it tried to tell me that consciousness was just an epiphenomenon—nothing but an impotent by-product of the brain. According to this view, mind is what the brain *does*, it has no substantive existence of its own. The "ghost in the machine" was reduced to nothing more significant than a hiss escaping from a steam engine. That did not sit well with me, either.

Next I turned to evolutionary biology. Whatever else might be going on in the world, the one thing I was most convinced of was the reality of my own experience. Among all the facts and theories of science, consciousness stood out like a shining beacon. It didn't fit in, yet it was the single most immediate datum of knowledge that I had. To my mind, consciousness was undeniable. If thinking and intellectual exploration needed a "given" to start off from, this was it. I figured that evolution might be able to show how consciousness came to be in the world.

As I scoured the literature looking for clues to where consciousness first arose in evolution, I noticed something very startling. Not only had psychology failed to address the subject matter essential to its science, *biology, also, failed to account for the origin or nature of life.* Science, in other words, could not fit either life or consciousness into its worldview. Together with matter, life and consciousness formed a triad of the most prominent features of existence calling for explanation and understanding. Science was wide of the mark on two counts. This didn't do much to reassure a recently committed, but curious, convert that, by pursuing science, I was on the right track.

Having assessed the evidence in evolution for the origin of consciousness, I discovered there was no point in the process where we could say, "Here, this is where mind begins." I concluded, therefore, that since consciousness undeniably exists in the universe today, it must *always* have been here, in one form or another. And with that, I took my first step on the long road to scientific and philosophical "heresy." (The second and decisive step in my heretical journey happened, as mentioned earlier in this book, shortly after I turned forty, when I revisited and embraced the views of panpsychism as espoused by Alfred North Whitehead.)

Anyway, at this early, questioning phase, science had failed me in two areas: (a) the origin of life and consciousness and (b) knowledge about experience and consciousness itself. If religion, and now science, had failed me, where could I turn to gain access to such knowledge? By this time, I had been paying enough attention to my own experience— for example, experimenting with different techniques for achieving altered states of consciousness—that I knew where I needed to look: beyond belief, beyond external authorities, to the authority of my own internal experience. But I didn't jettison my trust in science and the scientific method. I wanted to find a way to integrate or harmonize experience and scientific experimentation, to discover a way for the two to complement each other.

At this point, I began to dig deeper, beyond the belief structures of science, and started questioning its metaphysical foundations. Soon enough, I discovered an irony, if not a paradox, lurking at the heart of science. Beginning as a reaction to the superstition and authority of the medieval Church, science had introduced a new method for gaining knowledge, based on the evidence of data *experienced through the senses*. In other words, science turned away from authority and revealed knowledge to facts perceived by the senses—to *empirical knowledge*.

However, the paradox is that in its search for empirical knowledge, science has excluded from investigation—even from its picture of the world—the very basis by which scientists know what they know: their own experience. They have exorcized mind from their world picture, so it should come as no surprise that when they look for any signs of consciousness in science, it is nowhere to be seen. By definition, mind is outside looking on, or else it doesn't exist.

FROM AUTHORITY TO EXPERIENCE

Modern science emerged when naturalists and philosophers began to challenge the metaphysic of belief based on expert testimony. Instead of relying on the authority of Aristotle, St. Augustine, Thomas Aquinas, and the Church fathers, the new approach to knowledge in the seventeenth century, proclaimed by Francis Bacon in England and René Descartes in France, established sense experience and reason, respectively, as the criteria and methods for achieving knowledge. The scientific method was born from this union. And from this, a new form of belief arose. Instead of faith, which was relied upon by religion to anchor belief, science now honored a new god, that of objective, rational, sensory-based empiricism. The "empirical method" had arrived. From then on, belief would have to be validated by scientific evidence or else it would be discarded.

The irony is that the methodology of science has been so successful at delivering knowledge of the material world through a process of progressive specialization, compartmentalization, and fragmentation that ordinary people once again must turn to scientific "authorities" to tell them about matter and energy, and life and human behavior. In this sense, belief in the knowledge of science must also be based on trust. Scientific knowledge then becomes, for the masses, a matter of faith. If I talk of atoms, electrons, and photons, or of genes, DNA, and natural selection, or of ids, and operands, I must trust in the accuracy, honesty, and integrity of others to communicate to me the results of their work based on *their* experience in *their* experiments, for I have never experienced any of these entities, even indirectly. It is all secondhand knowledge to me. I take my science on faith, because the stories seem to fit. But I no longer *believe* them— not like I believe I am breathing.

And it is not just lay people who substitute faith for knowledge in science. Scientists, too, share this "unscientific" faith because a scientist is only a scientist within his or her own specialized field. With regard to physics, for instance, a biologist is just as much a layperson as an art teacher, priest, factory worker, or journalist would be.

If pressed on this, many scientists will openly admit that they take the other guy's science on trust and will point out that their trust is based on a belief in the efficacy of the scientific method. At this point the issue begins to get really interesting, contentious, and troublesome—because now the questioning must focus not on the scientific data, not on the theories, not even on the scientific method itself, but on the *metaphysical assumptions* underlying the whole edifice of science. This is where things get tricky, this is where many scientists tend to switch off, get confused, get excited, get defensive, and even occasionally get hostile. Whitehead noted: "Science repudiates philosophy. In other words, it has never cared to justify its truth or explain its meaning."

At this level of questioning, the very foundations of science are being scrutinized, and if they are found wanting, the whole edifice may come crashing down. Understandably, this can be threatening to people who have invested whole careers in a particular way of doing science. When a scientist's ego is enmeshed, even identified, with the structure of his or her science, the scientist will do almost anything to protect it. "Knowledge" gets redefined—confined to facts, evidence, or theories that fit the preferred metaphysical structure.

FROM SCIENCE TO *SCIENTIA*

To understand the significance of this redefinition of knowledge, we need to move deeper into our investigation of epistemology—the study of *how* we know what we know. What does it mean, for example, to say that any particular piece of information is scientific? The word "science" comes from the Latin *scientia,* which means "knowledge." It is a relatively recent addition to our vocabulary and we would do well to examine its implications.

We could, for instance, reexamine the foundations of science to see if it can and does yield the sort of information that we need to live lives rich in meaning, quality, and value. If science cannot meet this task, we are entitled to ask whether it deserves so dominant a place in our society, and whether it needs to be revised or expanded.

Science as currently practiced is failing us because it does not address the realm of inner experience, nor does it question the methodology that removes the observer's consciousness from the world being observed (see chapter 9, "*Knowing-1:* Shafts of Wisdom").[1]

To develop a true science of inner experience, of consciousness—a science of the soul—we need a radical revision of the epistemology underlying science. We begin by asking, "How does consciousness know what it knows?" "How can consciousness know itself?" We can go further and ask: "How does consciousness work in the world?" The fact of our own experience, the undeniable existence of consciousness, almost compels us to engage in this task.

In pursuing such questions, we will find ourselves overturning one of the very cornerstones of modern science: the *fundamental metaphysical assumption of universal physical causality*—the idea that all events everywhere and at all times in the universe are caused exclusively by physical processes.

The new epistemology must open the way for scientific exploration of phenomena relating to consciousness and inner experience. Until now, the metaphysical assumption of physicalism—that everything in the universe is ultimately made up of physical stuff—along with the methodology of objectivity and replicability, have prevented science from investigating mind.

Consciousness has been excluded from science on two major counts: First, *subjective experience* does not meet the requirement for valid scientific data and analysis because it is not public, physical, or objective, and therefore cannot be measured. Second, the assumption of universal physical causation precludes the possibility of *volition or freewill*—of consciousness having any causal agency, of intention having any effect whatsoever on the course of events in the world. Both of these scientific limitations fly in the face of our daily experience.

TRANSFORMATIONAL SCIENCE

In our quest to explore the basis of knowledge and belief, then, we encounter a dramatic gap between the beliefs of science and our own experience. We encounter, also, the centuries-old conflict between religious and scientific worldviews. Although some questions remain exclusive to each camp—for instance, science has nothing to say about the nature of God, and neither religion nor theology has anything to contribute to the study of, for instance, chemical bonds—areas of overlap emerge when we allow consciousness a place within science.

For example, both religion and science would be interested in the phenomena of meaningful coincidences, such as synchronicities, miracles, healing effects following intentional prayer, the sense of "second sight" or a "guardian angel" that seems to forewarn of danger, and other psychic phenomena. In addition, both science and religion would be interested in the phenomenon of states of consciousness, such as mystical or religious experiences, or "alternative realities."

Both science and religion also share a common interest in questions concerning the origin of the universe and the evolution or creation of life and human beings. These three areas will require agreement from science and religion if we are ever to develop a *scientia,* a form of science based on what William James called "radical empiricism"—leaving out nothing that falls within the range of human experience, and excluding anything that falls outside it.

Such a science would be bigger than knowledge-as-final-truth. Like a religion, or spirituality, based on experience rather than on the authority of dogma, the knowledge of this new science would also be beyond belief. Neither science nor religion, in this new worldview, would lay claim to ultimate truth, or be the ultimate arbiter of real knowledge. In the mutual co-causality of a self-organizing universe, truth will always be in flux, and knowledge likewise needs to evolve in phases. With this approach, we would have a much broader base of knowledge involving all four epistemological "gifts": an understanding of physical determinism (combining the Philosopher's Gift of reason and the Scientist's Gift of empirical observation and method); an appreciation of psychophysical synchronicities (the Shaman's Gift of participatory feeling); as well as a form of "knowing-through-being" involving acts of creative intentionality and the grace of communion (the Mystic's Gift of sacred silence and spiritual practice).

As long as we restrict knowledge to a combination of reason and sensory empiricism, we will remain trapped in the "catch-22" at the heart of science. *In order to have confidence in the scientific view of reality, we need an adequate epistemology. But an adequate epistemology implies a prior understanding of the mental processes underlying observation, and for that we need a scientific epistemology.*

Breaking out of this circular predicament will require a much more open and participatory approach to scientific research—especially when the object of exploration is consciousness itself. Indeed, investigators of consciousness need to be willing to be transformed, to be open to *metanoia*—a transformation in experience, in their sense of who they are, the nature of the world, and the relationship between the two.

It is important to acknowledge the nature of this transformational shift and its impact on epistemology—on the relationship between the knower and the known. The central issue in any rigorous investigation of consciousness concerns a shift from *concept-based epistemology*—models and metaphors derived from cognitive and intellectual modes of thought—to *more experiential modes of knowing*. Without this shift, it will be "business as usual" in science, albeit with new sets of concepts and new models, and we will remain stuck in the old concept-based epistemology—missing the essential point of consciousness study.

The nature of this transformation shifts epistemological exploration to a different level. It involves a different kind of knowing, a different way of knowing. It arises from knowledge rooted in the *being* of the investigator, dissolving the usual distinctions between knowledge and the knower. It is not knowledge as usually conceived in science, consisting of discrete facts resulting from precise measurements of selected variables. Neither is it conceptual or sensory knowledge. Furthermore, as an *experience,* it is not communicable solely through the typical media of words, formulas, mathematical symbols, and other images. Any such description is, at best, a metaphor or model of the experience, not the experience itself. Yet a skilled and trained scientist or teacher would be able to communicate the experience to students prepared and willing to undergo a transformational experience themselves.

Such an approach can break through the circularity of requiring a prior epistemological methodology in order to explore or develop an epistemology of consciousness. It lifts the exploration out of the closed-circuit of concepts in the mind of an observer observing the process of observation in order to know how he or she knows. When the knower and the knowledge become indistinguishable in the transformative crucible of experience, the conceptual loop is short-circuited and a new kind of knowledge emerges in lived experience.

If at this point it sounds like we are talking religion or spirituality as much as science or philosophy that is because the new epistemology we are indicating transcends that distinction when it comes to an investigation of consciousness. However, we are not simply talking religion any more than we are simply talking science. We are taking an approach to knowledge that combines a transformation in consciousness ("religious" or spiritual experience) with rigorous empirical investigation, reporting, and testing (scientific methodology). As always, the experience of consciousness itself will be ineffable (whether gained through religious or scientific practice); but that does not and should not exclude it from the domain of scientific investigation.

The transformation in experience that the scientist undergoes while exploring consciousness is essential for the kind of direct and deep insight required to gain knowledge of the psyche. Without it, the scientist would be blind to the phenomena and processes of our "inner worlds." Such "inner vision" is the starting point—the *sine qua non*—of consciousness science. It is the source of data that, later, the scientist can build into a communicable model. Like all abstract concepts and models, neither the recipe nor the menu is ever the experience of the meal. The model is not the reality, but it enables scientists to agree on translatable elements of the experience, and to communicate them in ways that may be further tested and explored.

However, as in any other scientific activity, there comes a point when, no matter how sophisticated, the theory must be tested empirically if it is not to remain an intellectual game. Consequently, the scientific process of data gathering, hypothesis and model formation, and empirical testing applies equally to investigations of consciousness as it does in any other area of science. The work of a theoretical particle physicist requires years of training to know how to devise experiments to test, say, theories of quarks or superstrings. Likewise, the work of the consciousness theorist requires dedicated and lengthy training in psycho-spiritual discipline in order to test conceptual models of consciousness against the sharp edge of direct experience.

TOWARD AN OPEN PARADIGM

The purpose of this reinvestigation of the epistemological basis of science is not to hasten the advent of a new paradigm. Such a shift would only displace the problem. It would mean substituting one set of beliefs (physical causality, reductionism, objectivity, determinism) for another set of beliefs (co-causality, synchronicity, holism, subjectivism, self-organizing principles). Even if the new paradigm were an improvement on the old, it would still confine us to a blinkered view of the world.

The aim of this work is to create epistemological openings for a multiplicity of worldviews. This does not mean opening the floodgates to an undisciplined hodgepodge of ideas and flights of fancy. I am not advocating "smorgasbord epistemology." The point is to create an open-ended paradigm unanchored within the confines of any *one* conceptual system, while being accessible to *all*.

The "open paradigm" (or "meta paradigm," as Peter Russell calls it) would rigorously and continually reexamine—*through direct experience*—its metaphysical underpinnings and, whenever possible, uproot any that seemed to be settling into a system of fixed beliefs. The aim of such an open paradigm would be to transcend all belief systems, while not negating any. It would recognize that anyone who engages the question "How does consciousness know itself?" must source the vitality and growth of their knowledge in *experience,* and move beyond the authority of belief. The open paradigm, then, is not a matter of any particular set of concepts—it is about experience beyond belief.

Next, we will focus on the topic of experience itself, and lay a foundation for the difficult task of exploring consciousness through words and ideas. We will find out how to avoid the greatest pitfall in this work by clarifying the different meanings people use when talking about "consciousness."

Part 2
Ways of Knowing

6

Meanings

Clarifying Consciousness

Let's begin with a simple equation—straight out of "Philosophy 101 for Dummies" (or from "Consciousness for Zombies"). I know I promised that this book would be free of mathematical formulas and equations, but this really is a *very simple* equation. It's the starting place for my philosophy—I'd even be bold enough to say it's the starting point for all philosophy.

If you want to know what consciousness is and how it fits into the physical universe this is where to begin:

The world = things + experiences of things.

Now that wasn't difficult, was it? That's the whole shebang, all it takes to make a world. That simple equation covers everything. Think about it. Is anything left out? I don't think so. If I were a god and my task was to create a universe, that's where I'd begin. Those are the only two ingredients I'd need: "things" plus "experiences" of those things. The "things" are physical objects made of matter and energy (such as stones and trees, thunder and lightning, houses and freeways, blood and bones) and experiences are what *know* those things.

If I wanted only a "zombie world," I'd just create things, period—with no beings to experience them. But that would be a very boring universe. If, however, I wanted a world that would keep me on my toes, I'd add in beings that could experience the things I'd created, and who could exercise free will. Otherwise, what would be the point?

Okay, so far so good. We've got *things* and *experiences*. But what kinds of things? Well to make my creation interesting I'd make *physical* and *nonphysical* objects—those kinds of things. Physical objects would be all those things made of matter or energy—from quarks to quasars, and everything in between. Examples of nonphysical objects would be mental contents (such as ideas, feelings, intentions). Are there any other kinds of things? I don't think so. That covers it for things. (Of course, by "things" I really mean "events"—processes.)

What about experiences? If things are objects (physical and nonphysical), what are experiences? Quite simply, experiences are what *know* the objects or events. So now we have a world of objects and experiencers—in short, *objects* and *subjects*. Objects are what we know. Subjects (that's us) are what do the knowing.

If you ever wanted to know what consciousness is, now you do. Consciousness is what knows or feels or is aware—of anything. Consciousness is what *knows*. It's what feels the flow of energy; it's what knows there's any energy at all.

The universe is full of energy flows, vortices, and vibrations—in a glorious profusion of forms and manifestations. But without consciousness, all this would be forever unknown and unfelt. Only because of consciousness can the flow of energy be felt, known, and purposely directed. Therefore, consciousness is the ability that matter/energy has to feel, know, and direct itself. It's that simple.

Next question . . . .

Well, perhaps it's not quite as simple as all that. But where else would you start? In my work as a philosophy teacher, I've seen how easy it is for people to become very confused about the nature of consciousness and its relationship to energy, to the physical world. This simple equation is one way I found to clarify what consciousness is and what it isn't; and it's not a form of energy. *Things* are made of energy. Consciousness is what *knows* or *feels* those things.

If it really is that simple, why all the fuss and confusion? Why book after book trying to explain what consciousness is? Well, part of the difficulty is that words are just not up to the task. We cannot catch consciousness with a net of language. Perhaps we can catch its shadows, its echoes, its afterimages, maybe even its scent . . . but consciousness itself, ultimately, is an experience beyond words. Best to be quiet, and silently experience it. I won't argue with that. But I have a book to write, and books require words; as a philosopher they are the tools of my trade. With this proviso, let's approach our quarry from a different perspective.

FISHING FOR CONSCIOUSNESS

Like all experience, but even more so, consciousness is ineffable. As soon as we begin to talk about it, it slides from our grasp like a slippery fish. Yet, using the net of language, we can go fishing . . . and with diligence, we may leave with something to fry (or to throw back).[1]

The word "consciousness" was first used in European philosophy by John Locke in the seventeenth century, and since then the concept has undergone radical evolution. Today, its meanings are multiple, and a great source of confusion in both academic debate and ordinary conversation. Such confusion and misunderstanding hamper clarity and progress in consciousness studies—as well as in philosophy of mind, psychology, phenomenology, epistemology, and ontology. But the confusion can be avoided—or at least significantly minimized—if we pay attention to how we use the term.

In the pages ahead, we will cover some well-worn ground as we survey different perspectives on consciousness. And as we move ahead, we should always keep in mind that beyond our explorations of language and ideas *about* consciousness, our venture will produce little but empty abstractions unless we also remember to pay attention to our own *lived* consciousness—unless we remember that we are also explorers probing our own inner world of direct experience . . . beyond belief.

When we try to define consciousness, we become like one of those figures walking on a paradoxical Escher stairway: While it seems we are getting down to basics, we always end up back where we began. When Güven Güzeldere, at Stanford University, turned to the *Oxford English Dictionary* *(OED)* for help with a definition, he found himself chasing his tail:

Starting with consciousness as an *explanandum* [what is to be explained] and following a lexical path of definitions from consciousness to perceptions, to awareness, to feelings, or to internal knowledge, one eventually finds oneself back with a definition that relies on "consciousness" as an *explanans* [an explanation].[2]

In other words, we need the concept of consciousness to explain consciousness—which, of course, explains nothing very much. Consciousness is . . . well . . . it is *consciousness!* With full-frontal tautologies like this we may well be excused for giving up any attempt at defining consciousness, and rest content simply with the unspoken *experience* itself. But then we would be very poor scholars of consciousness. Sitting in silence at home or in class, in the lab or in church, and moving deeper into the experiential mystery of consciousness— enlightening though that project may be—will not produce sufficient clarity for thinking or talking or for reading or writing about consciousness. If we wish to talk or write about consciousness, we need to get clear on the meanings of the words and concepts we use.

But we won't get stuck in *definitions.* Instead, as explorers, we will examine different uses and *meanings* of consciousness throughout history, and aim for a clearer and more coherent understanding of the kinds of pitfalls and dead-ends we are likely to meet along the way. We will work to create a map, signposting the lie of the land, and with this map in hand, we can hope to negotiate and navigate our way around the conceptual obstacles that inevitably confront us in the study of consciousness. Most of all, we will be on the lookout for distinctions in meanings to help orient our search.

In this chapter we will explore consciousness from two conceptual perspectives: The first will be an attempt to identify the core issue (or philosophical problem) regarding the nature of consciousness; the second will address different varieties of consciousness.

We will examine various meanings of "consciousness" and allied terms—such as "experience," "mind," "awareness," "intention," and "attention." (Some of the following meanings may seem familiar to readers of *Radical Nature.* I deliberately repeat them here because they serve as useful reminders of how important it is to be as precise as we can in our use of language when discussing consciousness. In my experience with thousands of students and conference audiences, it is clear that people need to hear these ideas and distinctions many times before they sink in.)

"ENERGY *FLOWS*. CONSCIOUSNESS *KNOWS*."

Because the word "consciousness" is notoriously difficult to define and is frequently a source of misunderstanding, it is important to clarify some of its basic meanings. The following will include both a simple "outsider's" and a more technical "insider's" clarification. (By "outsider," I mean someone relatively unfamiliar with the field of consciousness studies. By "insider," I mean someone who has thought about and has read material concerned with this field.)

Outsider's simple meaning. Back to our simple equation: The world (everything that exists) consists of physical energy and non-physical consciousness. Or, to reiterate what I stated earlier, the world equals things and experiences of those things. It's what philosophers mean when they tell us the world consists of "objects" and "subjects." Objects are made of energy or matter; subjects experience the energy and matter.

So, the world is made of "stuff"—matter-energy. Mind or consciousness is what knows, feels, or thinks about the "stuff." Consciousness is what *feels* the flow of energy through our bodies; consciousness is what *knows* there is any energy at all.

I like to help my students grasp fundamental points in philosophy by catching the essence of key ideas in what I call "bumper stickers"— so I tell them that at its deepest level, the world is made up of matter and mind, or energy and consciousness. Here's the bumper sticker that says it all: *"Energy flows. Consciousness knows."* Everything that exists is made of some kind of energy, and energy is always dynamic, always in flux, flowing from one part of the universe to another. But in addition to the objective "things" that flow, there is the subject that *knows*, or feels or experiences those things—that's consciousness.

Consciousness, therefore, is what enables us to feel, think, know, intend, attend, perceive, choose, and create . . . . It is the source of all meaning, value, and purpose in our lives and in the world. It is "interior," it is what enables us to feel and know who we are inside—distinct from our external, physical bodies.

Now let's go a little deeper, and examine two important, though different, meanings from an "insider's" perspective.

Insider's technical meaning. For some people, "consciousness" means more or less being awake, alert, aroused, aware—or, simply, being *conscious* as distinct from being *unconscious*. This is the psychological-psychoanalytical meaning. It is the kind of distinction we each encounter every morning—the difference between being asleep and waking up. But if we use this meaning, how do we account for the difference between a sleeping person and, say, a rock (or a dead person)? It doesn't seem sufficient to say that both the sleeping person and the rock are unconscious in the same way. While it is true that neither the sleeping person nor the rock is awake, it is not true to say that both lack all psychic or sentient capacity. The sleeping person is unconscious, but the rock is *non*-conscious. The unconscious person's body still responds to stimuli, it still senses and feels—it still has a psychic life—but the rock does not. (See appendix 5, "The Philosopher's Stone," for a discussion about whether rocks have consciousness.)

In short, then, being unconscious is not the same as being non-conscious. Being unconscious, our lives can still teem with sensations, imagery, and dreams. Unconsciousness, therefore, has a form of consciousness of its own; a form of consciousness never available to a non-conscious entity such as a rock. Psychological consciousness, therefore, is merely one variety (being awake) of a much broader and richer spectrum of consciousness.

Confusion about consciousness among those already engaged in its study often arises because people use the word to mean different things. Let's look more closely, then, at the distinction that helps avoid what is probably the most common confusion whenever two or more people come together to discuss "consciousness"—the distinction between the *philosophical* (or ontological) and the *psychological* (or psychoanalytic) meanings of consciousness.

Switched-on Consciousness

Philosophical meaning. Here "consciousness" is used to mean an aspect of reality radically distinct from "*non*-consciousness." Non-consciousness is the total absence of any experience, subjectivity, sentience, feeling, or mentality of any kind. The lights are totally out. There's nobody home. Examples often used to illustrate non-consciousness are objects such as tables, thermostats, computers, or rocks. In contrast, any entity that is a *subject*—that feels its own being—possesses consciousness. "Consciousness," in this sense, means the basic, raw capacity for sentience, feeling, experience, subjectivity, self-agency, intention, or knowing of any kind whatsoever. It *feels like something* to be a being with consciousness. The "lights" are on, there's somebody home.

Psychological meaning. In this case, "consciousness" is used to mean a state of awareness contrasted with the "*un*conscious"—for example, being awake and alert instead of being asleep or dreaming. Here, the light of experience is always on, though the luminosity may vary from very dim to glaring brightness—ranging from being psychologically "asleep" to full spiritual awakening. Even the psychological unconscious has something psychic or mental going on. To be unconscious is still to be sentient (worms and sleeping people still feel), whereas to be non-conscious is not (rocks and computers do not feel).

Clearly, "philosophical consciousness" is more fundamental because *no* form of psychological consciousness would be possible (asleep or awake) without at least some trace of philosophical consciousness being present. Examples often used to illustrate being unconscious include sleeping, dreaming, a coma, and may include the normal living state of creatures such as worms, starfish, and plants. In contrast, psychological consciousness typically involves phenomena such as cognition, perception, emotion, or volition.

And just to confuse things, a third meaning of "consciousness" is often popular in New Age circles:

Spiritual meaning. Here, "consciousness" is used to indicate a "higher" or "more developed" or "more aware" state beyond the ordinary awareness of day-to-day psychological consciousness. Phrases such as "we strive to be conscious beings," or "whatever you do, do it with consciousness" use the term in this spiritual sense. But clearly, from the perspective of the philosophical meaning, we don't have to strive to be conscious beings—we already *are* beings with consciousness.

This spiritual meaning of "consciousness" refers to a heightened state of self-awareness that involves increased ethical discernment.

Examples often used to illustrate spiritual consciousness include mystical experiences, unconditional love, purity of compassion, and egolessness. Since, in this case, the "lights" are also always on, spiritual consciousness is really a version of the psychological meaning (we could call it "psycho-spiritual" meaning)—where the light is approaching optimum brightness.

So, another way to think of these different meanings is to picture philosophical consciousness like a light switch. It is either on or off. If flipped up, the light is on and consciousness is present. If flipped down, the light is off and there is complete darkness, no consciousness at all.

On the other hand, we could picture psychological consciousness more like a dimmer switch. Once the power is on, you can turn up the brightness (i.e., consciousness) from dim unconscious to sparkling consciousness, or "enlightenment." In this case, the power is always on, it's just a matter of turning up or down the dimmer.

When we speak about "consciousness," therefore, it helps a great deal if we are clear about what we mean: Do we mean the *fact* of awareness contrasted with the complete absence of any mental activity whatsoever (philosophical meaning)? Or do we mean a *form* or *state* of awareness contrasted with being unconscious (psychological meaning) or contrasted with low moral or ethical sensitivities (spiritual meaning)?

The difference between the psychological and philosophical meanings of consciousness is crucially important. If we can keep this distinction in mind whenever a conversation about consciousness comes up, we will be well served in our search for coherence and clarity. But, as we might expect from the Güzeldere quotation above, the challenge before us is not quite so simple, and this first distinction is merely a starting point. There are multiple other meanings of consciousness besides these two.

For example, in 1880, British psychologist Alexander Bain struggled with thirteen different meanings of the term. And currently, the *OED* gives eight definitions of consciousness. Based on these, psychologist Thomas Natsoulas has written a series of articles exploring seven different meanings of consciousness.[3] As for the term "unconscious," psychologists English and English counted no less than thirty-nine different meanings.

No wonder the fish slips out of our hands! Every time we think we've caught it, it turns out to be a mere shadow or a reflection. The real creature swims through the cracks of language, all the while tantalizing us as it shimmers through our direct experience. We know it's there. We feel it moving through us moment by moment, but as soon as we shine the spotlight of inquiry on it, it slips away into the shadows, beyond the net of definitions.

But perhaps we can coax it a little if we give it a name that acknowledges its multiple meanings, its shimmering coat of many colors. Let's call it by a new name—an incantation perhaps—one we can invoke whenever we need to invite it into discourse. The name, I suggest for reasons that will become clear later, is the strange-sounding "SAPRIUD" (see chapter 17 "*Origins*: Evolution of Consciousness").

Now let's look at the meanings of other terms closely related to "consciousness."

Experience

In many ways, experience is synonymous with consciousness. However, some writers, such as philosopher David Ray Griffin, have expressed a clear preference for "experience" over "consciousness" as the most useful term for signifying interiority.[4] Griffin's rationale is that consciousness tends to carry the connotation of something like "self-awareness," something akin to the normal human state of being conscious (with the ability to form concepts, and to organize them along with perceptions into intellectual models). If consciousness were used in this sense it would mean *thinking*—rational cognition. To attribute consciousness in this sense to less evolved, less complex organisms, such as dogs, cats, fish, worms, or bacteria would, rightly, be easily dismissed as blatant anthropomorphism—projecting human characteristics onto other creatures.

Since Griffin, following Alfred North Whitehead, attributes subjectivity to all individual entities, all the way down to atoms and electrons and beyond, he prefers the term "experience." Experience, even in humans, is often preverbal and prior to cognition and conceptualizing—it is more akin to *feeling* than to thinking—therefore, according to Griffin, it is far less likely to conjure up notions of thinking tadpoles, bashful bacteria, myth-making molecules, self-aware atoms, enthusiastic electrons, poetry-making protons, or questioning quarks. For Griffin, "experience" is less loaded and comes with less human-sounding baggage, than "consciousness."

Given the ambiguous uses of consciousness to mean, for instance "self-awareness," "cognition," or even "conscious self-reflection" (as defined in many forms of psychology, and in many dictionaries), Griffin's distinction is valid. However, once we make clear that our use of "consciousness" means "primordial interiority," or "primordial subjectivity," the ambiguity is removed, and "consciousness" and "experience" may be effectively used interchangeably. Both refer to the capacity for feeling, for being a subject, for ontological interiority, the raw ingredient of all psychic, imaginative, emotional, mental, cognitive, and linguistic phenomena. In this book, I will use this broad meaning of consciousness and experience.

We may note, too, that "experience" carries its own ambiguity. For instance, we can use it in Griffin's sense to mean an entity's subjective feeling of its self, its own interiority, or we can use it in the sense of having accumulated skill or knowledge, being qualified, as in "so-and-so is experienced for this job." It is also often used in a third sense, meaning "something that happened to someone"—as in, she experienced an earthquake, or he had a romantic experience. All three are related, though by no means identical in meaning. The latter usages ("events that have happened to you") are limited cases of the first (which means "you are registering and feeling events happening right now").

Mind

Mind, too, is often used synonymously with consciousness—for example, in the phrase "philosophy of mind." However, there are good reasons for limiting "mind" to a specific subcategory of consciousness. If we define consciousness as "primal interiority," or all-encompassing experiential *context*, it may be useful to distinguish "mind" as the *forms* or *contents* that show up in consciousness. In this case, whereas consciousness itself would be "pure," subject without object, mind would be "consciousness of" something, for instance, a pain, an idea, a perception, a memory.

Mind is sometimes used in an even more restricted sense to mean "intellect"—the rational, cognitive aspect of consciousness—as distinct from, say, "emotion" or "feeling." Mind, in this sense, is more like a computer or information processor that mechanically runs its learned programs, its habits of thought and memory. If we go along with this usage, we may say, "mind is the activity and the contents of cognition."

In some schools of psychology, mind would equate with the ego, whereas consciousness would equate with the Self—although Jung and the Jungians did not identify "consciousness" with the Self.* For them, Self transcended consciousness (which tended to mean "egoic awareness"). Clearly, however, the Jungian "Self" must partake of the nature of consciousness in the philosophical sense—it has interiority, sentience, subjectivity, intentionality, purpose, value, meaning, creativity, and volition.

Awareness

Yet again, the term "awareness" is frequently used in place of consciousness, experience, or mind. And mostly we will use the term synonymously here, too. However, we may distinguish two particularly important aspects of awareness for philosophy of mind. These are "attention" or "attentional awareness" and "intention" or "intentional awareness." In philosophy, "intentionality" refers to consciousness that is directed at some object and is therefore similar to the second definition we gave above for "mind." "Intentionality" is, in this sense, essentially indistinguishable from "attention."

However, it may be useful at times to distinguish the philosophical use of "intentionality" from the more common usage of "purposeful" or "willful." When I say, "I intend to do something," I usually mean more than "I direct my awareness at it" (the philosophical meaning); I mean that I *engage my will* to bring about a particular outcome. The first usage we may call "attention" (receptively directed awareness, or "alertness"); the second usage we may call "intention" or "will" (actively and *causally* directed, or *projected,* awareness).

---

*In Jungian psychology (as in Freudian and all subsequent psychoanalytic-based psychology), "consciousness" means that which is contrasted with the "unconscious."

Attention

Attention, then, may be defined as "receptively directed awareness." It is consciousness that is "alert," that draws into itself meanings, messages, or information about the state of the world around it. Attention may also be "open" (alert but non-discriminating—the image of a sentry on duty, or a Zen meditator) or "focused" (alert and receptive to a specific and limited region of the immediate environment—the image of a cat stalking a bird).

Intention

By contrast, intention may be defined as "purposefully projected awareness." It is consciousness thrown out from the self into the world to cause some change or to gain some knowledge or information. It evokes the image of an archer shooting at a target or of a sprinter darting for the tape. Intention is, in this sense, the causal agency of consciousness. It is "will" or "volition."

Self

The above terms "attention," "intention," "will," "volition" all presuppose an agent or self who is responsible for directing awareness or attention. We may define "self" as the experienced identity of a particular stream of consciousness. Self is a continuity of identity through time. It is what distinguishes "this subject" (self) from "that object" (non-self). With a small "s," self refers to an individualized subjectivity; with a large "S," Self refers to consciousness as the intersubjective ground of being from which all individual selves arise.

So far, we have looked only at meanings of terms on the "consciousness" or subject side of the world equation. We should also look at some key terms on the other, physical object, side in order to get a clearer sense of what consciousness is *not*.

Body

Whereas self is a continuity of identity through time, body is a continuity of identity through space-time. It is experienced as the identity of a particular, individual *locus* of consciousness. Whereas self is usually experienced as individuated *psyche,* body is usually experienced as individuated *physis*. We may substitute the term "soma" for individuated *physis* permeated by individuated *psyche*. In this sense, soma is body with intrinsic feeling and is a locus of experience. It is a node of awareness and meaning in a web of larger environmental interactions and processes—a non-Cartesian bodymind, a being-in-the-world.[5]

In this chapter, we have examined key concepts in the philosophy of mind to establish a foundation for "mind talk" as an alternative to "energy talk" when developing a science of consciousness. In the next chapter, we will look at some additional meanings—including the meaning of meaning itself—that will guide us further in our quest to lay a foundation for consciousness science. We will pay particular attention to a class of anomalous phenomena known as "synchronicities"—mysterious events that pose one of the deepest challenges to the metaphysical assumptions at the heart of contemporary science. These anomalies, as we will see, may well be a kind of "wake-up" call from the universe— and their frequency may be a signpost of spiritual development.

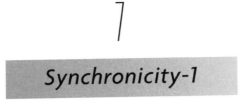

7

Synchronicity-1

Beyond Energy

Because. Because. Because. These three words conceal a world of difference—a difference that could radically alter or expand the way science gains knowledge of the world, and how we understand our place in nature. It's a difference that could bridge the gap between matter and mind, between mechanism and meaning, between science and spirituality. It's also a difference that could hold a key to understanding synchronicity—those strange "coincidences" that sometimes seem like messages from the gods.

What do synchronicities have to do with exploring consciousness? As we will see, they may be crucial clues to understanding not only mind but also the mysterious relationship between matter and mind. If, as I proposed in *Radical Nature,* the world is composed of matter that feels—of stuff that tingles with the spark of spirit all the way down to cells, molecules, atoms, and subatomic particles—then the world around us teems with sentient beings, themselves full of intrinsic meaning, constantly sending out messages as a kind of "connective tissue" that unites all of nature in a universal network of shared, participatory meaning. Synchronicities are the universe whispering to us, reminding us of our deep interconnectedness.

Synchronicity works, essentially, through *a sharing of meaning.* It is a nonmechanistic, noncausal phenomenon—that is, it operates without the usual relationship between cause and effect that lies at the foundation of scientific understanding. A clearer insight into the nature of synchronicity, as well as a deeper understanding of the relationship between meaning and mechanism, could open up a revolutionary new way of exploring consciousness that does not rely on reducing it to cause-effect mechanisms or attempt to explain it in terms of "energy."

Consciousness does not work like a machine. As we have seen, it is not a form of energy, and does not involve exchanges of energy. It cannot be a form of energy because it does not exist in space. (By definition, anything physical is made up of energy, and all forms of energy and physical existence have extension in space—that's why we can measure them.) Consciousness is not just "nonlocal," as many new-paradigm thinkers are fond of saying—it is *nonlocated*. It isn't located anywhere in space, and therefore it cannot be observed or measured. Consciousness has no objective reality; yet, of course, it is the most undeniable reality of all.

The key distinctive characteristic of consciousness is its subjectivity—its interiority, the "what-it-feels-like" from within. I do not need any objective verification that I am a conscious, sentient being. I experience and know the fact of my own consciousness directly. And, since you too are a conscious being, your first-person access confirms your own consciousness.

However, we are not confined to knowing just our own minds—as modern philosophy, following Descartes, would have us believe. In this book, I am making a case that when two or more sentient beings engage each other's presence they know and experience each other mutually through direct, unmediated, subject-to-subject communion, through second-person *intersubjectivity*. This second-person sharing of consciousness (sometimes called "telepathy"), likewise needs no objective confirmation, and cannot be understood or explained as an exchange of energy passing through space.

Not only will we fail to understand mind or consciousness, therefore, by searching for mechanisms; I am proposing, further, that we will not resolve the mind-body problem—or understand how mind and matter are related—by searching for a "mechanism" by which mind acts on matter, or vice versa.

Even more radically, I will propose later that it is probably not even the case that consciousness ever *causes* anything to happen in the physical world—despite all the recent claims of "new paradigm" thinkers that consciousness *is* causal. To be sure, in some mysterious way, consciousness is a "force" in the world—it is active, not just an impotent epiphenomenon. Consciousness works in the world in a way that can hardly be expressed in our language. But an understanding of synchronicity may help.

In this chapter, we will explore the notion of "be-cause" as it relates to science and synchronicity, to mechanism and meaning. We will follow with a discussion of three additional concepts that, I believe, are key to a proper understanding of synchronicity—meaning, mechanism, and causality. Finally, we will examine the definition of synchronicity most commonly quoted from Carl Jung, the psychologist who coined the term, and see how synchronicity may pose a major challenge to science and philosophy.

BECAUSE, BECAUSE, BECAUSE

"Because" is a familiar word, one we all use every day. But it's deceptive because it is actually three *different* words, carrying three different meanings. One meaning comes in response to "how?" questions—*how* something happened; a second meaning is in response to "why?" questions—*why* things are a certain way; and the third meaning . . . ? Let's look at meanings 1 and 2, first.

Because-1. Explorations of the first "because" are the stuff of science. Here, the foundation question is "How does the world work?" And the answers science provides are along the lines of "the world works the way it does *because* one thing causes another to happen." According to this view, the world is made up of events that are linked together by causes and effects. "Be-cause," here, means, "events linked by cause and effect." Because-1, therefore, is *causality* (a special kind of causality, as we shall see, called *mechanism*).

Because-2. The second "because" is the stuff of philosophy. It is prompted by questions such as "Why is there something rather than nothing?" "Why do we exist?" "Why is this (rather than that) the state of the world?" And philosophy answers by providing *reasons:* "Things can happen, must happen, or can't happen *because* of logical possibilities, necessities, or impossibilities." Because-2, therefore, means, "because there are reasons" (logical necessities) for any particular state of affairs.

Because-3. The third "because" is perhaps the strangest of the lot. It is the stuff of mysticism or spirituality. It, too, can be a response to "why?" questions. But the kinds of answers provided by mysticism tend to annihilate the questions posed. For instance, in response to "Why is the world the way it is?" or "Why am I not enlightened?" mysticism might answer: "*because* that's just the way it is." This "just-so" kind of because is actually no because at all. There is no reason, and there are no mechanisms or causes, that will provide satisfactory answers. Answers of the just-so kind require a leap beyond all "becauses" into a realm or state of awareness typified by an expansion of consciousness where instead of reasons or causes, the answer comes as a deepening of *meaning*.

What is so intriguing about Carl Jung's work in synchronicity is that it seems to involve events that may serve as a bridge between the three "becauses"—between the causes (mechanisms) of science and the becauses (reasons) of philosophy, on the one hand, and the "no-causes" (meanings) of mysticism, on the other. For synchronicity, as we shall see, seems to involve events that *cannot be linked causally* yet are conspicuously *connected through meaning*. Synchronicities are neither mechanisms explicable by (standard) science, nor are they purely "just-so" requiring mystical experience. They seem to hover above (below?), or intersect, the domains of scientific causality and spiritual consciousness. Perhaps they are gateways between these two worlds?

Whatever they are, synchronicities call out for explanation—yet by their very nature may in the end elude explanation. Instead of asking, "*how* can acausal connections (synchronicities) intersect the world of causal events?" we may need to ask, "*why* do synchronicities occur at all?" Instead of explanation, we may need to be content with a deepening of meaning and a sense of purpose. Is *that* their function: to remind us not to stay fixed in the realm of causes and reasons, but to be open to the possibilities for growth that may come with accepting "just-so"? At least in my own case, this has been their predominant effect.

EXPLANATION OR MEANING?

For about four hundred years, Western science has very successfully developed a detailed understanding of the way the (physical) world works. Based on the discoveries and theories of Galileo and Newton, scientific knowledge explains events as *mechanisms*—that is, in terms of impacts of bodies in motion (a worldview traceable back to the ancient Greek philosopher Democritus's notion of "atoms in the void"). Even today, Newton's laws of motion form the basis of classical mechanics taught in colleges and universities around the world. With the advent of Maxwell's field equations, the focus shifted from solid bodies in motion to fields extending into space, but the interactions between particles and fields were still described as causal "mechanisms."

Now that is changing. Discoveries in quantum physics, along with Jung's synchronicity and recent advances in consciousness studies, have revealed "holes" in the scientific assumption of universal causality and mechanism. As a result, since the early days of the twentieth century many historians of science (as well as millions within the educated lay public) believe that modern science and society are on the verge of a major paradigm shift—from a mechanistic worldview to something much more holistic, where mind or consciousness (and, in some cases, even spirit) is recognized as an active ingredient in the way the world works. We will look at implications of this emerging paradigm below, but first it will help if we understand more about the dominant role mechanism and causality play in the "old" paradigm—knowing where you *are* helps get you where you're going.

MECHANISM

In a completely physical universe, things can happen only through lawful, causal, or pure chance interactions of particles and fields. One thing bumps into another either through deterministic causal laws or by the probabilistic laws of chance and, by imparting some of its energy, causes the other object to move. In such a universe all there is is mechanism. All relationships are governed by these causal mechanistic laws.

Mechanism, in short, is nothing but interactions of physical causes and effects. That is, it depends entirely on contact or contiguity between physical bodies, be they particles or fields. Even electromagnetic and gravitational fields are understood to operate by transmitting energy over great distances at the speed of light. In electromagnetism, the energy is carried by photons, and physicists are still searching for the elusive "gravitons" believed to be responsible for transmitting the force of gravity. All action-at-a-distance or communication-through-the-void is ruled out. There has to be some physical *medium* carrying the energy or signals from one point in space to another.

That is why the force of gravity was such a headache for Newton. On the one hand, he discovered gravitation when the famous apple dropped on his head, launching a whole new era in science that explained so much about the physical world—from falling fruit to orbiting planets. But, on the other hand, neither Newton nor anyone else could find the medium that was needed to transmit the action of gravity. Somehow, even without an intervening medium connecting different points in space (e.g., the Earth and our sun), gravity seemed to be able to reach out across the void and make things move.

Ever since Scottish physicist James Clerk Maxwell developed the mathematical "field equations" to explain electromagnetism in the nineteenth century, modern science has assumed that the "medium" for transmitting energy is some kind of "field." Energy and information, then, are understood to move through space via disturbances or undulations in the field—in other words as *waves* or *vibrations*. But no one has ever discovered just what it is that vibrates or undulates in space to account for gravity. You cannot have a wave or vibration unless there is *something* to vibrate.

Newton and his followers were understandably perplexed because—despite everything else they knew about physical reality—gravity seemed to confirm that action-at-a-distance *is* possible and *does* happen. This seemed far too mystical and metaphysically problematic for levelheaded scientists to accept. When asked to explain how gravity could act through empty space, Newton refused to speculate: "*Hypotheses non fingo,*" he said—"I frame no hypotheses."

Centuries later, Albert Einstein proposed a radical solution. He said that gravity works the way it does, not because of some invisible, mysterious medium filling all of space, but because the very fabric of space-time itself bends or "warps" in the presence of matter. Planets orbit stars, and apples fall on scientists, he said, because they are merely following the curvature of space.

But even Einstein's "solution" depends on the notion of *causality:* Warps in space-time cause bodies to move along paths carved out by the masses of all objects in their vicinity. Meanwhile, physicists continue to search for the "holy grail" of gravitons to explain how "gravitational waves" interact with physical masses.

The search for the "missing" gravitons is yet another attempt to find a causal *mechanism,* and to avoid the prospect of action-at-a-distance. It is still based on the materialist belief that everything that exists is physical, and that physical events can happen only through exchanges of energy.

In a world composed entirely of "atoms in the void," of matter in motion, of particles moving through fields of force, no room is left for meaning, purpose, or value. Nothing can happen in such a universe through influences shared synchronistically—that is, through non-mechanical, *acausal* connections that do not involve exchanges of energy through space, yet do manage to communicate meaning. Before turning to meaning and its role in synchronicity, let's take a moment to look more closely at causality—the cornerstone of mechanistic science.

CAUSALITY

Causality, we have seen, is closely tied in with mechanism. However, mechanism, or what Aristotle called "efficient causation," is only one variety of causality. Near the dawn of Western philosophy, Aristotle had identified four kinds of causes—formal, material, efficient, and final—that are involved in every event. Take as an example making a chair: First, we have in our mind the *idea* (or form) of the chair (the idea triggers us into action). This is the *formal* cause.

Next, we find the wood we will use for the chair—the actual physical matter. This is the *material* cause (without which the idea or form of the chair could not be made manifest).

Then we set to work, using our muscles and skill to construct the chair. This is the *efficient* cause (the energy we expend in shaping the chair).

Finally, we do all that work because we have a goal or *purpose* in mind—what the chair will be used for. This is the *final* cause.

Remove any of these causes, Aristotle believed, and the chair would never come into being. This four-fold understanding of causality was accepted for millennia until the advent of modern science. Following Galileo and Newton, and their laws of mechanics, science eliminated all but one of the four causes. Only *efficient* causation survived, and with it the idea that only physical work, or *exchanges of energy*, can cause anything to happen in the world. This is the central dogma of mechanism, and it replaced the earlier medieval notion of "organicism," that everything is alive and happens for a reason; that all events unfold because of some idea, substance, and purpose. When I talk about "causality" in science, I'm referring specifically to efficient causality, and the assumption that all causes are ultimately mechanical exchanges of energy.

However, the ghosts of two of the "lost" causes still lurk in the halls of modern science, albeit under different guises and different names. Material causation, by which Aristotle meant the raw substance of a thing, has been replaced in science by modern-sounding notions such as "energy" and "fields of force" (which are believed to interact exclusively through "efficient" exchanges of energy between fields and particles). Formal causes, which refer to non-material forms giving shape to things and events, are now called "natural laws" or "laws of nature."* Formative causation has also returned via more controversial ideas on the frontiers of science, for example in psychologist Carl Jung's archetypes or biologist Rupert Sheldrake's morphic fields.

The one cause that science refuses to admit in any guise is "final," which refers to a teleological, goal-directed "pull" from some end-purpose (implying that nature's events unfold with *purpose* or inherent intelligence). These have been categorically dismissed by science as unscientific and unreal.

---

*I thank my friend Dr. Eric Weiss for this observation.

I mentioned earlier that the "old" paradigm of mechanism is undergoing a shift toward a more inclusive holistic worldview, where mind or consciousness (and therefore meaning and purpose) is recognized as a participant in how the world works. Let's now take a look at an important aspect of the emerging paradigm, particularly in relation to the role of causality.

A CHANGING PARADIGM

The prevailing scientific worldview, based on the concepts of mechanism and causality, began to change dramatically after the discovery of the quantum. Here, for the first time, science encountered empirical evidence for events that had no causal foundation (e.g., radioactivity or quantum jumps of electrons within atoms). Such events "just happen," according to standard interpretation of quantum theory. They are completely uncaused and are, therefore, instances of pure chance (or pure creativity, depending on how you like to view such things).*

Nevertheless, despite this shift in paradigm, quantum theory is still called "quantum *mechanics.*" Modern science has remained wedded to the ideal of discovering underlying mathematical laws or descriptions (e.g., probability equations, wave and matrix mechanics) that can account for the sometimes bizarre and profoundly counterintuitive phenomena that occur in the quantum domain.

From classical Newtonian and Maxwellian physics, to Einsteinian relativity and quantum mechanics, modern physics—and therefore modern science in general—is committed to discovering and explaining *how* the world works. And this "how" is invariably some version of mechanics, of bodies (particles) or fields (waves) in motion and interacting *through an exchange of forces.* Ever since Einstein's demonstration of the equivalence of matter and energy ($E=Mc^2$), descriptions of mechanical impact have shifted from accounts of material pushes and pulls to accounts of exchanges of energy. But

---

*The collective behavior of *large groups* of quantum events can be predicted with great precision *statistically.* However, individual quantum events, being random, are unpredictable. For individual quanta, the rule still holds: no cause, no predictable effect.

whether Galilean-Newtonian pushes and pulls, Maxwellian fields of force, Einsteinian warps in space-time, or quantum interactions . . . some form of contact through *energy exchange is a foundational assumption. Mechanism reigns supreme.*

But already, within science, there is a problem with this assumption: On the one hand, the laws of thermodynamics demand that every event involves energy transfer; on the other, one of the most daunting paradoxes in contemporary quantum physics is the phenomenon of *nonlocality.*

Experiments have confirmed that two quantum particles are *correlated* (that is, they match each other's behavior) even if separated by great distances. Change the spin on one, and the other *instantly* changes its spin accordingly. This happens even if there is insufficient time for any energy or signal to pass between them. Scientists say that the particles are separated by "superluminal" distances, which means that no light signal (no energy, no information) can pass between them in the available time; and yet their behaviors are correlated—*as if somehow each knows what the other is doing.* In other words, quantum nonlocality means that parts of the universe are correlated (or "meaningfully connected") *without the possibility of any mechanism to account for their connection.*

This raises the specter of "action-at-a-distance" or "correspondences" (a notion in medieval magic that early science made great efforts to disprove). Now, with quantum nonlocality, "spooky action-at-a-distance" (as Einstein called it) has reintroduced a hint of "magic" and "correspondences" back into science. The discovery of nonlocality in quantum physics, along with the discovery that quantum events are uncaused, has inspired various authors and scholars to pay more attention to occurrences of synchronicity and the idea that events may be linked across time and space through *meaning* rather than mechanism.

Since meaning plays such a key role in synchronicity, let's now take a closer look at what we mean by "meaning."

■

THE MEANING OF MEANING*

Meaning is closely related to mind, to psyche. It is difficult to imagine how there could ever be any meaning in a purely material, wholly objective universe. What meaning would such "meaning" have? In a universe without consciousness, without an experiencing psyche, all would be blind matter, the random-deterministic dance of "atoms in the void." Nothing would be significant.

In materialistic science, meaning is reduced to mechanism, to explanations of causal physical relations. When a particular model or theory is said to correspond with empirical data, with how phenomena in nature are observed to interact (i.e., cause-effect measurement), we say we have scientific explanation (for example, kinetic energy of molecules "means" heat). But such a definition of meaning as causal explanation leaves something out of what we normally mean by meaning, something that has to do with significance, something that resonates in some way with our experience of self.

Meaning involves intentionality in the sense of directed awareness. It is awareness that refers to something beyond itself with which it participates in some way. If a particular event means something to me, it is because my consciousness "reaches out" and draws it into my field of being (or, alternatively, it reaches out and attracts my consciousness). When one thing means some other thing, at least part of its being is *about that thing*.

As a useful working definition of meaning we might pursue the following: Meaning is the significant relationship between the experiencing self and the event or situation being experienced. (Below, I define "significance" as "the quality of relationship between self and something that is not-self . . . it depends on the fit between self and its environment.") This strong sense of "meaning" includes a deepening of self-understanding and our felt relationship to the world. It is about

---

*Readers of *Radical Nature* will find this section familiar: I have repeated here much of that discussion on the meaning of meaning because it is so central to the topic of synchronicity, and because I do not assume that every reader of this book will have had the advantage of having read the first volume in this trilogy.

communication and information flow (not to be confused with energy transfer)—a non-mechanistic in-*forming*.

As a locus of being or experience, the self as bodymind is in constant communication with its environment, constantly exchanging energy and information in multiple forms—food, air, water, light, sound, smells, radiation, ideas, emotions, concepts, and so on. We are constantly sharing messages with the world around us, picking them up in our bodymind, processing or metabolizing them, and expressing some residue back out. We call this process "life."

The significance of this exchange of messages—this discourse with our environment—depends on the quality of relationship between self and not-self. In short, it depends on the fit between self and its environment. If the bodymind-self cannot receive, process, or feed back information or energy with its environment, it experiences a "misfit," and its ability to develop or grow is at stake. If the misfit is sufficiently acute or chronic, the individual will die.

The significance, or meaning, of the messages, then, is ultimately a matter of the organism's growth or survival. *Meaning is the experienced fit between self and its environment.* The key word here is "experienced." Meaning is a first-person, subjective phenomenon and cannot be accounted for merely by "functional fit"—that is, third-person, objective relations between parts of a system. As the self opens up to respond to more environment—whether physical, mental, or spiritual—the experience of self expands and more of what was not-self is incorporated. Ultimately, when the sense of self expands to encompass the entire realm of being, as mystics tell us, the distinction between individual self and the cosmic Self, or the Cosmic I, disappears. The entire cosmos, then, resonates with meaning.

FROM "HOW" TO "WHY" THE WORLD WORKS

Before delving into the meaning of synchronicity, let's pause at this point to review the ground we have covered in this chapter. Having posed modern science's central question, "How does the world work?" we saw that science's answer is: "The world works *only and always* by *exchanges of energy*"—that's what "mechanics" means. Whenever we encounter a mechanical explanation, we know some energy exchange has taken place.

The entire edifice of science is built on the premise of mechanism or mechanical causes—that all events in the world always and only involve exchanges of energy. Within this worldview, it is impossible that any event could take place without some transmission of energy.

But, as we have also seen, anomalies exist as well. With the discovery of the quantum, some "happenings" in the world apparently do not involve exchanges of energy, or at least are not wholly accounted for in terms of energy exchanges. And these anomalies require us to ask, not only "*how* does the world work?" but also "*why* does the world work the way it does?" Whereas "how" questions require answers in terms of mechanical causes, "why" questions require us to look for purposes or reasons—for *meanings*.

This was Carl Jung's great discovery, and his great contribution to modern science. He noticed that some events in his own life and in the lives of his patients could not be accounted for in terms of mechanical causation, but instead manifested connections through *meaning*. He called such connections "synchronicity."

If we examine Jung's most familiar definition of synchronicity, we can see if instances of this phenomenon really do pose the kind of challenge to standard science that Jung believed they do.

WHAT IS SYNCHRONICITY?

Jung defined synchronicity as "a *coincidence in time* of two or more *causally unrelated* events which have the same or *similar meaning.*"[1] Why should such an idea be a challenge to the modern scientific worldview? Let's take his definition step by step.

Coincidence in time. First, the notion of "coincidence in time" is, by itself, unproblematic. All sorts of things happen to coincide at the same moment. Right now, for instance, while these words are being typed, a plane is taking off somewhere, waves are breaking on a beach in Australia, and a comet is heading toward the sun. Countless millions of other events are happening together at this and every moment. That's inevitable in a pluralistic universe. Simultaneity, or coincidence in time, is an unremarkable fact of reality. There is nothing strange or scientifically challenging about events "coinciding in time."

Causally unrelated. Perhaps the problem is with "causally unrelated"? Clearly, we have no reason to suspect that my typing the previous paragraph could have any influence on a flight take-off, on surf crashing in Australia, or on the trajectory of a comet. And, likewise, all of those events are causally independent. On its own, each event, of course, is the product of a chain of causes and effects. But, *precisely because they happen simultaneously,* and are separated by distances, none of those events could possibly affect any of the others. They are "causally unrelated," and that's exactly what we would expect both logically and scientifically. So, no problem here.

Similar meaning. If there is a challenge, then, does it lie here, where two or more events have the "same or similar meaning"? But why would *that* be a problem? All sorts of things share similar meanings. For example, my typing fingers, the plane taking off, the breaking waves, and the orbiting comet all share the meaning of "motion." Or, cows chewing the cud, celebrants feasting at a wedding, bacteria ingesting decaying cells, all share meanings of "food" and "digestion."

If these examples seem too weak, consider four scenarios, given the following: I have three dimes and two quarters in my pocket—a total of five coins. Two cars and three trucks on the highway add up to a total of five vehicles. Both sets of objects share the meaning "five."

Scenario 1: Suppose I took the five coins out of my pocket *at the very instant* those five vehicles passed by my house, would that be synchronicity? They "coincide in time," are "causally unrelated," and share the "same meaning." But this would hardly qualify as Jungian synchronicity. What's missing?

Scenario 2: Suppose, now, that as I took the coins out of my pocket, they fell, scattering on the floor, and at that very instant the five vehicles outside my house crashed into each other. Again: simultaneity, causally unrelated events, and shared meaning. But, again, hardly synchronicity. Why not? What's missing?

Scenario 3: Take it further. Suppose that for some reason I was angry, I took the coins out of my pocket, threw them against the wall, and at that same instant the five vehicles outside my house piled into each other. Again the two events coincide in time, are causally unrelated, and share the same meaning (fiveness). Are we getting warmer? And if so, why? It's hardly the added ingredient of drama, since surely that was also present in scenario 2.

What's missing in all three scenarios is a *linking* of the two events. It is not enough that they coincide in time, or even that they share a similar meaning—for both of those situations can be accounted for by *chance*. It "just happened" that there was a pile up of the vehicles outside as I threw the coins. And it "just happened" that there were five coins and five vehicles. We would describe the simultaneity of these two events as a "chance coincidence."

Let's say, however, I threw the coins out my window and they hit the driver of one of the cars who swerved and rammed into one of the trucks, triggering a chain-reaction pile up. Clearly that could count as a connection between the two events. But it would be a *causal* connection. Our second criterion is that the events must be causally unrelated, that they be *acausally linked*.

And here, I believe, we meet a weakness in Jung's definition quoted above. It is not enough that the simultaneous events be "causally unrelated," they must be also *acausally* connected. Being "causally unrelated" is not the same as "acausally connected." The first is an *absence* of causality; the second is a *presence* of acausality.

The negation of something (say, the extinction or nonbeing of X) is never sufficient to affirm the existence of something else (say, the presence or being of Y). It is always possible that X could cease to exist without Y coming into being. As noted above, the mere absence of causal relatedness (i.e., causal unrelatedness) between the five coins and the five vehicles, does not even imply, never mind necessitate, the presence of acausal connection between the coins and the autos.

And as we've seen, all sorts of simultaneous events are (and must be) causally unrelated, but it would be completely unwarranted to claim they are, therefore, acausally connected. Any such universalizing claim would make the notion of acausal connection empty and meaningless. The problem, or the mystery, occurs when we are presented with evidence that two simultaneous events *without any possibility of a causal (mechanistic) relationship* are, nevertheless, *connected*. Here, because they are causally unrelated *and* connected, the connection must be *acausal*. The problem is to account for *how*, in the absence of causality, they could possibly be connected. Jung proposed such events are linked through meaning. But is the presence of shared meaning a sufficient condition for "connectedness"?

In all three scenarios, both events (coins and autos) were linked by the number five. They shared the meaning of "fiveness," and to that extent they were related. But in any of these cases, was this a *meaningful link?* Did the link deepen our understanding or experience of ourselves or the world in some way? Although we could say that the coins and the vehicles were "linked" by the meaning "five," we would be tempted to say this was just a "chance linking," a "chance shared meaning," and therefore a very weak "link" indeed.

There is, it seems, a difference between mere "shared meaning" and a "meaningful link." But what is this difference? And how does it give synchronicity its trademark distinction? What is it about true synchronicity (if there really is such) that lifts it beyond mere chance coincidence and chance shared meaning? What missing ingredient would compel us to accept a coincidence of causally unrelated meanings as an instance of synchronicity and not just chance?

Whatever this "extra ingredient" is, it seems we need to add it to Jung's initial definition of synchronicity (see Appendix 1 for a more comprehensive list of Jung's definitions). In addition to a "coincidence in time" of two or more "causally unrelated" events that have the "same or similar meaning," I propose that the differentiating ingredient is a numinous quality—an *experience of the numinous*. Numinosity is the "charge" we experience when we find ourselves involved in events we suspect are unrelated by cause yet are acausally related through a meaning that transforms us in some way. Now try this:

Scenario 4: Suppose, this time, that I wrote down the dates from all five coins, and that *after the fact* of the auto pile up I discovered that five people injured or killed in the crash were born the same years as the five dates on my coins. Here, any suggestion of "chance coincidence" or "chance meaning," would *feel like* a stretch. (Or it would bestow on chance a quality of orderedness that would be self-contradictory.) Instead of chance, the overwhelming feeling would be a sense of hidden order or pattern, accompanied by a tone of eeriness, a wondrousness, a mysteriousness, an inexplicable sense of *meaningful connection* between those five coins and those five people, *at that shared moment in time.* The sense of inexplicable meaningful connection and coincidence, combined with a knowledge that this could not be due to any *thinkable* causal connection, would be accompanied by an unmistakable sense of numinosity: *Some deeper, higher, or wider pattern enfolds these otherwise apparently unconnected events.*

The numinosity characteristic of scenario 4 is due, I believe, to a sense that the perceived meaning is *more than personal*—more than subjective projection. *The meaning somehow transcends any individual psyche (or psyches) involved and is as much a part of the* objective *situation. The meaning is sensed to be* inherent in the *material world* as much as *in the human mind* that perceives the meaning. Both matter and mind seem to cooperate, even conspire, in the unfolding of events—as if "persuaded" or coaxed by some deeper, larger pattern that gives order and arrangement to the ways of the world (including our individual parts in it).

This is what Jung is pointing at with his notion of synchronicity, where mind and matter are "guided" together by the deeper formative matrix of the archetypes.

THE CHALLENGE TO SCIENCE

If synchronicity is real—and Jung amassed many compelling examples that demonstrate its validity—it poses a profound problem for modern science because it challenges the hegemony of causality. Scientific explanation is predicated on the notion of cause-effect relationship. Without the premise that every effect is preceded by a determining cause, science would be unable to predict any outcome. Without prediction, science would be unable to control. Without control, scientific experiments would not work. Without experiments there would be no science. In short, the ideal of nomothetic science—of science aiming for and discovering universal laws—is unthinkable without causality.

But, as we have seen, one of the key hallmarks of synchronicity is that its constituent events are *acausal.* If synchronicity is true, then, the entire scientific enterprise based on causal laws comes sharply into question. But perhaps the situation need not be quite so drastic. It remains possible that acausality could exist alongside causality (as, indeed, *prima facia,* seems to be the case), and that both are related through some form of complementarity. Perhaps both are "at work" in the universe. However, even in this case, we would still want to know how science would move beyond *universal* mechanism, and expand, or open up, to include synchronicity within its worldview.

Ironically, the deep challenge facing science may, in the end, turn out not to be synchronicity but *causality itself.* Despite its foundational role in science, and however obvious it may seem to common sense, causality remains profoundly problematic philosophically. Although mechanism has produced great successes in science and technology (judged, of course, according to criteria inspired by mechanism itself), it may yet turn out that its foundational assumption, causality, will prove to be a metaphysical fiction. And perhaps the limitations, dangers, and failures of mechanism when applied to living and sentient systems will be overcome only when attachment to "nothing-but" causality is given up, and some other, noncausal, principle is seen to be more (or comparably) fundamental.

Science has made great strides in understanding nature in terms of efficient causality. However, when science attempts to expand its reach beyond the physical world into the inner world of consciousness—the inadequacies of this mechanistic paradigm are starkly revealed. And the shortcomings show up, too, in other areas of science. Limiting causality to mechanical causation, as we saw in the case of quantum physics, means scientific causal explanations fail to account for all of the data.

The same is true in other sciences, such as evolutionary biology, neurosciences, psychology, and cosmology, where other anomalies require alternative explanations. The Institute of Noetic Sciences has published a series of reports from its Causality Project addressing this particular issue.[2] In addition to alternative forms of causation (perhaps revisiting Aristotle's four causes), the indeterminacy of quantum physics and the concept of synchronicity in Jungian psychology suggest an even more radical break with mechanism and causality.

It may be that the universe operates and holds itself together through other *noncausal* processes, such as meaning, in addition to the dynamics of mechanism. For example, Jung's hypothesis is that a more accurate and adequate model of reality is one where both mind (*psyche)* and matter *(physis)* are aspects of some underlying "psychoid" continuum. Throughout the entire continuum, mind and matter interpenetrate each other, though in differing degrees depending on where an event occurs on the "reality spectrum."

For instance, at one end, *physis* would be predominant, and here causality and mechanism would operate as, indeed, physicalist science has discovered. However, at the other end, where *psyche* predominates, causal mechanism would be replaced by acausal connections through meanings or synchronicities. At points in between there would be varying admixtures of causality and acausality, of mechanism and meaning.

Meaning, mechanism, causality—a further exploration and understanding of these key concepts could help to clarify the relationship between consciousness and the physical world, and explain why the worldview of mechanism cannot account for consciousness or meaning. We need to look more deeply into the meanings of these words, as well as arrive at a deeper understanding of synchronicity and acausality, if we are ever to develop a science of consciousness.

To live in a world where science is brought back to consciousness would be to live in a world where the technology of mechanism is complemented by the significance of meaning—a world that is both useful and meaningful. In such a world, our practical uses of technology would be guided by the wisdom of knowing our deep interrelatedness with the whole environment in which all our actions and being are embedded. In such a world, science would be imbued with a sense of the sacred.

Such a "sacred science" will come about only when the trance of explanation exclusively in terms of efficient causality is broken; when our culture—including science—opens up to different modes of relationship and connection between events that involve sentient beings. A first step in this direction occurred some two hundred years ago when British philosopher David Hume shocked the scientific world with his devastating critique of causality (see next chapter pages 112–14). But a second step is also needed; a step that not only highlights the shortcomings of efficient causality, but that also takes us beyond it. This step was taken by Carl Jung in his theory of synchronicity.

Let's now examine Hume's critique of causality to see how, together with the process cosmology of Alfred North Whitehead and the quantum physics of David Bohm, it forms a launching pad for a new perspective on synchronicity—offering a new understanding of consciousness and its place in the physical universe.

8

Synchronicity-2

Reality without a Cause

In the previous chapter, we saw how Carl Jung's discovery and description of synchronicity challenged the deeply embedded idea of *causes*—that the world works by exchanges of energy, and that only mechanisms can make things happen. Synchronicity, we saw, presents a potentially paradigm-breaking challenge to science.

But long before Jung, British philosopher David Hume in the eighteenth century had startled the world of science out of its "dogmatic slumbers" when he drew attention to the fact that no one has ever seen a cause, and therefore the entire foundation of science, which *assumes* causality, rests on highly questionable and possibly fictional foundations. Hume's wake-up call echoed through the halls of science, and it took one of the greatest philosophers of all time, Immanuel Kant, to come up with a solution.

However, as we will see, Kant's "solution" may not be the saving grace of science it was once believed to be. Hume's critique of causality lives on and has gained force from Jung's synchronicity, the arrival of quantum physics, and the emerging field of consciousness studies. Together, these three bodies of knowledge have reignited the fire of Hume's critique, posing a profound challenge to modern science while at the same time offering a solution to philosophy's age-old, and supposedly unsolvable, mind-body problem. In this chapter, we will see that the "connective tissue" between these three disciplines is the process philosophy of Alfred North Whitehead, and how it opens the way for a revolutionary approach to the perennial mind-body problem.

HUME'S CRITIQUE OF CAUSALITY

David Hume's (1711–1776) startling analysis of causality, and its provocative challenge to science, hinges on what we can *know*. It is, essentially, a problem of epistemology: We can never know, or perceive, a cause. His critique is thoroughly sensationist; that is, it is based on the assumption that all knowledge begins with and arises from the senses. Hume emphasized a distinction between sensory impressions and ideas: "Sensory impressions are the basis of any knowledge, and they come with a force and liveliness that make them unique. Ideas are faint copies of those impressions . . . . [But] what *causes* the sensory impression? . . . to what impression can the mind point for its idea of causality?"[1]

According to Hume, our minds can have no true knowledge of causes, including those responsible for sensations, because we never have an experience of cause as such; instead, all we ever have are discrete sense impressions that occur one after another. Only through an association of ideas—a habit of mind—do we come to form an idea of causation. In actuality, all we ever know through perception and observation is a *pattern of events,* a sequence where one event (let's say striking a billiard ball with a cue) is always followed by a corresponding event (the ball moves). Noticing the constant (or repeated) conjunction of such events, Hume pointed out, we then *infer* that the first event caused the second event. In other words, we *assume* that the cue caused the ball to move. But no matter how carefully or precisely we observe the sequence of events we never actually see an event we call the "cause."

Think about it—or, better yet, try it out for yourself: If you attend very closely to what happens what you will see is that the cue moves (event #1), then it strikes the ball (event #2), and then the ball moves (event #3). Nowhere do you actually see an event we call "cause." All you see is a *sequence* of events, and "cause" is not one of those events. You may be tempted to think that event #2, cue-striking-ball, *is* the cause, but really all you see is one event following another event—and you *assume* that cue-striking-ball *causes* the ball to move. But for all you know, what actually happened is that the moment the cue struck the ball, the ball just happened to move (or decided to move!) out of the way; or perhaps some other chance arrangement of the universe had foreordained that whenever a stick hits a ball, the ball would move. What you witnessed *could be* some kind of preestablished harmony and not a result of causality.

Hume's bottom line is that we never *perceive* a cause. Causes are not something the senses can detect. They are always something added by the mind to whatever we happen to see. And, if causes do exist, we are incapable of knowing them. In a nutshell, Hume's position is:

- All knowledge is "caused" by sense impressions on the mind;
- but knowledge of causality itself is impossible because the (presumed) cause linking sensations and ideas is not itself a sensation;
- therefore, all knowledge is suspect because the very basis of knowledge is mere assumption—the assumption of causality; the assumption that an external world causes sensations and that sensations cause ideas in the mind. That we have ideas in the mind, there is no doubt; and that ideas are dependent in some way on sense impressions seems equally certain; and, in turn, that sense impressions are dependent in some way on events in the external world is also reasonable to assume. All this underlies what we call "knowledge."

- But, Hume pointed out, such knowledge is built on a chain of unsubstantiated assumptions linking the various stages in what we believe to be knowledge. At bottom, all we ever know are the ideas in our own minds. What—if anything—these ideas "represent" we cannot know.

The possibility of scientific knowledge, and the whole edifice of science, including the magnificent achievements of Galileo and Newton, suddenly became vulnerable to Hume's devastating skeptical critique. His severe analysis of causality, and its implicit undermining of the status of scientific knowledge, roused German philosopher Immanuel Kant (1724–1804) to come up with a response—waking him from his "dogmatic slumbers," as he put it.

Kant's solution (later echoed by Jung) was that causality is intrinsic to the mind (like the categories of space and time) and is one of the very *conditions of experience*. We know causality, Kant said, not because we can perceive it "out there" in the world, but because it is part of the fabric "in here," in our minds. But this solution transplants causes from the external world and transforms them into purely subjective events. Furthermore, unlike with Jung, Kant's philosophy had no room for acausal experience.

CAUSALITY FROM ACAUSALITY

Taking our cue, then, from Jung and his concept of synchronicity, and linking it to Whitehead's process philosophy, we have an alternative to Kant's solution—one that restores causes to the world of objects or actual occasions. But it does so with a twist.

First, Whitehead argued compellingly that we can best get a handle on the relationship between mind and matter—between consciousness and the physical universe—if we switch from thinking of the world as though it were composed of substance, of "things." Instead, he said, the world is constituted by *processes*—processes that move forward by leapfrogging "mental poles" (subjects) and "physical poles" (objects). What we understand as material objects are really expired subjects— summed up in the phrase "past matter, present mind."[2]

At every new moment a new subject comes into being through a process of literal self-creation. Each subject is a purely creative act. And every subject always exists in the present moment *now*. But the duration of each moment is so infinitesimally short that just about as soon as it arrives, it's gone—slipped into the past. The "now" never stands still; it is always vanishing into the past, to be replaced by the next new moment of "now."

Likewise, each momentary subject—each center of consciousness or subjectivity—completes itself almost the instant it comes into being. It "expires" and becomes an object to be grasped, or "prehended," by the next moment of experience, the next subject. But the new subject is shaped by the pressure of its immediate (and distant) past, and so each new subject preserves continuity with its predecessors. (A good thing, otherwise we might not recognize ourselves to be the same person from one moment to the next.) So our bodies—as repositories of all our expired "prior" moments of experience—play a crucial role in preserving our sense of self-identity.

This "pressure" of the past on the present "now" subject—of objects conditioning and shaping the momentary sense of self—according to Whitehead, is the ultimate source of our notion of "causality." All other uses of the term are derived from this (usually unconscious) *felt* experience of the past determining our present. But this determinism is not the whole story. It is always accompanied by the creative self-agency of a new "now" subject that organizes or "informs" the constituting objects. (In this way, the metaphysical position of materialism, and its counterpart mechanism, is avoided.)

The present—this moment *now*—is the source from which all manifest reality springs. It is the abode of consciousness and the ever-replenishing well of creativity that both sustains the world and introduces true novelty and open-ended possibility. The "now" is an existential opening, the doorway though which the unmanifest becomes manifest (both as subject and object, as mind and matter). Depending on our worldview, we might call this opening the domain of quantum potential, zero-point energy field, or the channel for spiritual creativity. (German existential philosopher Martin Heidegger called it the "clearing" through which Being shows up.)

All past—all that ever existed—was once present. All objects were once subjects. All matter was once mind. But mind cannot exist without matter—the present is inextricably coupled to the past, as subject is to object. Always surfing on the crest of time, the present carries the weight of the past. It is the cutting edge of history. It holds the past together—without the present, the past would evaporate into nothingness. Without the past, the present would have no form. Past and present, subject and object, mutually implicate each other.

In Whitehead's cosmology, the world consists of "organisms"—these inextricable couplings of subjects and objects, of minds and bodies. Organisms are subjective objects, experiencing bodies, composed of *matter that feels*—from subatomic particles to atoms, molecules, cells, plants, and animals.

Every organism is a hierarchy of its constituent suborganisms (e.g., cells in a body, molecules in a cell, atoms in a molecule, etc.)—

what systems theorist Arthur Koestler called "holons" (meaning every part belongs to a whole, and every whole is composed of parts—that is, all organisms, all beings, are "part-wholes").[3] Externally, a holon or organism is perceived as an object; internally it is experienced as a subject. Every holon, therefore, tingles with the creativity and subjectivity of its hierarchy of *present* elements. Simultaneously, each present subject (at each level) tingles with the pressure of its own objective past—the matter or objects that compose its associated body.

This "tingling with subjectivity and creativity" we call "choice" or "freewill." And this "tingling with the pressure of the past" we call "causality."

However, this "causality" is quite different from our usual billiard-ball notion of one thing causing another to move by imparting some energy to it. Rather than an exchange of energy, as typically understood in mechanism, what's happening is a sequence of experiencing subjects blinking in and out of existence. And this "sequence of subjects" retains its sense of continuity by a process more accurately described as a passing on of meaning, than a mechanistic exchange of energy.

We might say that our original intuition of causality is the communication of meaning from the past—from objects, expired subjects—to the current *now* experiencing subject. It is the *felt* exchange of meaning. Based on this felt intuition, scientists and philosophers projected the notion of causality onto the world of objects, as though the relationships between objects could be understood without reference to any experiencing subject, as merely an objective exchange of energy. Hume threw science and philosophy into a crisis when he revealed that causality could not be objectively observed.

The alternative to Kant's solution, then, is that rather than assuming everything we know about causality has its origins in some innate mental category that automatically and inevitably shapes our understanding of the world, what we believe to be a process of cause and effect between objects is ultimately an *acausal* synchronistic sharing of meaning between subjects (or between now-subjects and expired-subjects). In short, causality is an *intersubjective* experience of shared meaning.

In then end, then, even causality is ultimately an *experience* of the pressure of the past. It loses its sense of energetic exchange and turns out to be, rather, a sharing of meaning.

Looked at this way, we can see how Jung's synchronicity can give us a glimpse of what Whitehead meant by causality. *The connection between matter and mind is ultimately a connection via meaning rather than mechanism.*

This is not to deny that causality, understood as exchanges of energy between objects, never occurs. It may, but we can only ever know about it because our mind, our subjective experience within the "now," prehends, or grasps, meaning passed on from prior, expired, momentary subjects. We feel the pressure of the past, and we interpret this as "energy" undergoing a process of cause and effect.

What I am proposing here is that alongside the causality we attribute to objects, the world also produces patterns of connectivity that are fundamentally linked by meaning. I agree with Jung that when subjects and objects (mind and matter) are involved in a synchronistic event the deep acausal nature of reality reveals itself to us.

Jung wrote his landmark book *Synchronicity: An Acausal Connecting Principle* with physicist Wolfgang Pauli, one of the early founders of quantum theory. They likened the acausality of synchronicities with the then new and thoroughly baffling notion that quantum events are uncaused. Typically, quantum acausality is described as randomness. And one of the great puzzles is how the familiar world of order all around us—the constancy of nature even amid perpetual change—could be built on a completely random series of events. Yet that is precisely what quantum theory had revealed.

The standard explanation in modern physics for how a world of order could arise from utterly random quantum events is *statistical probability.* In complex macroscopic systems the randomness of countless trillions of quantum events remains deeply buried in matter. Yes, each individual quantum event is random, we are told, but *collectively* the randomness is mostly canceled out, and the world of material objects evolves as a network of highly probable objective events. So, nothing about our world is, or could be, ever completely certain— instead, we live within a network of highly probable events that are themselves built on intrinsic quantum uncertainties.

Not all contemporary physicists could bring themselves to accept this bizarre state of affairs. And great physicists such as Albert Einstein and David Bohm took a different tack. Einstein declared that "God does not play dice with the universe," and Bohm developed a detailed alternative mathematical formalism for quantum mechanics that included a deep underlying order directing the apparently random quantum events. Bohm said that every manifest quantum event is surrounded by "pilot waves" that guide or direct the unfolding of quantum processes. Bohm called this deep underlying dynamic the "implicate order." (We will discuss this further in chapter 13, "*Dialogue: Consciousness and Cosmology.*")

Bohm's quantum cosmology—especially his notion of the pre-quantum implicate order—made a radical break with standard physics and materialist philosophy. Bohm was saying, in effect, that below the level of the quantum lies a deeper, innate intelligence that he referred to as "purposeful holomovement" (a phrase that will become more meaningful when we come to chapter 13). In other words, Bohm was presenting a thoroughly panpsychist cosmology—a metaphysical worldview that acknowledges the presence of some kind of consciousness (or "intelligence") all the way down to the deepest levels of physical reality. Consciousness, purpose, meaning, Bohm is telling us, are embedded in the very roots of what we know and experience as the manifest physical world. Matter/energy itself is sentient, intentional, and creative, and this may hold the key to the age-old "mind-body problem."

MIND-BODY INTERACTION

Synchronicity, as an acausal connection through meaning, may offer us a radically different approach to understanding two related problems that have befuddled philosophy and science for a long time: the famous "hard" problem of how mind and body are connected, and the "causality problem" of explaining how mind could cause the body to move.

Let's look at the causality problem first—how mind causes the body to move. We are all intimately familiar with this: You choose to wave your arm and it moves. Somehow, it seems, the *mental* act of choosing has the power to move something *physical*. This is a complete mystery to science.

For one thing, just *how* does a nonphysical event (making a choice) get translated into a physical event (moving a body part)? How is it possible for a thought or an idea to be transmuted into physical action? Even if we could understand how consciousness might be transformed into energy, it would still violate the first law of thermodynamics (also known as the Law of Energy Conservation), a cornerstone of modern physics, which tells us that energy can neither be created nor destroyed. Yet every time we choose to move our bodies we are apparently introducing some *new* energy into the universe. That's a problem for science.

But there may be a way out—if we give up the old idea of mechanistic causality involving exchanges of energy. We'll come back to the causality problem in a moment, but first let's see how solving the mind-body problem is tied up with solving the problem of the causality of consciousness. With three simple "keys" we can unlock these perennial riddles.

First key: realizing that *knowing* is not a form of energy—it is *awareness* of energy. Just remember the slogan, "Energy *flows*. Consciousness *knows*."

Second key: Matter/energy is *intrinsically* sentient—just remember *matter feels*.

Third key: Matter/energy possesses *self-agency*. Because it is sentient (and consciousness is *first-cause*—see below), matter/energy *moves itself*.

Put the three keys together and we have our solution to the mind-body problem: *Consciousness is the innate ability of matter/energy to know and move itself purposively.*

There is no dualism of mind moving body, and therefore no mysterious mind-body interaction. I'm drawing attention to a rather obvious and familiar fact: *Our bodies move themselves—guided by our consciousness.* It is the body's own consciousness that *chooses*, and the body moves accordingly. Bodies move themselves because they are *sentient, knowing,* and *volitional*—in other words, bodies tingle with consciousness.

The whole notion of mind-body "interaction" is a hangover from Cartesian dualism. There is no interaction, I'm proposing. Does the shape of a tennis ball "interact" with the substance of the ball? Does the past "interact" with the present? Does the number four "interact" with four cows in a field? When we speak of "interaction" in this context, not only are we objectifying consciousness but we are also reifying it, and even physicalizing it. At the very least we are "*substantifying*" it—doing what Descartes did: conceptually turning mind into a substance.

For mind to interact with matter, they both would have to share a point of *location in space*. That's just not possible for mind because *subjectivity* isn't that kind of reality. Consciousness is what *knows* or feels the flowing of energy, and it doesn't interact with energy to know it—because *consciousness is the innate knowing of energy*. There is no interaction because interaction requires two things to interact. I'm saying there really is only the one reality: *sentient energy.**

This avoids breaking the first law of thermodynamics because consciousness does not mysteriously introduce new energy into the universe. From this viewpoint, it is a categorical error to think of "mind moving body," or "consciousness creating energy," or "thought converting to action"—these are all hangovers from Cartesian dualism.

The matter of our bodies (in our cells, molecules, atoms, etc.) is itself sentient, and it "communicates" with the consciousness of our unified embodied "self." I'm confident that something like this is happening, and I'm also confident that it's not *causal*, not in the way Descartes implied. Instead, I'm proposing that the relationship between "my" sentient body and the sentience of "my" constituent cells, molecules, atoms, etc. is *intersubjective*—involving a sharing of *meaning* rather than an exchange of energy (mechanism). And it's a two-way

---

*The situation is different if we talk of *subtle* energy interacting (such as *ch'i* or *prana*) with physical bodies. This is not at all comparable to the mind-body hard problem. It is quite conceivable that subtle energy, like electromagnetic energy, is *vibrational*—in fact I'm almost certain that it is. And just as the high vibrations of a guitar can "interact" with the low vibrations of a standup bass, or just as ultraviolet light can interact with objects reflecting the visible spectrum, or just as radio waves can interact with TV receivers, I see no conceptual difficulty imagining how subtle vibrations might resonate with lower-frequency bodies.

communication. I can get my cells to move (e.g., by moving my body through conscious choice) and they can get me to move or act (e.g., through what we might normally understand as "unconscious" processes. Intuition may be communications between our cells and our conscious "self").

In neither case (communication from cells to self, or from self to cells), is consciousness *causing* my body to move. Rather, "we" share meaning and intentions, and the matter associated with the shared consciousness (i.e., my body) then moves itself directed by the purposes expressed in "my" "collective" consciousness.

Furthermore, I'm saying that this intersubjective process or communication is happening "all the way down and up." Ultimately, the consciousness of "me, my cells, I" is relaying the intentions of the Universal Self or Cosmic I. This is what directs or in-forms the movements of the entire body of the cosmos—and all "our" movements are steps in that cosmic dance.

A DEEPER CAUSALITY?

Blending the metaphysical insights of Jung and Pauli with Bohm's, and viewing them in the context of the mind-body and causality problems, we come full circle in some sense. We can begin to see that the "acausality" of synchronistic events may actually be expressions into manifestation of deep unmanifest cosmic meaning. We may, as Einstein and Bohm did (and as Jung and Pauli did not) understand this as a completely different kind of "causality"—the causality of *choice* and *creativity.*

So, yes, there may be a kind of causality at work at the most fundamental levels of reality—even within synchronicity—but it is not a causality of mechanism, objective exchanges of physical energy. Rather, it is a causality of *first-cause* sourced in the inner cosmos of the psyche, a subjective causality of intentionality, a causality of volition—what we might call a truly creative act of the whole unified cosmos, a creative act of Spirit.

And because it involves the whole cosmos of interpenetrating mutually creating and mutually sustaining subjects, we could call it an *intersubjective* causality of shared meaning and purpose. If this is so, then the idea that synchronicities are "messages from the gods" takes on new significance. Indeed, they would be expressions of the deep intelligence of the whole cosmos flaring up, usually at moments of personal existential crisis—"divine" clues or reminders of our profound interconnectedness and ultimate unity.

In short, there may well be a deeper (or higher) consciousness—a cosmic consciousness with its own powers of choice and causality—of which our apparently individual consciousness is always just an expression. In that case, the mind or consciousness that "chooses," for example, to move my body would not be "mine" at all. It could be that all apparent individual acts of free will are really ways the Cosmic I has of moving bodies in space-time. Of course, again, it's not the Cosmic I that is "causally" moving our bodies, but our bodies "giving voice to the cosmos," expressing the will of the Cosmic I. Likewise, synchronicities would be "whispers" from the cosmos, telltale signs that we are part of a larger intelligence. None of this involves anything "supernatural"; it just expands our notion of what is "natural."

How can we learn to pay attention to these "clues from the gods"? By now it will come as no surprise to hear that opening up to the meaning of synchronicities takes us beyond the grasp of reason and the senses. We need to develop other ways of knowing. We need to be willing to take an epistemological leap beyond words and ideas—a leap that involves some risk because more often than not it takes us through the fires of transformation. We need to be willing to open up to different "shafts of wisdom"—the topic of our next three chapters.

9

Shafts of Wisdom

Two philosophers, one a scientist from the West, the other a sage from the East, were sitting on the bank of a river discussing the nature of the world. The scientist reached down and scooped up a handful of sand:

"This is the stuff of the world," he said as he let the grains slip through his fingers and vanish into the water. "Particles of matter." The sage smiled, then without a word stood up and walked into the flowing stream.

"The world is like this," he said, standing to his waist in the river. The scientist looked up, and slightly amused, asked, "You mean the world is basically made of water?"

"No, I don't mean that," replied the sage. "I mean the world is like this . . ." and he moved his arms slowly through the air as if following its unseen pattern of currents.

The scientist, a little puzzled, inquired: "If you mean it is made of air, or perhaps of whatever air and water have in common, then in reality you agree with me, for both air and water are made of molecules and atoms, like the grains of the sand."

The sage shook his head. "The world is not made of anything. There is nothing—no-*things*, just activity."

"But what is it that produces the activity, just what is it that changes?" the scientist asked.

"That's my very point," said the sage. "We are now asking similar questions. And we must answer, it is the *whole world* that produces the activity. The whole world moves from within itself—don't you agree?"

Modern physics has now revealed that the fundamental sub-atomic entities are not solid "things," but events—dynamic patterns and processes—and that means *change*. Nature is not static; it does not stand still for scientists to discover its laws, like a photographer capturing an image on film. If we wish to discover fundamental laws or principles of nature we should look into the nature of change to discover what accounts for the regularities of the world of matter and for the unpredictable, creative irregularities of consciousness. What, for example, is the relationship between consciousness and change, between choice and time, between matter and dynamic form?

Eastern spiritual traditions constitute a large body of knowledge based on the idea that nothing is constant, everything changes. In Hinduism, for example, this vision is expressed as the cosmic dance of Shiva, in Buddhism as the ceaseless flux of *dharmas,* the moment-by-moment becomingness and vanishing of the world. In Taoism, the nature of these changes is explained in terms of interaction between *yin* and *yang*—a principle that Western scientific minds can find difficult to grasp because it involves intuitive as well as rational sources of knowledge. In fact, as we shall see, it even involves forms of knowing that transcend intuition.

To grasp the full implications of the yin-yang principle, one must go beyond rational arguments and logical analysis, and be open to alternative "shafts of wisdom"—including intuition, insight, and a form of paradoxical knowing best described as "not-knowing" or "no-knowledge." Another term for this is "paradox consciousness," which involves a form of knowing prior to, and transcending, abstractions or any separation of subject from object.

We will look more closely at this paradoxical form of knowing in chapter 11. But first, it will help if we acknowledge how current scientific knowledge is limited, and how opening up to different ways of knowing could clear the way for a truly radical science of consciousness—thereby helping to bridge the gap between science and spirituality.

PATTERNS THAT FIT

Modern science, using the powerful gifts of reason and sensory empiricism, has undoubtedly given us a large, highly organized, and complex body of knowledge. Science allows us to understand, for example, aspects of nature as diverse as why rivers flow into the ocean, how birds can fly, how life may have evolved from inorganic matter, how to produce electricity; from what goes on inside an atom to how a living cell manages to stay alive and reproduce itself, to the age, weight, and size of the Earth, and how it moves around the sun, to how the sun manages to give off so much energy for billions of years, to how the universe may have begun and how it may end.

That is really a wonderful store of knowledge though, of course, in no case is it complete. And some of the explanations may turn out eventually to be wrong. Nevertheless, science helps make sense of the world we see around us; it makes sense of our experiences. Scientific theories and "laws," then, are ways of correlating experiences and, as such, are essentially orderly descriptions of patterns we observe in nature. The more the patterns fit together, the more we believe we know what's going on.

The same process of pattern formation occurs in the development of other disciplines that attempt to uncover truth and meaning: mysticism, religion, art, or mythology, for instance. In this fundamental way, science is not so different from these other bodies of knowledge. Whether in science or in mysticism, the test for truth or understanding is not the independent proof of details, but their coherence and ability to grow within the larger pattern of existing knowledge.

The closer we zoom in on a "single" fact, the more the surrounding matrix or pattern is blurred. Every so-called fact is known always and only as part of a larger pattern of data—what we really understand is the *pattern*. We cannot even know if there are *individual* facts or events.

To satisfactorily grasp the pattern, we need more than sensory data analyzed by reason and logic—we need also to *intuit* how the pattern holds together. There are just too many fine details, connected by too many complex relationships, for any one person to hold it all in awareness using rational concepts. An intuitive element is always involved, aiding us in grasping the pattern as a whole (or at least relevant parts of it). Take, for example, the idea of "an electron" as a "fact." Everything we know about an electron depends on a complex matrix of knowledge about other aspects of particle physics, electromagnetic theory, quantum theory, relativity theory, . . . plus a whole lot else besides.

Truth, then, any truth—scientific or mystical—must be related to the larger pattern, not to isolated details. In short, what we know in science are not "objective facts" but rather patterns that emerge from correlating scientific concepts.

Whitehead recognized this:

> The notion of the complete self sufficiently of any item of finite knowledge is the fundamental error of dogmatism. Every such item derives its truth, and its very meaning, from its unanalyzed relevance to the background that is the unbounded universe.[1]

And because the background pattern of knowledge changes constantly, the truth and meaning it expresses change or develop, too. This is true for science, as it is for art and mysticism. In each case, truth is not a mere gathering of facts; it is a relationship between the knowing subject and the rest of the unfolding universe.

Science, therefore, is not different from mysticism or spirituality because its knowledge is purely logical rather than intuitive. In fact, the history of science yields many examples where great discoveries resulted from flashes of insight, where reason was short-circuited by intuition. A few well-known examples will illustrate this.

INTUITION IN SCIENCE

Freidrich von Kekulé, a professor of chemistry in 1865, had a dream vision of a molecular structure that has since become one of the cornerstones of organic chemistry. He tells how he fell asleep one afternoon beside the fire and had a dream where atoms were dancing and twisting about in snakelike motion. Then one of the snakelike chains of atoms swung around and bit its own tail. Suddenly, "as if by a flash of lightening" he awoke and realized he had discovered that the structure of the benzene molecule was a closed chain or ring of atoms—like a serpent biting its own tail.

The great French mathematician Henri Poincaré developed one of his more important discoveries, known as "fuchsian functions," by a series of flashes of intuition. He had spent fifteen days of difficult work trying to prove that the fuchsian functions could not exist. One night, however, he could not sleep. His mind buzzed with ideas that collided until pairs interlocked. By morning, he had discovered the first of the fuchsian series.

Shortly afterward he went on a geological excursion and forgot all about his mathematical work. At one stage, as he was boarding a bus, he realized with another burst of insight that the mathematical formalisms he had used to define the fuchsian functions were identical to those of non-Euclidean geometry. Poincaré subsequently had a series of similar "flashes of insight" and recognized that a common factor in the creative process was a prolonged period of prior unconscious work.

German mathematician Karl Friedrich Gauss, whose work helped pave the way for Einstein's theory of General Relativity, had spent four years working on a particularly difficult theorem. Then one day he, too, had a sudden inspiration that solved the enigma.

Einstein, too, acknowledged that his sense of certainty relied more on imagination and intuition than on sharp logic and bare facts. At one time, he was so convinced of a theory because of its internal beauty that when some evidence emerged that contradicted his theory he was unmoved and said, "the facts must be wrong."

A striking feature of his early papers on relativity is that they contain little mathematics. He preferred to express his ideas in words describing simple thought experiments, rather than in abstract mathematical symbols and equations. He had an unusually keen capacity for insight and arrived at his results by instinct and intuition as to what they *should* be. In forming his concepts, he made use of those intuitive glimpses that could not be expressed in words or any language. These "glimpses" were *experienced* rather than "understood" or "known" in any communicable sense. Einstein *felt* his thinking.

Scientists, like mystics, go beyond the facts not for the sake of idle speculation but because they must—if they are to make any sense at all. Intuition clues us into the whole (or at least to the larger pattern of events and their connections), and then we try to bring the intuition "down to size" by applying analytical tools of reason and logic to formulate manageable and testable hypothesis. But, as we saw, by focusing on some isolated experimental variable, we inevitably blur knowledge of the contextual pattern. We gain something from precision but also lose some of the holistic value contained in the original intuition.

Like the rest of us, scientists use intuition to "connect the dots" between so-called facts. For example, as we saw in the previous chapter, the very notion of causality, the bedrock of mechanistic science, is *never* observed as a fact. It is purely an intuition. Likewise, objectivity in science is something of a myth. The experimenter is never isolated from the experiment (otherwise how would he or she gain any knowledge?), and he or she inevitably interferes to an indeterminate degree, with what is being observed. The "facts" of the experiment are not "out there" shielded from the researcher's subjective influence as if behind some thick plate glass of objectivity. Scientists, like mystics and artists, inevitably *participate* in the acquisition and expression of knowledge.

CAN YOU PROVE IT?

There can be no final, objective truth in science, and no such thing as "proof." A classic illustration will make this clear. Let's say you want to test the hypothesis "all swans are white," and you set out to prove your statement by observing as many swans as you can. Ten swans. One hundred swans. A thousand. A million. A billion . . . and in every case they turn out to be white, just as your hypothesis predicted. You might be tempted at this point to believe that you have proved your hypothesis. A billion data points, and they all confirm the prediction: "All swans are white."

But then someone suggests you go to Australia, and there you discover a black swan. Despite the previous millions or billions of confirming instances, all it takes is this *single* observation to refute or disprove your hypothesis. *No matter how many confirming instances support a hypothesis or theory, it is always possible that the next observation will be different and refute it.*

Of course, the researcher could declare: "Yes, we have discovered a large black bird in Australia that *resembles* a swan. But, because it is black, by *definition* it cannot be a swan!" However, this would be a slippery way out. A more truly *scientific* response would be to test the black bird further to see if, for example, its genetics actually do match those of white swans. If the DNA does match, then the hypothesis is disconfirmed (*all* swans are not white). And if it doesn't match, *this time,* the possibility still remains that the very next, or some future, observation will reveal a genetically true *non-white* swan. No amount of data can ever *prove* that the hypothesis is true without exception. The best we can hope for are observations that support or disconfirm the hypothesis, allowing us to refine it. Bottom line: Science cannot prove anything; it can only *disprove.**

I emphasize this point not to downplay the importance of science, but to challenge the notion that the scientific method of sensory empiricism, reason, and logic is some kind of epistemological Excalibur that alone can slash away the veils of ignorance and reveal truth. Instead of proof, we should aim for clarity, rigor, accuracy, and integrity in how we gain knowledge, and in how we communicate it.

DIFFERENT WAYS OF KNOWING

In this and subsequent chapters, therefore, we will explore different ways of knowing, to see how they may complement scientific knowing—and how they may contribute to developing a *science of consciousness.* The following discussion of epistemologies is partly inspired by the work of Chinese scholar R. G. H. Siu, whose *The Tao of Science,* an essay on Western knowledge and Eastern wisdom, is an insightful analysis of the comparative values and validity of rational knowledge and intuitive knowledge.[2]

Knowledge is a continuum because it is a reflection of the continuum of nature onto consciousness. But when restricted to logic

---

*In my experience as a teacher, it is commonplace for students to think that science is about *proving* facts conclusively, and that leaves them with a wrong impression of what scientists are actually doing. It also leaves many of them with the idea that scientists are motivated by some dogmatic urge to "prove" this or that, closing off all possible alternatives. People feel uncomfortable with this, and I try to point out that their discomfort is based on a misunderstanding of what scientists are actually doing in practice.

and rational analysis, based on a view of the universe where "causes" and "effects" are regarded as separate phenomena, nature is represented in our consciousness as separated facts and discrete entities—consequently, the continuum of knowledge is fragmented into little bits. This is the process of abstraction by which science selects and focuses on particular details in the search for exactness and certainty.

The conventional aim of science is to build up a detailed picture of nature from these fragmented bits of knowledge (like a pointillist or impressionist painting) all linked together or classified according to common properties and characteristics. This method has considerable experimental value, but we should keep in mind that the little pieces from which the scientific world picture is constructed are abstractions.*

The precision sought by science does not exist in nature, where there are no exact and discrete entities corresponding to scientific concepts such as electrons, atoms, molecules, genes, cells, organs, and individuals. Someone accustomed to a causal and rational mode of thought may object that exactness *can* be observed in nature. For example, we could point to a single tree and maintain there is just one tree—no more, no less. Or we could point to our own body and say "I am one, just one, individual."

But could we look at the ocean and point to one wave and define

---

*In a perceptive observation, my colleague Martin Schwartz, Ph.D., of the Departments of Microbiology and Biomedical Engineering, University of Virginia, remarked: "Actually this process is not uniquely scientific, it is our *commonsense* view of reality. Watching my children when they were young, I had the strong impression that they learned about permanent 3-D objects from experience—they were not born to it. For example, what we know as a "chair" (or any other object) is a concept, built out of many discrete experiences. This issue brings home how so-called facts are irretrievably linked to concepts and the entire realm of rational knowledge is a *network* of interlocking facts.

"But I have to disagree on one point: Abstraction is *not* responsible for chopping up reality; abstraction is unification, seeing hidden likenesses shared by different experiences and giving those likenesses a name. Seeing a shape from different angles and calling it a chair unifies those experiences. I think that the error is seeing the fundamental units of reality as objects instead of experiences."

its boundaries? Where does the wave begin, where does it end? You may object that this is not a fair comparison because a wave is not so much a "thing" as a process. And you would be right. A wave is a process, but so is the tree and so is your body. There are no "things" distinct from processes.

Just like the ocean wave, the tree and human bodies have no sharp boundaries. Where does the oxygen that you breathe become "you" and no longer a separate gas? At what point is the sweat on your brow something other than "you"? What about your breakfast, is that you yet? Organisms, whether human or tree, are constantly exchanging matter and energy with their environments. There is no exact line of separation.

If we could see to the minuteness of a billionth of a millimeter, where does the tree begin and the inanimate world end? Can we say exactly when or where a molecule of carbon dioxide (roughly ten millionths of a millimeter) being absorbed by a leaf becomes part of the living chloroplast in a leaf cell? The tree is constantly drawing salts from the soil into its roots, and resin oozes from the cells of the bark. Just as an electron is an abstraction representing an uncertain process, so too the concepts of a single, separate tree or an individual human being, are abstractions.

Exactness and precision are available only in theory. If we want knowledge that reflects nature's unbroken continuum, then the gaps between the abstractions need to be filled in by other shafts of wisdom that do not rely on analysis, causality, and objectivity.

THE MYTH OF OBJECTIVITY

Science is considered objective because its knowledge is open to inspection, and is assumed to be independent of any individual viewpoint. But this objectivity is more apparent than real. It relies on the assumption that it is possible to separate subject and object, and to study them independently (introspection and contemplation for subjects and empirical science for objects). This is false for a number of reasons.

First, the observer (subject) interferes in an unascertainable manner with the object of investigation.* Not only is the boundary between subject and object an illusion, but both subject and object are constantly influencing each other, and there is no way the subject can subtract or extract him- or herself from the environment of the object to arrive at "purely objective" knowledge. The "actualities" are there for everyone, but because of their inherent uncertainties, no two people can observe the same event.

To counteract this, multiple observations are made, and concepts and theories are formed based on probabilities. However, each observation is experienced by each individual observer, not by the scientific community or by society at large. Scientific concepts and theories, therefore, are arguably hardly more objective than those of other bodies of knowledge such as metaphysics, mysticism, or art.

And the publication of scientific theories in journals and books does not make science a public affair any more than the publication of metaphysical treaties or descriptions of mystical experience. Yet scientific knowledge is considered public on the basis that, being the product of rational analysis of objective evidence, it is communicable between people. This "communicability" is supposed to distinguish scientific from mystical, artistic, or religious knowledge. But just how much scientific knowledge is communicable and to whom?

It is fine in theory to say that scientific knowledge published in journals and books or online is there for everyone to inspect and acquire. However, scientific knowledge is *not* open to universal public scrutiny. Not just anyone can pick up a book on, for example, "the biochemistry of cytodifferentiation" and understand it. Someone who understands and learns from such a specialist publication is unlikely to gain much information from another journal in another specialist discipline, say, particle physics. By focusing more and more on finer details abstracted from nature, scientific knowledge has become increasingly obscured in a maze of specialist disciplines.

---

*In physics, this is referred to as "the measurement problem." Every time a measurement is made on subatomic particles, for instance, the very act of measurement changes what is being measured. For example, the photons of the light needed to observe an electron have enough energy to knock it off its path.

KNOWLEDGE, RUMOR, OR FAITH?

As R. G. H. Siu pointed out, the rate of specialization in science is exponential. In the eighteenth century, it was still possible for a well-read citizen to comprehend the entire spectrum of the sciences and a lot more besides. Back then, one could have been an authority on mathematics, astronomy, as well as philosophy, art, and theology. But now, specialization has increased so much that no one person could possibly read through even a fraction of the published literature. No one researcher could possibly have an inkling of what researchers in all the other fields are doing. To get at all this knowledge, and to correlate it into a coherent description of nature is nowadays impossible.

And even if there were some super genius who could get it all together, how much would that person really know? How much *knowledge* would have been communicated in contrast to rumor or hearsay evidence, no matter how "authoritative"?

Given the need for highly specialized scientific training, and given the interdependence of data within the highly complex matrix of scientific knowledge as a whole, it is progressively more and more difficult for anyone to assert that they actually *know* how the data they observe find their place within the larger context or continuum of knowledge. Instead of possessing scientific *knowledge*, I'm arguing that most scientists actually rely a great deal on *rumor* or *faith*. I know this sounds provocative—but I think it is valid, and it highlights a state of affairs rarely acknowledged within the scientific community.

It is one thing to read, and even understand, what researchers have published within some specialized area of science (let's say research into something as basic as electrons). But, *without the scientific "initiation" involved in learning how to operate the research equipment and, therefore, being able to "see" or experience the data for oneself*, the "knowledge" remains secondhand and must be taken on trust (or "faith")—that's what I mean by "rumor."

So, even if our "super genius" could comprehend *all* data published in every journal, he or she would still be dealing with nothing more than sophisticated and authoritative "rumor" *unless or until he/she actually performed the experiments personally*.

How, then, can scientific knowledge, which consists of an increasing number of specialized disciplines—each focusing on esoteric details abstracted from nature—be considered a public affair, universally communicable? The vast majority of people are excluded from scientific knowledge because of their unfamiliarity with the subject matter, and that's why science is no more objective or "public" than the knowledge of mystics or shamans. Each requires a process of rigorous training or *initiation* before the knowledge is available.

The methods of initiation may be different—logical analysis and empiricism in science, intuition and insight in mysticism—but the availability of scientific knowledge and mystical knowledge is the same. Anyone could dedicate him- or herself to learning a particular spiritual practice as easily as learning the protocols of a particular science.

The point I'm emphasizing here is that the scientific "public" is a select group of initiates. Young students of science must learn the ropes for themselves, guided by reason and logic, just as aspiring mystics must develop meditation and other spiritual practices, guided by extra-rational experience. Each can be helped along the way by teachers who already have the relevant knowledge, and who can indicate the path to progress. Either way, there is a learning curve, and if one doesn't follow that curve then the knowledge (scientific or spiritual) remains "esoteric" to the uninitiated. In each case, until the students go through the initiation process themselves, the knowledge remains just rumor. Scientific knowledge, therefore, is no more *communicable* or *testable* than spiritual knowledge; it is no more objective in the sense of being open to public scrutiny.

I am not implying that there is *no* difference between science and spirituality. Clearly there is—otherwise we wouldn't need two words to name identical disciplines. Of course there are differences—science focuses its beam of inquiry exclusively on third-person *objects;* spirituality focuses on first-person (or second-person) experiences. The *targets* of the respective disciplines are different; and the *procedures* for gaining data are different, too (because the "targets" are different). Nevertheless, the *essential methodology* is the same in both cases: Given the requisite training for both, spiritual data are just as observable as scientific data as we will see in the next chapter.

10

Knowing-2

Radical Science

While I was writing the previous chapter, a colleague of mine, Dr. Martin Schwartz who is a research scientist at the University of Virginia, pointed out what he believes is a crucial difference between science and spiritual knowledge—science, he said, is more public and objective. For example, anyone can see the needle on a voltmeter (a device for measuring an electric charge) and, therefore, many people can read it and agree on what they observe. By contrast, mystical experiences are not open to public view, and, therefore, offer no possibility of objective consensus. His point is that it is *easier* to access and test objective, scientific data than subjective, private spiritual experiences.

His objection is understandable and should be considered. So, let's look at this example a little more closely. Yes, anyone (with functioning eyes) can see a voltmeter; but not everyone (e.g., a New Guinea tribesman or a four-year-old child) will understand or be able to meaningfully *interpret* what the voltmeter is indicating. Similarly, it is also true that anyone (with "inner vision") can observe or reflect on their own consciousness; but not everyone (e.g., a typical materialist scientist or a four-year-old child) will be sufficiently skilled at detecting, understanding, and meaningfully *interpreting* the subtleties and shades of their first-person experience.

What is "easy" is what we are familiar with, and in our culture we have been educated for hundreds of years to use and trust our senses and reasoning faculties to know, understand, and navigate our way through the world. However, other cultures, while, of course, also using their senses, do not share our Western bias for sensory verification—that what can be seen, touched, heard, smelled, or tasted is the best or only guide to what is real. They also use, trust, and cultivate other non-sensory ways of knowing such as feeling, intuition, and intersubjective presence.

CULTURALLY CONDITIONED KNOWLEDGE

I believe it is a cultural and historical accident that modern Western (scientific) societies place greater emphasis and trust on senses such as vision, hearing, and touch rather than on attending to subtle shifts in consciousness (and our language reflects this bias). I'm not denying the biological, physiological, and evolutionary factors in this perceptual bias. Survival demands and contingencies have certainly selected for sharp senses.

But if we are willing to expand our cosmology or metaphysics to allow for (at least the possibility of) more subtle realms of being (perhaps involving *ch'i* or *prana*) as other non-Western cultures do, then "survival" takes on a much broader significance because it would involve abilities and capacities for discerning the relationship between our biology and these subtle realms. Shamanic healing, for instance, is less (if at all) concerned about chemical or biological agents, and very concerned about subtle agents such as "spirits," "souls," "energy beings." Developing the perceptual skills for discerning these subtle beings, and developing appropriate language for communicating *with* and *about* them is often a priority in such cultures.

Many different cultures, throughout millennia, have held the metaphysical belief (not shared by modern Western scientific societies) that the health, well-being, and survival of our biological bodies are intimately dependent on the health and integrity of our "subtle bodies" and relationships with "spirits." They believe in what I have elsewhere called a "continuum ontology"[1] (sometimes referred to metaphysically as the Great Chain of Being—Spirit-Soul-Mind-Body-Matter), where "higher" or "more subtle" realms inform or "manifest" what happens in the "lower" realms.

The advent of psychoneuroimmunology in Western science is a recognition that mind influences the health of the body; shamans go a step further and tell us that soul influences mind, and further still that spirit influences soul. In some Western accounts of these traditions this progression from Spirit to Soul to Mind to Body (Life) to Matter is called "involution." Involution is seen as a complement to evolution, which reverses the process: moving from matter to life to mind (and that's as far as modern science has reached or is, so far, willing to go).

I think it is important, therefore, to acknowledge the strong influence culture has on how we perceive and understand the world (as we saw in chapter 4, "*Paradigms*: Intention Creating Reality," "believing is seeing"—our perceptions are conditioned by our conceptions). I see no reason to exclude the practices of science (which are also culturally and socially conditioned) from this influence. The scientific notion of *paradigms* is a now widely recognized version of this phenomenon.

Bottom line: What is "easy" in one society or culture (e.g., looking at, seeing, and understanding a voltmeter) may not be so easy in some other culture; and conversely, what may be "easy" in that other culture (e.g., attending to, observing, and understanding subtle energies or "spirits") may not be so easy in ours.

Nevertheless, I am aware that the audience for this book is likely to consist of Westerners, or of people educated within a culture heavily influenced by Western science. For such people (and I include myself), it is clearly the case that gaining knowledge via our five physiological senses is often much easier than by paying attention to subtle shifts in consciousness. In *our* culture, it is easier to gain information about physical objects (either systematically through science or casually by just using our senses) than it is to acquire knowledge of inner states of personal or intersubjective experiences.

One of the intentions of my "radical consciousness" trilogy as a whole is to highlight differences between standard scientific practices (focused on the physical world) and spiritual and/or shamanic practices (focused on nonphysical realms)—to draw attention to the *gaps* between science and these other ways of knowing, and then to offer *ways to begin building bridges* across those gaps.*

---

*I thank Dr. Martin Schwartz for his diligent reading of this and the previous chapter, and for urging me to emphasize the differences between science and spirituality and my attempts at bridge building.

I want to emphasize, again, that I am not ignoring the enormous value science has to offer society. I enthusiastically credit science for its really remarkable store of knowledge about the physical world, and for a truly effective *methodology.* But I believe it is important to highlight shortcomings that constrain the *restricted* version of that methodology practiced by most mainstream scientists—for example, operating on the assumption that only data gathered via the senses and analyzed using reason and mathematics can count as "true science."

We will now explore what I believe to be the *core essence* of the scientific method—a research methodology not based on an assumption of sensory empiricism. In fact, as we will see, I'm proposing a "radical science" that embraces spiritual and shamanic disciplines, giving us rigorous, *testable,* knowledge of the inner cosmos of consciousness to balance and complement our knowledge of the outer cosmos of matter and energy.

THE POR METHOD

It is commonly assumed that science is different from other forms of knowing, such as spirituality or shamanism, because science employs a unique methodology for gaining knowledge. For example, as we've seen, science is assumed to be objective, and to confine itself to exploration of the physical world—the world of *objects.* Spirituality and mysticism, on the other hand, are assumed to be "merely" subjective explorations of the interior world of consciousness.

Science is considered unique because it *tests* its knowledge—it conducts *experiments.* In volume three of this trilogy, I will discuss the issue of science and consciousness in much greater detail. But for now, I want to briefly explain why the assumed "uniqueness" of science derives from a deep misunderstanding about the essential nature of the scientific method.

Yes, it is true that, *as currently practiced,* modern science confines itself to the exploration of physical objects and therefore does not (and cannot) investigate consciousness. As long as science restricts its methodology to a combination of sensory empiricism and rational analysis (relying on the three "M"s of materialism, mechanism, and measurement), then we cannot have a science of *consciousness*. Quite simply, consciousness, being nonphysical and non-objective, is not amenable to this restricted scientific method.

Therefore, if we want to have a true science of consciousness the methodology of science will have to radically change to expand beyond the three "M"s. We will need to develop a *radical* science. And, as it happens, at its heart, science is already sufficiently "radical"—scientists just need to acknowledge it. The essential core of the scientific method will not have to change.

The essence of "radical science" is what I refer to as the "POR" method—short for "Procedure," "Observation," and "Report."* It is "radical" because it outlines an investigative methodology that can be applied to *any* form of rigorous inquiry—not merely to third-person, measurable, objects that are the focus of current science but also to first-person subjective private experiences and to second-person inter-subjective shared experiences (that are central to spiritual and shamanic practices and traditions). Here are the three essential elements of any rigorous (radically) scientific method:

Procedure—an agreed upon set of protocols for conducting the inquiry. This ensures both consistency and rigor if followed correctly.

Observation—as the investigator conducts the procedure he/she observes and records whatever registers in his/her experience (these are the research *data*). They may be sensory experiences of third-person objects, or first-person subjective private experiences (e.g., in medita-tion or other spiritual practice), or second-person intersubjective, shared experiences. In every case, the "data" are what show up in *expe-rience.* (There is no other way to acquire scientific data.)†

Report—having followed the procedure and observed the data in experience, the researcher *reports* his/her findings to a community of peers (e.g., via peer-reviewed journals). This allows other researchers

---

*Ken Wilber has summed up this three-part approach to knowledge as *injunction, illu-mination,* and *communal confirmation.*
†More than a century ago, philosopher William James called it "radical empiricism"—accepting as valid "data" any and all phenomena that show up in experience, and *only* those.

who have similarly adequate training in the procedures and observational methods to replicate the experiment and to *test* if the results confirm or disconfirm the findings in the original report. (An alternative way to describe this essence of "radical science" is: Protocol, Record, Test; or Procedure, Observation, Communication.)

The POR procedure involves all three investigative perspectives of objectivity, subjectivity, and intersubjectivity:

Procedure is a third-person *objective* "recipe" (set of protocols); available for anyone to follow;

Observation is a first-person *subjective* event—every scientific investigator necessarily attends to what shows up in his/her experience in order to get the data (all data originate in someone's private experience);

Report is a second-person *intersubjective* sharing or communication of information (data/experiences) among a community of qualified peers who can replicate and test the original experimental results.

Using this POR methodology, scientific knowledge would no longer be confined to objects in the physical world; instead, we would have an expanded or "radical" science capable of investigating the inner world of subjective and intersubjective experiences. By focusing on and applying the core essence of the scientific method, we can begin to bridge the perennial gap between science and spirituality. Further, the POR method could open science to a much vaster realm of knowledge beyond merely human consciousness.

INTERSPECIES SCIENCE

Something else often overlooked as a result of the dominance of rational thought in science is that the "public" science speaks of is confined to the consciousness of human beings. At first glance, this point may seem obvious and trivial. From the scientific or rational viewpoint, of course, all other animals and the plants are excluded from the public to which scientific knowledge is communicated. For how would you communicate the theory of relativity to a dog, or transmit the concept of genetic mutation to a drosophila fly or peavine?

These creatures can't think; they have no rational faculties. The sharing of knowledge is limited to human consciousness because other creatures are incapable of understanding. If the dog could think rationally enough, it would understand. The knowledge is there, and it is not because of any defect in its communicability that it cannot be shared with the dog (or any other species).

But just how true is all this?

Rather than saying that because the dog cannot think rationally, and that the failure of communication is due to him, we could equally suggest that it is precisely *because* scientific knowledge is so heavily loaded with logical analysis and rational exposition that it is limited to human consciousness. The situation could be described as follows: Because scientific knowledge is expressed in rational and causal terms, it is incapable of being communicated to the dog—that is, it is not translatable into information the dog's brain or mind can assimilate.

But there are other forms of knowledge that can be shared. We can communicate grief, anger, or joy to the dog, and it can communicate with us. The knowledge of the friendship between the dog and its human companion is mutually shared. And anyone who has seen cattle, sheep, pigs, or chickens on the way to the slaughterhouse cannot have helped noticing that the unfortunate creatures seem to *know* that the butcher, or some other ghastly fate, is waiting for them. These are extra-rational forms of knowledge that are not confined to human consciousness.

Rational analysis, as we saw, derives from abstracting bits and pieces from the continuum of nature, and rearranging them according to some theory or model. But this process of gathering separate bits of knowledge does not reflect the basic integrity of nature. Extra-rational knowledge, which goes beyond the realms of human consciousness, arises from the continuity of nature. It is not abstracted from the rest of nature but emerges spontaneously in suitably prepared minds—the feeling-based preconquest kind of consciousness discussed in chapter 2.

Despite its pretensions to "universality," science excludes all other creatures and inanimate matter from what it deems to be its universal public, because rational knowledge can be communicated only between humans. And, as we have seen, the men and women who do share scientific knowledge are a select and restricted group. Is it any easier to communicate the latest news on, for example, superstring theory to an indigenous tribesman in the rainforests of New Guinea, than to inform your dog about the protein in his meat?

INTUITION BEYOND REASON

Scientific knowledge cannot rightly claim to be more real, more representative of nature, because it is "objective and open to public scrutiny" than extra-rational knowing, which is "subjective and confined to the mind of the knower." It would be false and prejudiced to claim that "real" knowledge can be acquired only through logical concepts and reason applied to sensory data, a prejudice that would lead to the false conclusion that knowledge arrived at through means other than reason is irrational, consisting of empty imaginings.

In a personal communication, Dr. Martin Schwartz, whose views on science were mentioned at the beginning of this chapter, noted: "The question of reliability is central to the issue of public versus private knowledge. Pure rational thought or scientific research goes wrong often enough. There are plenty of published papers that are wrong; well known examples of incorrect theorems in math; and faulty data or analysis in science. However, the knowledge is sufficiently public that other suitably trained mathematicians or scientists can see what's wrong and correct the mistakes. Intuitions and other kinds of knowing, in contrast, are private, so it is not as easy for others to test or correct them."

His point is well taken. However, using the POR method, it would be possible for an investigator to report data acquired through intuition so that sufficiently trained peers, following the requisite research protocols/procedures, and observing their own intuitive data, would be able to *test* them and correct any faulty intuitions. It all hinges on *reportability*.

It is true that, by its very nature, intuition is often not translatable into language (i.e., rational concepts) and so may not be reportable and testable. And yet . . . what if intuitive data are reportable in other ways—for example through poetry, dance, music, or art? Wouldn't these be ways to report *and test* intuitive data?

I agree: *Interpretations* of intuitions are notoriously problematic—at least, linguistic or conceptual interpretations are. But what if intuitions were not filtered through the mesh of reason or language and instead were directly and spontaneously *enacted* and *expressed* nonverbally though the body? What if, for instance, dance or *ta'i ch'i* movements could be used to communicate intuitions? Isn't this what the sage at the beginning of this chapter was doing?

The point is that these other forms of knowing are not irrational— they are *extra*-rational. They are *beyond* reason, consisting of experiences not susceptible to rational analysis. To dismiss these other forms of knowledge would be to remain restricted to the rational. And to attempt to analyze and rationalize them would be to attempt to judge something that lies beyond reason by means of reason itself—and *that* would be irrational.

The processes by which intuitive knowledge and insight arise in consciousness cannot be satisfactorily described in rational and causal language. Whereas logic and reason can be expressed in coherent patterns of speech, intuition cannot be systematized in a comparable way. Rather, appropriately, intuition must be grasped intuitively. Because of this fundamental difference between rational thought and intuition, they have been considered two opposing and mutually exclusive modes of knowing. Those who favor logic and reason emphasize the imprecision and lack of definitiveness of intuition (which they find confusing), while those who prefer to rely on intuition are dissatisfied with the limitations of reason and often point to the many unsolvable paradoxes that laugh in the face of logic.

However, they are not mutually exclusive. As we saw, intuition goes hand-in-hand with reason in scientific discovery. It is continually filling in the gaps between the abstracted bits of knowledge produced by logic and reason. The ability to infuse intuitive understanding at each step of rational analysis is a prerequisite for scientific knowledge. Intuition, with its spontaneous comprehension, can grasp the interrelatedness and continuity of nature. Instead of priding ourselves on our rational abilities to the exclusion of other forms of knowing, we would all do better by being more open to the flow of knowledge through the other, extra-rational, shafts of wisdom—especially the paradoxical form of knowing that Taoists referred to as "no-knowledge."

And that's what we will look at next.

11

Knowing-3

Beyond Intuition

When logic and reason fail, intuition often takes over. But just as reason is limited, intuitive knowledge can be too. At this point, we must go beyond both modes of knowing and lose ourselves in the ever-changing continuum that we cannot know, only experience. This is the realm of "sage-knowledge" or "no-knowledge," as Chinese scholar R. G. H. Siu translated it from the Taoists. I have called it "paradox consciousness."

PARADOX CONSCIOUSNESS

No-knowledge is not really knowledge as understood in the West, where "knowledge" usually involves the selection or abstraction of specific details, and, typically, also assumes the duality of subject and object.

Paradox-knowledge, or no-knowledge, makes no such distinction. It involves an understanding of what the Chinese call *wu*, or non-being. *Wu* transcends all ideas and conventions. There are no separate entities and distinct phenomena—these are the objects of ordinary conventional knowledge. And, of course, *wu* cannot be such an object. To appreciate *wu*, one must forget all distinctions and definitions, and experience the silent spontaneity of no-knowledge. The scientist or philosopher who relies solely on rational knowledge becomes an artificial *spectator of* nature.*

---

*Reason automatically and necessarily *objectifies*—a result of the subject-predicate grammatical structure of language. And mathematics, as a process of symbolic abstraction *par excellence*, doesn't avoid this difficulty, either. Mathematics has no way of

Conversely, if a scientist opens him or herself to no-knowledge, to paradox consciousness, he or she becomes *a participant in nature* and shares the ineffable understanding *of what is*. All true intellectual creativity springs from the deep shafts of wisdom that connect this ineffable region with some rational synonym.

But just as there is no method for translating intuitive knowledge successfully into rational language, the ineffability of no-knowledge makes it even less susceptible to translation. Since no-knowledge is experiential, beyond the abstract objectivity of rational discourse, something inevitably is lost in translation into rational terms. To compensate for what is lost, one must rely, paradoxically, on one's own ineffable awareness of the ineffable. To achieve this awareness, one must put aside the segmented "facts" and "events" that are the objects of rational and logical thought, and allow the ego to fuse with or to dissolve into the wordless silence of no-knowledge.

To a confirmed rationalist, this may sound like muddled nonsense. But to dismiss it as such is to betray the uninitiated view that, as Siu put it, cannot distinguish between "having no knowledge" and having "no-knowledge." The former is simply a state of ignorance; the latter can be a state of enlightenment. To criticize and analyze no-knowledge from the basis of its translation into rational language is to miss the point that the translation itself is not no-knowledge. Such criticism arises from mistaking the description for what is described. No-knowledge is not something that can be thought about and analyzed. It is to be experienced.

The rationalist who refuses to open up to this ineffable shaft of wisdom sees nature as a challenging mystery, full of puzzling paradoxes to be broken apart piece-by-piece using the tools of logic and reason. But the mysteries and the paradoxes cannot be dissected and deconstructed. They must be entered into, engaged with fully by the whole human being—embodied action, rational mind, intuitive soul, and *wu* spirit. Paradoxically, the paradox remains, yet once inside the paradox, it dissolves into "what's-so."

---

including the *subject*—at best, it can include a symbolic placemarker in its equations for the subject, or at least for the consequences of the subject's inevitable participation (the psi symbol [Ψ] in quantum mechanics is a case in point).

THE "LANGUAGE" OF NATURE

No-knowledge is not restricted, like rational knowledge, to human consciousness. It is common to all nature and is communicated wordlessly between human and mammal, bird and reptile, trees and flowers and insects, and between the molecules and atoms of the oceans and the winds. It is the language of nature, the embodied language of our ancestors when they sang with the symphony of the wild, and shared its subtle messages—before the stones fell silent.

No-knowledge is the voice that informs us how nature appears to itself, not as it appears to the abstracted gaze of some rational mind, a scientist's or otherwise. It is through no-knowledge that the Taoist artist captures the "bambooishness of the bamboo." As Siu expressed it: "With rational knowledge, one is in tune with the scientific man; with intuitive knowledge added, one is in tune with the total man; with no-knowledge added, one is in tune with nature."[1]

PARTICIPATORY KNOWING

No-knowledge is a form of knowing where the "knower" merges with, or participates with, what is known. Because of this extrarational aspect, it is not easy to convey its essence in purely rational terms. But it has its rational aspect, too, and this can be discussed in terms of logic and paradox. However, describing this state of awareness in rational terms cannot convey its full meaning, which can be attained only by direct *experience* of the phenomenon, by non-mediated immersion in the experiential moment.

The main value of rational discussion of such knowing is to point out that rational knowledge cannot be the full story and that, with an awareness of the limitations of reason, one can benefit from other sources of knowledge. For example, the Taoist sages have emphasized that to understand or appreciate the wisdom of the yin-yang principle we have to go beyond intellect and reason—and even beyond intuition.

A rational objection to the principle would be that, like psychoanalysis or Marxism, it is not falsifiable, and therefore not much use to science. But that kind of objection misses two important points. First, unlike psychoanalysis and Marxism, the principle does not claim to be "scientific" in the sense that it is the product of reason and sensory empiricism. Second, because it involves no-knowledge, it goes beyond, while including, reason as a means of apprehending the world.

To criticize the principle rationally in an attempt to invalidate it would be a categorical error. Its rational aspect can be fruitfully criticized rationally; but it would be irrational to criticize its non-rational aspect rationally. Reason isn't much help to us in understanding paradoxes; but, like nature itself, the yin-yang principle does not shy away from paradoxes. Nothing is ever wholly yin or wholly yang, each always contains the germ of its opposite.

None of this is intended to devalue the power of reason. In fact, in my written works and college lectures I emphasize the importance of a rigorous application of reason to understanding the mind-body problem and other philosophical and scientific issues. But by now it should be clear why I think we need to cultivate other ways of knowing—alternative epistemological gifts such as feeling, intuition, and no-knowledge—particularly if we wish to develop a rigorous (and radical) scientific approach to exploring consciousness. And by far the most radical way of knowing is this paradoxical path to wisdom called "no-knowledge."

A VIA NEGATIVA

The methods for gaining rational knowledge, on the one hand, and no-knowledge, on the other, are very different. Rational, scientific knowledge is acquired by positively emphasizing the phenomenon under investigation—by abstracting and isolating it from the continuum in which it is embedded.* No-knowledge, on the other hand, is acquired by the opposite or negative method of *not* separating the phenomenon from the continuum. No-knowledge does not point out, or describe, the phenomenon; instead, by using a negative method of illuminating the shadowy character of phenomena that relate to it,

---

*This reductionist methodology is one way of doing science but is not the only way. In many areas of research, systems approaches are gaining favor.

but are not it, the ineffable features of the phenomenon filter through the shafts of wisdom and emerge in our consciousness.

An analogy might help here: Throughout the 1980s, a popular fad was to experiment with a perceptual anomaly known as "defocalizing." People would show up at parties with pictures that looked liked nothing more than meaningless dots and patterns, but if you stared at the images obliquely for some time, suddenly, a *very noticeable* stereographic 3D image (of a dolphin, a lion, the Taj Mahal, or whatever) would jump out of the page. You never succeed in seeing the image by staring directly at the picture; you have to "loosen" your gaze, and learn to stare with your peripheral vision. For most people, the image eventually appears. Something like this "oblique attention" is the way to open up to "no-knowledge." It's a via negativa.

However, the positive and negative methodologies are not contradictory or mutually exclusive. The positive approach always contains an element of implication and uncertainty, and the negative approach must be balanced by a degree of rational interpretation in order to be useful in practical affairs. For the sake of simple explanation, I have discussed rational knowledge, intuitive knowledge, and no-knowledge separately; however, they are all parts of the one continuum of knowledge.

PRE-PERSONAL AND TRANSPERSONAL KNOWING

No-knowledge is a form of knowing that both precedes and transcends reason. However, this does not imply an identity between pre-rational and post-rational knowledge. That would be committing a "pre/trans fallacy" (to use Ken Wilber's term)—conflating pre-egoic *participation mystique* with trans-egoic spiritual, or mystical, experience. The two forms of knowing are different, though they do share common qualities. Let's look at this more closely.

The first is pre-personal, the second is transpersonal; both are *extra*-personal—neither takes the isolated, individual subject as the focal point of knowing. In the pre-personal state, consciousness has not yet evolved to an awareness of subjective individuality. It is still shared with and arises out of the group. It is *intersubjective*.

The second is transpersonal, having passed through, transcended, and included knowledge and distinctions gained through individualized personal experience. Transpersonal consciousness is experienced as a co-creation among mutually interpenetrating inter-subjects. It is *interpersonal* and intersubjective, in a way that the pre-personal cannot be (because there are not yet any "persons"). The commonalty that both forms of knowing share is intersubjectivity—a mutual, non-rational, participation among experiencing centers, or nodes, of consciousness.

I am, therefore, not advocating a conflation of pre-rational archaic magical thinking with post-rational mystical experience—even though the terminology used to describe both states of consciousness involves words such as "communion" and "unity." We may characterize the archaic experience as *embodied in a world of animated matter;* individuals felt themselves and their world to be alive, all part of a great matrix of interdependent bodies, experiences, and events. The poet Wordsworth wrote of a sense of "something deeply interfused," so perhaps we can borrow his insight and speak of "archaic interfusion"—distinct from the mystical experience of "spiritual unity." Our pre-rational ancestors lived in a world where matter and spirit, body and mind, were deeply interfused. They *felt* the world long before they thought about it, or could transcend such thoughts.

Valuable though I believe the pre/trans distinction is, I am not concerned with it in this chapter. I want to emphasize, rather, the *extra-rational* nature of "no-knowledge," and leave the evolutionary issue aside for now. I am not equating "no-knowledge" with mystical experience, though it is clearly an attribute of that state of consciousness. Nor does one have to be a mystic to be in the state of "no-knowledge."

Your dog's consciousness is a prime example of what it's like to have "no-knowledge," but I would not say your dog is a sage. However, a sage with "no-knowledge," having transcended rational knowledge, could very well be in a mystical state. Whereas the dog would not know what it's like for a sage to have no-knowledge, a sage with no-knowledge would know what a dog's no-knowledge is like. For simplicity, we might distinguish between "low"(pre-rational) and "high" (post-rational) no-knowledge.

SACRED KNOWING

Another way to approach no-knowledge is to say that the conscious-ness of the knower "tunes into" the consciousness of the object. And, if we mean this literally, not simply as an epistemological figure of speech, but as an ontological reality, then we are saying that nature itself, at all levels, is imbued with consciousness.

In short, the notion of paradox consciousness implies a number of rather controversial propositions:

1. *That we can attain an intersubjective, even viewpointless, epis-temology.* That some forms of knowing involve transcending both first-person subjective and third-person objective points of view. This is what is meant by "knowing a thing as it appears to itself"—a thoroughly postmodern, non-Kantian idea.
2. *That knowing and being can blend into a single activity.* This is what is meant by "tuning into the consciousness of the object," literally becoming it by experiencing its experience.
3. *That "objects," therefore, are "subjects," too.* In other words, what we consider and perceive to be "objects," physical parts of nature, are experiencing beings in some sense like ourselves. And—
4. *That, therefore, matter is in some sense experiential.* Nature, lit-erally, has a mind of its own and is constantly communicating with itself—*including us.*

With these four propositions, we have opened the way to a new approach to understanding a number of profound and perennial episte-mological and ontological problems—for example, the problems of "other minds," how mind and body are related, free will versus determinism, causality, and choice, and how subjects can know objects. It's also an approach that takes us far beyond the problems of Cartesian dualism.

I have tried to indicate in this chapter that the "paradox" approach also provides a *methodology* for a much more participatory philosophy of mind and science of consciousness, wherein the philosopher/scientist's consciousness actually undergoes a transformation by engaging with the mind-body issue. Such a participatory methodology has profound implications for *all* our relationships—private, personal, interpersonal, professional, environmental, metaphysical, or spiritual.

Fundamental to all of this is the ontological implication of the fourth proposition: that matter is in some sense intrinsically experiential—that matter *feels*. This is a key theme throughout *Radical Nature*, and it implies that a breakthrough in philosophy of mind and a science of consciousness will involve a radically different view of what we mean by "matter" or the "physical," a view that returns soul to matter, and a sense of the sacred to the cosmos.

In this chapter, we have discussed the deep and intimate relationship between our methods of knowing nature and nature's own modes of being. Specifically, following Siu's notion of "no-knowledge," as a way of relating to nature beyond both rational and intuitive knowing, I have been proposing that we learn to cultivate a radical form of knowing—called "paradox consciousness." It is a way of being-in-the-world in which the knower knows nature the way nature knows itself. Paradox consciousness is knowing through not-knowing, an ineffable state of knowledge where the subject becomes the object; where knowing and being blend into one.

I mentioned above that one of the radical implications of no-knowledge or paradox consciousness is the attainability of an *inter-subjective* way of knowing, where it is possible to know the other as the other is experienced by him-/her- or itself. This second-person way of knowledge—knowing through relationship—is the central theme of this book. But before moving deeper into an exploration of inter-subjective consciousness, however, I want to set the historical context in the next chapter by elaborating further on the meaning of *embodied* consciousness.

12

Grounding

Embodied Meaning

Clearly, we are embodied beings—and our flesh, blood, bones, and brains are the media through which we experience ourselves and the world. As human beings, we are grounded in our bodies—they are our vehicles for the practical business of getting on with living.

We know from direct experience that we cannot uncouple mind from body (except conceptually). Often when I make this assertion to new-paradigm-oriented audiences, someone will quickly raise the issue of "out-of-body-experiences" (OBEs). It's such a common objection, that I should address it here before moving on.

I'm not ignoring reports of OBEs. Many such reports, though anecdotal, do sound authentic and reputable. And in a number of cases, the reports seem to involve knowledge that could not have been acquired through normal sensory channels. So, from these reports, it certainly *looks as if* the mind or consciousness of these OBE subjects was located somewhere other than the person's body. However, I'd like to point out a couple of things about OBEs and consciousness.

First, since consciousness is *nonlocated*—it is not located *anywhere* in space—it should come as no surprise that the mind could have access to information unavailable to a particular body, which *is* located in space. Second, from the perspective of panpsychism, all bodies always have their own interiority. It is possible that an OBE event involves an "identity shift" in consciousness from the familiar physiological body to what in some traditions is called a "subtle body."

Again, evidence from various cultures suggests that something like a subtle body exists (e.g., the Chinese notion of *ch'i,* Indian *prana,* Japanese *ki,* Polynesian *mana).* Such subtle bodies may exist in fields of subtle energy that extend far beyond the normal physical body and even beyond its associated electromagnetic field. Given the panpsychist perspective, these subtle bodies would also possess their own form of consciousness. If this were the case, an "OBE" might be more accurately termed an "ABE" (another, or an "alternative," body experience), or an "SBE" (subtle body experience), where the locus of identity of consciousness has temporarily shifted from the flesh and blood body to the more diffuse and less constrained subtle body.

With this caveat, then, our ordinary, day-to-day, lived experience confirms the panpsychist assertion that body and consciousness always go together. Whenever we attempt to divorce them, we create a psychological or physiological pathology (or both). We can know our body only through the process we call "mind," through the action of consciousness. This is almost so obvious it may seem redundant. Of course, we can gain knowledge about the body only if we use our mental faculties: Knowing cannot take place without consciousness. But such "obviousness" is actually a hangover from our Cartesian inheritance. For we cannot know the body through our mind without, at the same time, knowing consciousness through our body. In a very literal sense: The body knows itself—it *feels.*

This was seventeenth-century French philosopher René Descartes' blind spot. In formulating his famous *cogito*—"I think, therefore I am"— he dismissed the empirical groundedness of being in his body. Without a brain, without a body, his consciousness would not have even come up with the idea of doubting anything, never mind everything—the starting point of his revolutionary philosophy. He was correct to point out that he could not, without contradiction, doubt his own consciousness—and, therefore, declare that he existed at least as a thinking being.

Yes, Descartes was correct to conclude that consciousness existed because the very act of doubting or denying consciousness automatically, and inevitably, *demonstrates* it. Quite simply: It takes consciousness to doubt or deny anything—including itself!

But he was mistaken on three other critical points. First error: making the unwarranted claim, "therefore, I am a thinking *thing.*" Nothing in his meditations could have revealed his thinking (his feeling, his consciousness) as an object or a thing—because, as we have seen, consciousness is not an object, it's a *subject* that *knows* or *feels* objects. Knowing or feeling is not a thing; it is an experiential process. A more accurate statement would have been "I am a thinking subject" or "I am a *knower.*" Better yet, and more simply: "I am thinking," or "I know." But that would have been a tautology: "I think, therefore, I am thinking." He could have said, "I am a thinking *being,*" or improved it to say, "I am being thinking," and that would have been almost correct—except for his next mistake.

Second error: Nothing in his meditations would have supported his proclamation "*I am a thinking thing.*" He could not have discovered the "I" that is doing the thinking for the very simple reason that it is not discoverable through thinking or observation. Anyone practiced in meditation knows this: The "I" never shows up as a content in consciousness because *it is* consciousness. It is the observer, the witness, the context. And even if one could turn the beam of inquiry or witnessing back on itself all that would then show up would be the subject-become-object, the "I" transformed into "me."

The mind most definitely (and perhaps unfortunately) has the ability to construct its own self-image—the "ego." But the ego-image, the *concept* of "I," is not the real *witnessing* I. A century and a half after Descartes' great "discovery," German philosopher Immanuel Kant settled the issue when he showed, using the rigor, power, and precision of reason, that the "I" is nowhere to be found in the world of phenomena. Rather, it is an inhabitant of the eternally inaccessible domain he called the *numenon.* In other words, the "I" (or consciousness) is not itself a constituent of the mind.

Before Kant, British philosopher David Hume had also pointed out that no matter how hard or meticulously we search for it, we can never locate or identify the "self" that we believe ourselves to be. Yes, lots of mental contents show up, but the self is never among them. And, of course, a similar conclusion lies at the heart of Buddhist psychology and spiritual inquiry in the doctrine of *annata* or "no-self." Descartes, therefore, was wrong to conclude, "*I* am thinking," because no such "I" ever shows up. *The self is nowhere to be found.* The most he could have correctly concluded would have been: *"There is consciousness,"* or "there is thinking." But just *who* is doing the thinking is beyond the grasp of thinking itself.

Third error: Descartes believed that he could consistently and coherently doubt *everything* except his own consciousness. As noted earlier, this was the starting point of his revolutionary philosophy. It was revolutionary because, until then, Western metaphysics had been dominated by the authority of the Church and the ancient philosophies of Plato and Aristotle (and by that time, mostly Aristotle). Descartes, unlike most of his contemporaries, was not content to rely on the "authority" of scripture or ancient philosophy. Heroically, he wanted to find things out for himself. So he set himself the task of wiping the slate of history clean, and then looking to see if he could find a firm starting point for a whole new philosophy and science. His method, famously, was to employ rigorous and systematic doubt. In other words, rather than taking ancient knowledge on faith, he would begin by *doubting everything*.

Descartes was a skeptic in the truest sense, and he employed his method of radical doubt to dissolve away everything he believed he knew or had been taught. Under the pressure of his relentless doubt, everything crumbled—everything, that is, except consciousness. And "everything" included his own body. He saw how it was possible that even his body could be merely an hallucination in his mind induced by some powerful super "demon" intent on deceiving him. How could Descartes decide whether his body was real or merely a mental figment, as often happens in dreams? (He paid particular attention to his dreams.)

Descartes was right to doubt his body—to wonder whether it was real or imaginary. But he overlooked the fact that even if his body had no more reality than a phantasm conjured up in his or some Deceiving Demon's dream, the nature of that reality would be the nature of his body. He would still have a body, even if it were only a "dream body." The empirical fact is that whatever the true, ultimate nature of our bodies—whatever the ultimate nature of matter (whether physical or imaginal)—we, as living human beings, have no consciousness separate from our bodies.

Like Aristotle's *hyle* and *morph*, and the Chinese *ch'i* and *li*, body and mind go together—*always*. The actual fact is that without his body (imaginal or biological), Descartes would not have been able to engage in his meditations. He could doubt all he liked, yet he had no option but to act *as though* his body were real. His doubting was always *performatively* embodied. He could *doubt* his body, but he could never *claim* it was an illusion—not without falling victim to a performative contradiction.

Perhaps Descartes would have been closer to the mark and could have saved Western civilization from four-hundred years of epistemological and ontological dualism—not to mention the pathological consequences of the mind-body split—had he declared, instead of "*Cogito, ergo sum* (I think, therefore, I am)": "*Sentio, ergo corpus sum* (I *feel*, therefore I am embodied)" Or simply: "There is embodied feeling."

ORIGINS OF THE MIND-BODY SPLIT

Ever since Descartes separated *res extensa* (matter) from *res cogitans* (mind), Western philosophy and science have followed his lead, and split knowledge of the world into a collection of dualisms. The most fundamental of these has been the separation of mind and body. This split has had a deep and pervasive impact on our understanding of and attitudes to who we are as human beings. It has affected, for instance, how we relate to our environment, how we view the processes of illness and healing, and how we look for meaning in the world.

Other dualisms follow from this split—for example, subject/object, idealism/realism, empiricism/rationalism, organicism/mechanism, holism/reductionism—and they all link together like bolts and bars in a conceptual scaffolding on which we hang our experience of reality. In the history of science and philosophy, the West has tended to favor one side of each dichotomy at the expense of the other. Following the lead of its founding fathers—Bacon, Galileo, Descartes, and Newton—Western science has come down on the side of objectivity-rationality-mechanism-reductionism. In such a world, matter dominates mind—despite the absurdities and contradictions of striving after an "objective" science where the experiencing subject has no place.

In an attempt to redress the balance, new movements in science and philosophy have emerged in the West in the past few generations. We have witnessed a growing scholarly and popular interest in the "new sciences" of quantum physics, systems theory, ecologically oriented biology, chaos and complexity theory, cognitive-neurosciences, as well as a rising tide of attention focused on the "noetic" sciences and consciousness exploration.

Although this movement to restore a balance between mind and materialism is clearly needed and welcome, anyone participating in or even taking the view of an interested observer needs to pay attention to a potentially dangerous underlying assumption: In our attempts to heal the split between mind and body we may be inadvertently solidifying a false dichotomy. *In order to heal the split, we must first of all believe that there even is such a thing.* By focusing on mind or consciousness while excluding or ignoring the body, we continue, therefore, to add support to the old Cartesian dualism.

MEANING BEYOND THE MIND

Belief in the separation of mind and body may be at the root of many of our current problems in science, in medicine, and in our personal experiences of alienation from nature. This dualism is an intellectual inheritance peculiar to the West. It is not part of the metaphysics, cosmology, religion, philosophy, or mythology of many other traditions. The Chinese, for instance, do not make such a distinction—they have no word for "mind" in their language. In their view, all things are formed by the interplay of *ch'i* (matter-energy) and *li* (*organizing principle*).

By contrast, when we in the West introduced the mind-body split, we created a kind of metaphysical and experiential schizophrenia that has not only alienated human beings from nature but has alienated us from important parts of ourselves. In the West, we are educated to look for meaning in and through the mind—through a combination of intellect, reason, abstraction, intuition, and insight.

Meaning for us is in the mind. And so, whenever we are troubled by existential crises—Why are we here? Who or what are we? How are we related? What happens when we die?—we turn to the mind for explanations or solutions.

However, when we elevate mind to the position of creator and protector of meaning, we neglect the wisdom of the body. According to a number of body-oriented, "somatic," disciplines—such as Rolfing, Alexander Technique, Feldenkrais—the body is a repository of meaning. From the viewpoint of "embodied awareness," organisms are in continual communication with their environment, adapting and responding to signals, signs, symbols, and messages outside their skins, taking in and expressing out a continual stream of meaning. In somatics, it is more accurate to speak of the "bodymind" as one entity, one process. The duality of distinct and separate body and mind is replaced, here, by a unity of *organism*.

MESSAGES IN THE FLESH

In somatics, the entire organism is considered an "organ of perception," to borrow a phrase from the eighteenth century German scientist-philosopher Goethe. Instead of "body" or "mind," we can speak, both literally and metaphorically, of a "body of experienced meaning." We could equally speak of the "experience of embodied meaning," where, through interacting with our environment, our organism literally incorporates messages into the substance of its flesh.

These embodied meanings live in us, and when we fail to pay attention to them, we experience ourselves dislocated from the world. We feel we do not fit in. We feel alienated not only from our social and natural environments, but from our own sense of self. The somatics movement is responding to this need by teaching people to *"listen"* to their own bodies for messages and meaning. The body is an information processor; but it is much more than that. It is a *meaning processor*—it processes the constant stream of subliminal messages flowing into the body from the environment, integrating them with our felt experience, continually orienting us within the fields of matter, energy, and information swirling around and through us, so that we can distill a sense of direction and purpose. The body informs us about how we fit in.

When we neglect to listen to the body, to heed the signals that this "organ of perception" is transmitting, we are likely to become uncoupled from the larger system in which we are a part. We become a misfit, in a literal sense: We no longer fit the ecological body, and we pay the price in distress and disease. Somatics disciplines are designed to counteract this unhealthy alienation, by teaching us how to listen to the wisdom of the body, to become more whole and environmentally integrated.

PRINCIPLES OF EMBODIED AWARENESS

Listening to the body can teach us a number of important lessons. For example:

- We inhabit an *ecological body*. The *feeling* body extends beyond the skin and is constantly exchanging information and meaning with its environment.
- The body is an *organ of perception*. The whole body, including the skin, muscles, bones, and all the internal organs, is sensitive to changes, to *messages*, from the environment.
- The body is a *discourse of meaning*. Continually in communication with the environment, the body is actually in dialogue with the world. The body participates as a "conversation for meaning" or "discursive formation."[1] We can learn a great deal about ourselves, the world, and our interactions, by attending to meaning embedded in and flowing through the body's message systems.
- Health and illness are functions of the organism's fit—its *somatic fit*—within the flow of energy and information exchanged between the environment and the organism's body.
- Healing involves *listening to the body*. Unlike conventional behavioral medicine that aims for *controlling* the disease processes (whether through drugs, surgery, biofeedback, or visualizations and imagery), somatics and embodied awareness advocate *listening* and embracing the body's natural processes such as breathing, muscular-skeletal alignment, kinesthetic styles, and insights that arise from within the body's movement itself.
- Healing, therefore, involves a *partnership with the healer*. In

addition to guidance and treatment from the doctor or healer, the patient must also take responsibility for attending to the messages and meaning within his or her own body for clues on how to facilitate the healing process.

- Medicine is shaped by the *history of the body*. Medical practices are determined by the historical meanings attributed to the body. Throughout history, views of the body have changed, with each period producing its matching medical paradigm.[2]

- *Organisms strive for meaning.* Ingesting and metabolizing meaning are as critical to an organism's survival—its successful environmental fit—as its nourishment from food. In other words, the body of experienced meaning is shaped by the experience of embodied meaning.

These principles may help to position somatic disciplines, and distinguish them from other therapies. On the one hand, many conventional behavioral therapies that focus on adjusting or controlling the anatomy or physiology, and even those that focus on posture or movement, but pay little attention to the person's experience, tend to reinforce reductionism and Cartesian dualism. On the other hand, psychotherapies, such as hypnosis and analysis, tend to treat the person without acknowledging the reservoir of meaning embodied in the organism, in its muscles, bones, nerves, organs, and cells.

EMBODYING MIND, ENSOULING MATTER

To counteract the pathological schism between body and mind, we need a different conception and understanding of who we are as human beings. Beyond Cartesian substance dualism, we need to work toward a new synthesis in which we embody mind and ensoul matter. Descartes' error was to identify consciousness as a kind of substance, and not to recognize it as a process or as dynamic form *inherent in the body itself.*

As I noted in *Radical Nature:*

The paradox is that we must speak of this unified reality of "body-mind," of "form-process" in dualistic terms. The singular nature of the ground of being is, ultimately, unrepresentable and ungraspable. We may hint at it with words such as "psychoid," "archetypes," "entelechy," "essence," "Self," "Spirit," or "Tao"—but once conceived or uttered, such words block out the light of being itself. Our languages can only point like fingers at the moon. The "what is" does not stand still—any more than the "now" has any meaning beyond the momentary flow of experience. Yet it is all we have and are.[3]

In this chapter, we have focused on the body as a "meaning processor," noting that it is in constant communication with other bodies that make up its environment—extending to other people (personal and professional relationships), other animals (our pets and those we "husband" and eat); with plants and minerals, with the beautiful body of the Earth itself, and, ultimately, with the great body of the cosmos we will forever inhabit.

In the next chapter, we will begin to explore an unusual way of being with our own bodies, together with other people—a way that can lead to profound psychospiritual healing. It's a mode of communication completely overlooked in conventional education yet is possibly the most important element for any true *learning*. We will learn how this form of communicative practice and training can help us to *listen* with our bodies, and how to use our flesh, nerves, and muscles, blood, breath, and bones, to *know* by "feeling our thinking" how we are relating, moment-by-moment to the world around us, including other people.

We will discover how this way of being together can heal the mind-body split, the chronic fragmentation between consciousness and the physical world. Viewing them from a wider cosmological perspective, in the work of quantum physicist David Bohm, we will see how he integrates physics, cosmology, psychology, and social relations. His work in both physics and consciousness—especially his form of "dialogue"— provides both a metaphysical context and a methodology for exploring consciousness as fundamentally relational and intersubjective.

13

Dialogue

Consciousness and Cosmology

A group of about twenty people sits in a circle—some with eyes closed, some looking around at colleagues' faces, others apparently absent-mindedly staring at patterns on the floor. For hours they sit like this, often in silence. Then someone speaks, and it's as if she has opened her throat to let the universe flow into the room. A sense of deep meaning ripples through the participants, connecting them—they feel it in their bodies—and in this state of shared consciousness something both ordinary and extraordinary has been revealed: truth.

For years, I have been deeply impressed by the effectiveness of Bohmian dialogue as a method for exploring consciousness. In many of my classes at John F. Kennedy University, I include sessions devoted exclusively to this second-person approach to consciousness studies. Almost without exception, I'm moved and surprised each time at how deep people can go in shifting from our typical modes of thought to embodied, authentic self-expression, even in periods as short as a couple of hours. I'll summarize here some of the main introductory points I give to students about the dialogic process, including a thumbnail overview of David Bohm's life work to help set a cosmological and metaphysical context for dialogue.

Besides Bohm's contribution to consciousness studies through his method of dialogue, he has secured his place in the history of ideas and science as one of the twentieth century's geniuses in the field of quantum physics. Unlike most mainstream quantum theorists, and as mentioned earlier, Bohm did not accept that quantum events are purely random. In this, he agreed with Einstein that "God does not play dice with the universe." Like Einstein, he believed that behind the apparent randomness of quantum events there is a deeper, hidden pattern—he called this the "implicate order." Bohm's great contribution to quantum physics was to work out, in detail, an alternative mathematical expression for quantum events that accounted for all the observed, empirical data yet did not require us to believe that all the order and beauty we see in the world around us is the result of mere random quantum jumps.

Although other physicists acknowledge that Bohm's mathematical theory is as coherent as the standard "Copenhagen Interpretation," which describes quantum events as purely random, few physicists have followed his lead—presumably because of the profound cosmological and metaphysical implications of his model. Bohm's version includes mathematical expressions for what he called "pilot waves" that "guide" the apparently random quantum interactions—in other words, something very like *intelligence* is at work at the deepest levels of physical reality.

Bohm's cosmology is radical when viewed from the perspective of mainstream science: He believed that a complete theory of the cosmos must take account of consciousness. This must be so because clearly consciousness is an undeniable reality in the universe. Without it we would know absolutely *nothing*. All knowledge of the universe—in science, in philosophy, in art, in religion, in mysticism, in ordinary daily life—exists only because consciousness is present to experience and register the existence of the physical world. A complete cosmology, then, must include the *knower* as well as what is known. We need a cosmological story that has a place for the *storyteller*.[1]

According to quantum physics, all of reality is the result of an unimaginably vast number of tiny events—happening every single moment from the birth of the universe to this very moment *now*—where *actual* reality "collapses" out of a domain of quantum possibilities or probabilities. In the quantum wonderland, various potential states of reality coexist simultaneously (often referred to as "quantum superposition" or "quantum entanglement") described in a set of mathematical equations called the "wave functions," developed by Erwin Schrödinger, one of the founders of quantum physics.

Schrödinger immortalized a famous thought experiment (now called "Schrödinger's Cat") where it is possible for a "quantum" cat to be both dead and alive at the same time. He described a system consisting of a cat in a sealed box, with a vial of poison and a quantum device set up to crack open the vial and release the poison. Because the release mechanism is determined by a quantum event (for example, the emission of a radioactive particle from an atom), we would have no way of predicting when or if the device had been triggered, and so would have no way of knowing whether or not the cat is dead or alive. According to quantum theory, the only way to know would be to make an observation by looking in the box.

Nothing particularly strange there, you might think. However, what is bizarre is that quantum theory tells us that before we look inside the box, the quantum event that would trigger the device has *both happened and not happened!* This is because, in the quantum domain, all the probabilities exist simultaneously, as though "suspended" together. So, as strange as it sounds, the cat is both alive and dead *until someone looks.*

Until that moment of observation, all the quantum possibilities exist simultaneously. Only when an observation is made is the set of probabilities "collapsed" into a single actual event—an event that would result in the cat being either dead or alive. The quantum wonderland is a "both/and" world.

In other words, what we experience as the "real" world is built up from countless quazillions of such collapses from quantum probabilities to actual reality—*happening every moment.* And such quantum collapses happen only when a quantum system is observed. In fact, quantum theory is telling us, the world comes into existence only because it is observed. *By whom?* It must be by some experiencing entity, an entity with consciousness—because no matter how ingeniously we may design our experimental instruments, the chain of events that culminates in an observation must involve an *experiencing* observer. An "observation" without consciousness would not be an observation.

Thus, physical reality requires innumerable moment-by-moment "collapses" (of the quantum wave function); each of these "collapses" requires an observer; each observation requires consciousness . . . so consciousness (in some highly mysterious way) collapses the quantum wave function. In short: *Consciousness creates reality.*

Recognizing this, David Bohm reminds us that quantum theory compels us to accept that the scientist, as observer, is a *necessary part* of every quantum experiment. The quantum physicist is, therefore, a *participatory* observer. And this fact alone dissolves the assumed barrier that separates the object (the physical quantum system) from the subject (the scientist's consciousness). Bohm concluded, therefore, that quantum theory's recognition of inevitability of a *participatory observer* erodes the assumed separation between subject-object, knower-known, inner-outer.

Of course, if we accept the worldview of "panpsychism" or radical naturalism, where all matter is sentient, where consciousness "goes all the way down" to the smallest quantum of physical reality, then the "observer" that collapses the wave function need not be a human scientist. It could, in fact, be Schrödinger's cat itself (or, indeed, it could be the fleas in the cat's fur, or even the molecules in the glass vial, or one of the atoms in the poisonous chemical, or in the radioactive quantum device). Thus, panpsychism provides a solution to the mystery of how it could be that the universe evolved for billions of years before any human being (or even a single cell) was present to make observations that would collapse the quantum wave functions and create an actual world from the set of quantum probabilities.

Bohm, again like Einstein, believed that behind the domain of the quantum, and beyond relativity and the four forces of physics, reality is fundamentally a *unified field.* Furthermore, he said, the knower is an integral element in that field. In other words, *reality* (including energy, matter, space, time, and consciousness) is ultimately an *undivided whole.*

Underlying manifest physical and mental reality, he said, lies a deeper reality of an *unmanifest* matrix that gives rise to both matter and consciousness. Manifest reality (both matter and mind) is *enfolded* in the *unmanifest.* Manifest reality is the *explicate order*; unmanifest reality is the *implicate order.* Thus, something of the nature of mind or intelligence, a purposeful ordering, is embedded in the most fundamental fabric of reality.

Deep down below the level of the quantum wonderland itself, the implicate order contains the "seeds" of all knowing and intelligence, and it is here that we find the purpose or aim enfolded in the pilot waves that guide the unfolding of quantum events. In short, according to Bohm, the implicate order is the source of manifest subject (consciousness) and manifest substance (matter-energy). Subject and substance arise from the pre-quantum implicate order.

Furthermore, said Bohm, the implicate order is inherently *dynamic.* And because it is also "whole with intelligence"—a unified field he called the fundamental *holomovement*—at its deepest levels, reality is an inherently *purposeful process.* For Bohm, three terms characterize the essence of his cosmological philosophy: "whole," "movement," and "meaning." All attempts to relate to the world, to others, through analysis or fragmentation, through fixed things or ideas, or explanations in terms of mere mechanisms, seriously distort reality, and result in epistemological, psychological, and social pathologies. We need to find ways of seeing and knowing the world from the perspective of wholes, process, and meaning—and not get stuck in attachment to our partial fixed beliefs, many of which are unconscious.

BOHM'S COSMOLOGICAL PSYCHOLOGY

Given this perspective, it was natural enough for Bohm to develop a form of psychology and philosophy that was rooted in, and deeply consistent with, his cosmological physics. He taught that all our thoughts and beliefs are static habits of mind—a kind of "fossilized consciousness" operating within "the known." Deep reality, the implicate order, by contrast, is *unknown* by thought. Thoughts, he said, cannot comprehend the unmanifest, implicate order. Thus, all thoughts inevitably distort reality.

This is a profound insight, with immense implications for science, philosophy, psychology, education, and social institutions. Our entire educational system—from kindergarten to graduate school—is founded on the assumption that progress in knowledge relies on our ability to continually refine our ability to hook our ideas, beliefs, and thoughts to things and events in the world in ever-more accurate ways. This is the *correspondence* theory of knowledge and truth: Our thoughts and ideas are "right," true, and useful to the extent that they correspond with, or reflect, the way the world is put together. It's almost commonsense in our society. How else could we learn to know the world and how we fit in?

But Bohm asks us to consider a different approach: Only the *process of thinking* (not static thoughts, ideas, concepts), experienced moment-to-moment, can participate in "knowing the unknown." If we want to know reality, we must get beyond our static habits of mind. We must learn to focus less on how we hook our thoughts and ideas together, and instead pay increasing attention to where the thoughts come from, to *how* thinking arises in our bodies. (By "thinking," Bohm meant what we would normally call "consciousness," or "awareness" with all its multitude of experiences—he did not mean merely the process of cognition, which is what he meant by "thought.")

Bohm was always pointing out that the process of *thinking* is very different from the forms of *thought*: Thinking is *experienced*, thought is *conceptualized* (or verbalized). Reality is (or can be) revealed through awareness of thinking itself. It's not *what* we think, but *how* we think that matters. The separate, isolated "thinker of thoughts" is an illusion, he said. All there is really is the flow of the holomovement that manifests in thinking.

As one of Bohm's students, Renée Weber, noted: Immense amounts of "cosmic energy" are invested in the illusions of "thinker" and "thoughts." Diligent practice is needed to dissolve the illusion of "thinker" (psychological death), and when successful, vast "energy" is liberated.[2]

But here we encounter a paradox: The more we talk or think about reality or "truth," the less it is revealed. According to Bohm, thinking *about* reality never gets us there; our thinking *is* reality. This is not to say all reality is thinking, but that one way reality shows up is in thinking. So next time you meet a friend on the street you might ask, not "How are you?" but "*How* are you thinking today?"

Here's a little "koan" to help you grasp what Bohm is getting at: "Thoughts about thinking are not thinking; nor is thinking about thoughts thinking. Not even *thinking about* thinking is thinking. Thinking is thinking."

It's as if *you* are not thinking, but thinking is "youing"—the cosmic holomovement is thinking through you (or is "thinking you"). Therefore, as all the great spiritual traditions teach us, in order to "get at" reality, "you" (the ego) must get out of the way. The path to knowledge is through *emptiness* (or no-self). When "consciousness-as-knower" vanishes, "reality-as-known" (or "reality-as-is") arises. Without the "I," thinking (i.e., consciousness) functions in the deep structure of the implicate order and has access to information embedded in the whole. Thus pure thinking has access to the whole cosmos through the implicate order.

Ultimately, what matters to Bohm is whether and how "thinking our thinking" transforms us. His philosophical physics is a pragmatic ethics: Unless we can develop as moral beings, all thinking and dialogue are wasted—wasting the breath (spirit) of the cosmos. And since pure thinking is beyond concepts and words, *silence* is the optimum mode of "discourse" or "dialogue" for deep knowing.

BOHMIAN DIALOGUE

"Bohmian dialogue" is a form of communication devised by David Bohm in partnership with spiritual teacher Krishnamurti. It is a way to explore the possibility of experiencing *group consciousness*. Unlike other forms of communication such as conversation, discussion, or debate, dialogue does not involve any agenda beyond the simple aim to explore consciousness collectively. It is designed to see if we can discover the sources of "fragmentation" in our thoughts and beliefs (reflected in various forms of fragmentation in society), and what we can do to restore wholeness. In essence, dialogue is a way for a group to "think and feel" together—to collectively explore the spontaneous unfolding of meaning.

Dialogue honors the profound power of silence as the source of wisdom. We are encouraged to "feel our thinking"—to pay attention to the feelings in our bodies (what Bohm called "proprioception") as messages that inform our thinking and our thoughts. In the previous chapter, "Embodied Meaning," we emphasized the importance of grounding our thinking in the body, which is a constant source of meaning and messages from the world around us. Bohm's dialogue and proprioception underscore the importance of learning how to feel these nonverbal messages pulsing through our bodies.

Bohmian dialogue always begins in silence, and from that moment on there is (typically) no group leader or facilitator. Whatever surfaces from the silence of the group and individual consciousness is the substance of dialogue. Each participant is responsible for the communication of the whole group until the end of the session. In training sessions, a facilitator may occasionally step in to draw attention to a learning opportunity or to call the group back into dialogue (if, for instance, it might be slipping off into some other form of communication such as conversation, debate, or discussion).

There are no rules in Bohmian dialogue, yet certain procedures seem to facilitate group communication. These include: Only one person speaks at any time. Anything can be spoken. Nothing is "off limits." We do not speak to force a point, to win an argument, or to contradict what someone else has to say. We listen openly, suspending all evaluation and judgment and prior "expert knowledge." We listen to what others say as a "revelation" from someone else's viewpoint (which otherwise would forever remain unknown to us). We listen carefully (with our bodies as wells as with our ears and minds) for meaning and do not get caught up in analyzing words or ideas. We listen for, and acknowledge, assumptions (our own and those of others).

We speak (*if* we have something to say) because our viewpoint is also a valuable contribution. Our silence, too, can be a contribution. In dialogue, we pay attention to the group process or dynamics—to the movement or flow of consciousness through the group—so that when we speak we do not close somebody else down. *Nor do we suppress our own speaking.* And Bohm was clear that the purpose of dialogue is not to provide answers or solutions . . . participants come together simply to openly explore consciousness, and how it arises and changes within the group. Perhaps most important of all, in dialogue we are invited to listen, not so much to the words, but for the *meaning* of every communication.

Bohmian dialogue is an opportunity to experience the subtle arising of consciousness through each of us individually and through the "organism" of the group as a whole. It is a way to deeply feel the source of our thinking, to learn to listen for meaning, and in doing so to transcend the limitations of our individual minds. It is about being in relationship in such a way that we discover new ways of knowing that draw on the potentially inexhaustible wisdom of collective consciousness.

In the previous chapter, having discussed the importance of embodied consciousness as a way of knowing, and having here introduced dialogue as a methodology for exploring second-person consciousness, we will now sharpen our focus on this relationship-and-feeling based approach to consciousness studies. The next chapter will briefly introduce some key ideas in this largely overlooked perspective, emphasizing the importance of "being present" for and with others. Then, in the following chapters, we will dive deeper into the central theme of this book: intersubjectivity.

Part 3
Collective Wisdom

14

Participation

Engaging Presence

Let's set the scene with a little research fable: A brain surgeon and a mystic debated for days about the nature of consciousness, about how it is that human beings ever know or feel anything. The brain surgeon described the mind as a kind of "enchanted loom," a dynamic play of electric sparks and chemistry swirling over the surface of the brain in awesome patterns. For her, consciousness was the "poetry of chemistry," with measure and rhythm, a dance of energy in the cortex of the brain.

The mystic saw it otherwise: He, too, was enchanted by the marvelous details the surgeon described, and thought how fascinating it must be to manipulate such energy swirls, especially if, at times, it helped heal someone. He had no doubt that the brain surgeon did good work in the world. But none of what the surgeon worked on came close to uncovering the essence of what it *feels* like to be a human being. For that, the mystic urged, "I have to 'look inside.' The brain is outside, but feeling is 'inside,' and I find my way to consciousness by practice and discipline, through contemplation and meditation. It is as much in the heart as in the brain," said the mystic, evoking the disbelief of the surgeon.

After many days and nights looking at the question of consciousness this way and that, from the "outside" and the "inside," the two researchers failed to agree. One insisted that consciousness could be studied only by studying the brain—she favored *objectivity;* the other, equally persuaded of his position, would not be shifted from the view that consciousness must be studied from *within*—he favored *subjectivity*.

One day, after many weeks of friendly dispute, the man and woman finally looked each other deeply in the eyes and realized they were in the presence of a force they were creating *together*. Suddenly, the whole issue shifted. Something imperceptible, but very real, caught them in its power. In a moment of mutual realization, it hit them: *"There is somebody home."* Each now showed up for the other, a living, full-bodied, full-spirited *presence,* and they stood in the clearing of this deep realization, and smiled: "Consciousness is more than something objective or subjective—it is *intersubjective."*

Like the surgeon and mystic, we all come to know consciousness in at least three ways. But, often, the third way goes unnoticed.

■

Being intensely engaged in relationship with another is one of the greatest joys of being human. It is, perhaps, the most vital manifestation of consciousness. Yet it is an aspect of consciousness that, for the most part, has been conspicuously overlooked in philosophy of mind and the emerging field of consciousness studies. This approach to consciousness calls for a shift of perspective—from looking at the world as a collection of objects, or even as a collection of subjects, to a view that sees *relationship as fundamental.*

The deep foundations of consciousness in interpersonal relations have not been completely ignored in the West, however, as we will see in some detail in the following chapters. For example, philosopher-theologian Martin Buber earlier this century recognized the importance of the "I-thou" relationship and, more than two thousand years ago, it was the essence of the great dialogues of Socrates, at the foundation of Western philosophy.

Socrates' method of questioning—while engaging the normal rational cognitive faculties—was directed at the *soul* or essence of the other person, a process that often left that person with a feeling of great discomfort, and sometimes of transformation. Socrates was a master at penetrating behind perceptual and emotional surfaces to the deeper, core "presence" of the other. To be in dialogue with Socrates was to find one's precious opinions and certainties, which were based on appearances, dismantled and shattered—and then, as a result, to discover some deeper truth about oneself. See, for example, the famous encounter between Socrates and the slave boy in the *Meno* where, by a process of engaged questioning, Socrates draws out of the uneducated slave a "recollection" of knowledge of geometry that the boy didn't know he knew.

Reading Plato's dialogues, it is clear that Socrates was engaging his students in an approach that drew forth their innate knowledge by reaching into their soul's essence. He was passionately on the hunt for knowledge (an epistemological quest). We could equally say, however, that Socrates was hunting for "virtue" (an ethical quest)—a quality of the soul that emerges when the unconscious, emotional structures of the mind come into alignment and right relationship with our conscious cognitions; when instinct informs intellect, when the mind is open and responsive to its deeper dynamics. For Socrates, such virtue was true knowledge and transcended individual beliefs, emotions, and will—as though it were more accurate to say, "knowledge or virtue is knowing *us*, rather than we know *it*." This knowing, as we learn from Bohmian dialogue, emerges or flows through meaningful, sincere, and open encounter. At such times, when "I" and "you" meet each other fully, we become vessels or channels for knowledge and virtue—for wisdom that transcends what either of us separately possesses.

This same methodology of *engaged presence*—recognizing and experiencing the interrelationship between "I" and "you"—can also be called on to reveal the nature of consciousness itself (an ontological quest). It is this last aspect that has been missing in consciousness studies.

All three quests—for knowledge (what's "true"), for virtue (what's "good"), for being (what's "real")—are intimately related, of course. The point I want to emphasize here, however, is that even though Western philosophy has given a lot of attention to epistemology and ethics, it is precisely the degree to which it has moved away from the Socratic dialogic influence that the second-person perspective has been sidelined as a way of exploring the nature of consciousness—sidelined but not entirely silenced, as we will see in some detail in the next chapter.

FROM "IT" TO "I" TO "YOU"

The most common approach to the study of consciousness in philosophy and science (at least in Western academic disciplines) is from the *third-person* perspective; that is, consciousness is studied as an *object* like other objects in the world—such as stones or stars, fishes or foxes, bones or brains. But the scientific study of consciousness as an object completely misses its essential nature—whether as a behavioral property of organisms (psychology); or as a mysterious by-product of electro-chemical activity in brains and nervous systems (neurosciences); or as computer simulations using complex software programs in "artificial intelligence," combined with studies in linguistics and anthropology (cognitive science); or as micro events in tiny subneuronal structures called microtubules (quantum physics).

From these perspectives, "consciousness" is a *thing*—and as we now know, that's not really consciousness at all. What these scientists study are *correlations* of consciousness—that is, they study physical and biological processes in nervous tissue that *accompany* mental events. But as every good philosopher knows, and as every good scientist should know, *correlations are not consciousness*. No matter how complex or subtle, third-person processes or objects never explain first-person *experiences*. For example, the most sophisticated scientific analysis of a cavity in your tooth would never reveal your experience of pain. *Consciousness is not an "it"—it's an "I" or a "you."*

We should note, here, that although Western philosophy and science have based their common worldview on third-person perspectives, a very different approach has been integral to non-Western traditions. For instance, Islamic philosophy has a long history, from medieval times to today, in which an epistemology of *presence* plays a central role.[1] This "presence"—a nonsensory prehension of the being of the "other" (whether Allah, human, or animal)—is the *felt* enfolding of the "other's" being into a unity that transcends the dichotomy of separate subject and object.

Some Western philosophers, and mystics throughout the world, recognize that the most significant characteristic of consciousness is its subjectivity; it should be studied from the *first-person* perspective. In this view, consciousness is unique among phenomena. It is the only aspect of reality that presents itself as a *subject,* as an "I." Subjects, unlike objects, come to the world with interiority, with a point of view. Investigators taking the first-person perspective recognize that any comprehensive exploration of consciousness must include the investigator examining his or her own experience. The beam of inquiry is turned back on itself, and the study of consciousness becomes a matter of self-exploration.

The *second-person* perspective is a third alternative. In this view, consciousness is neither an "it" nor merely an "I." It involves *you,* or some other second person—it involves dialogic relations between two or more experiencing subjects. From this perspective, consciousness arises (or at least is informed and altered) when two or more subjects encounter each other and participate in some way in each other's being—what existentialist theologian Martin Buber called an "I-thou" relationship. It is *conscientia*—consciousness as "knowing with" another—that is, intersubjective or interpersonal consciousness. It is the consciousness experienced, for example, when two lovers share the knowing of their love for each other.

WHY INTERSUBJECTIVITY IS TRANSPARENT

For centuries, both objectivity and subjectivity have been investigated as ways of knowing. But Western science and philosophy have, for the most part, ignored intersubjectivity—particularly as a way of exploring consciousness. However, as already noted, it has not been completely ignored. In the next chapter, I will introduce a handful of scholars who have attempted to focus on this conspicuous oversight in Western philosophy in general and in philosophy of mind in particular. With these few exceptions—such as psychologist George Herbert Mead, theologian Martin Buber, and contemporary scholars such as Jürgen Habermas in Germany and Francis Jacques in France—I know of no philosopher in the Western tradition who has systematically approached the problem of subject-world relation, and particularly *the question of consciousness,* by invoking the *second-person perspective* as an alternative to the first-person perspective of subjectivists and idealists, and the third-person perspective of the objectivists and materialists.

In 1996, the *Journal of Consciousness Studies* published a paper, "Turning the Hard Problem Upside Down and *Sideways*," by two authors, Piet Hut (an astrophysicist) and Roger Shepard (a psychologist), that raised the possibility of a second-person point of view. In a couple of paragraphs, they suggested this perspective as a possible angle on the "explanatory gap" between brain and mind. But they did not develop the idea. Nonetheless, their paper demonstrates that the notion of second-person study of consciousness was already "in the air" in consciousness studies.

They noted, "The fact that we can and do interact with others is an aspect of conscious experience that is at least as important as the possibility that we humans have of reflecting on our own experience."[2] This last idea, almost a throwaway in their paper, is perhaps among the most important insights for the future of consciousness studies—provided it implies intersubjectivity in the sense of nonphysical engaging presence that does not require language or some other form of behavior or exchange of physical signals.

Ken Wilber should also be included as a scholar who recognizes the importance of dialogic relationship in any comprehensive study of consciousness. His detailed four-quadrants model includes a place for "interior-social," another term for intersubjectivity. However, unlike Habermas, Jacques, Buber, or Mead, intersubjectivity has not been a central concern for Wilber, even though he has recently been giving it additional attention. Furthermore, Wilber has tended to reduce intersubjectivity to a form of linguistic exchange (which gives it a third-person, objective, meaning—the weakest type of meaning—and hardly true intersubjectivity at all).

For a long time, I have wondered why this second-person perspective (of mutually engaged subjects) has not been studied in greater detail—particularly since we use all three ways of knowing (objectivity, subjectivity, and intersubjectivity) in one form or another pretty much all the time. We all perceive and interact with *objective* external material objects; we all feel what it is like to be a *subjective* being from within; and we all participate and communicate *intersubjectively* with other human beings, and (at least some of us), with other animals.

I suspect that this oversight is an example of a "fish-in-water" syndrome. We tend not to notice the second-person perspective because it is right in front of our noses every day. It's the medium in which we most naturally live. For the third-person perspective we need to set up controlled (and artificial) laboratory experiments to induce (at least the illusion of) a separation between observer and observed, and thus we step back, or step out of the stream of natural living and human interaction. This stepping-back allows us to notice the third-person perspective in action—because it's not "normal." Similarly, for the first-person perspective: In meditation (or other contemplative or introspective disciplines) we "withdraw" from the "normal" world, enabling the subjective perspective to show up in contrast.

But normal day-to-day living, interacting with and encountering other people, is the usual medium for consciousness. The mutuality of shared-perspective is at least available to us throughout the day in every encounter (even if we actually rarely consciously engage in it). Like first- and third-person perspectives, the second-person perspective can be another mode of *conscious inquiry*—where consciousness (and the reality that consciousness reveals) can be investigated as a process of mutual "taking account of" the other(s). Something different happens in consciousness when we engage like this. As we saw in the previous chapter, physicist David Bohm recognized the potential for relational, feeling-based consciousness exploration in his approach to "dialogue."

Clearly, our language already presents us with *three*, not just two, options—first, *second*, and third-person pronouns, "I," "*you*," and "it." And the second-person perspective, both theoretically and experientially, is a logical and natural bridge between the apparent dichotomy of the knowing subject and the world of objects—between "I" and "it," between interior "I" and exterior "other."

When I communicate with *you*, particularly in a face-to-face encounter, something about who I am and something about the world shows up *through you*—and vice versa. The "I" that encounters you (as the locus of another "I") is different from the "I" that encounters the world as a conglomeration of "its." Who I am can be revealed (at least partially) through my encounter with you, whereas I-as-"I" remains entirely unattainable if I encounter the world as merely a collection of "its." I (as subject) am never reflected in things (objects), only in other "I"s such as you. The "I" that can show up as an object either in first-person introspection as "me," or in third-person analysis (as in standard materialist philosophy of mind and psychology) is never truly "I" (as experiential subject) but only "me" or "it" as a spatio-temporal object.

SECOND-PERSON SCIENCE

Whether in dialogue with a group or in one-to-one relationships, there is something about the nature of consciousness that requires the *presence* of the "other" as another subject that can acknowledge my being. When I experience myself being experienced by you, my experience of myself—and of you—can be profoundly enriched and transformed.

The point is that consciousness "shows up" as a co-creativity between or among the participants. If we pay attention to this, we see that the implications range from, in philosophy, prompting us to reconsider our basic ontology—from discrete physical substances to a more process-oriented relational ontology of interpenetrating experiences (as in Whitehead), to, in science, providing a different way to approach the problem of other minds, or even possibly elucidating the mystery of parapsychological phenomena (telepathy, for instance, could be understood as an intersubjective sharing of meaning between individual subjects who are physically remote from each other).

As an epistemology of "presence," second-person intersubjectivity opens the way to a deep exploration of *relationship*—an approach that could take science beyond epistemology of objects, beyond methodologies of objectivity, measurement, and quantification, and beyond a preoccupation with mechanisms. As in first-person methodologies, the emphasis in second-person science would be on *engagement* rather than measurement, *meaning* rather than mechanism.

Psychologist Carl Jung spoke of the "psychoid" realm, an ontological domain prior to the differentiation of matter and psyche. At this unmanifest level, psychoid "tendencies"—Jung called them "archetypes"—give form to specific manifestations of mind (images, ideas, emotions) and of matter (quantum particles or forces). The archetypes give shape to events we consider mental and material. If we pursue this line of thinking, then, we may suppose that when two or more people engage each other's presence telepathically, or when an observer "interacts" clairvoyantly or psychokinetically with an observational system, what is actually happening is that some archetype is activated that *shows up* as a meaningful relationship (second-person), as the observer's intention or meaning (first-person), and the pattern of objective events (third-person). As we saw in chapter 7, "*Synchronicity-1: Beyond Energy,*" in such cases of psi, there may be no causal effect between mind and mind, or between mind and matter. Instead, we might say, there is an "archetypal expression"—what Jung called an acausal, "synchronistic" event.

To sum all this up in a phrase: We could say that standard third-person inquiry leads to a science of external bodies, first-person inquiry to an interior science of the mind, while second-person engagement leads to *a communal science of the heart.*[3] Whereas the ultimate ideal of objective knowledge is control, and the ultimate ideal of subjective knowledge is peace, the ultimate ideal of intersubjective knowledge is relationship—and, dare I say it, love.

But we rarely hear about this in modern philosophy or science—even in consciousness studies—because so much of what we are taught comes to us wrapped in the constricting garb of a particular myth, as we shall see in the following chapter.

15

We Are the World

The myth: We are all lone subjects in our own life's drama. Everything around us, including other people, consists of objects that form the set and setting for our part in the Great Play. Each of us is an individual. We look out on the world from unique centers of subjectivity, and we act on the world as individual centers of intention and will. We are like atoms with individual and separate nuclei. As we encounter or collide with others, we begin to form relationships—"molecules of connection."

This is the myth of the modern mind: *separateness and individualism*. We could call it "The Lone Ranger" myth of consciousness. The cult of rugged individualism has found its fullest expression in the American dream of the pioneering "lone hero" who can battle against all odds, pushing back frontiers—in science, in commerce, in sports, in entertainment—and establish him- or herself as a power center, a force to be reckoned with. It is a myth that draws nourishment from, and gives power to, such hallowed scientific principles as "survival of the fittest," and economic systems such as capitalism advancing to the mantra "might is right."

It is a legacy of the paradigm we have inherited from Descartes and Newton, and the philosophers and scientists that followed them. It is the myth of subjectivity—the myth that ultimately *we are alone*. The myth is that we are separate individuals—isolated, self-contained bubbles of Cartesian egos—who just happen to form relationships in response to the forces that shape our lives, like atoms coming together by chance.

Even our minds and our relationships are believed to be governed by the same Newtonian laws and forces that rule the physical world.

Yes, undeniably we are subjects—and, yes, we *are* centers of potent subjectivity. Each of us experiences our own interiority. Each of us looks out on the world from our own unique point of view. Each of us values the privacy of our own invisible and inalienable minds. And each of us cherishes our unique sense of self-agency, our freedom to choose and act as we will—to place ourselves in relationship to other, similar, egos or subjects.

But that is only part of the story.

Another paradigm—emerging in systems theory, quantum science, consciousness studies, and from the perennial philosophy of the world's spiritual traditions—tells us something different. It tells us we are more. In this new story we are definitely not alone. In fact, we don't form relationships, *they form us*. We are constituted by webs of interconnection. Relationship comes first, and we emerge as more or less distinct centers within the vast and complex networks that surround us. In this new view, we are nodes in the complex web of life. Each of us is a meeting point, a center of convergence, for countless threads of relationship. We are moments in time and locations in space where the universe shows up—literally, as a phenomenon (from the Greek *phainomenon,* "to appear" or "to show up").

In other words, in this "new story" we emerge as subjects from intricate networks of interrelatedness, from webs of intersubjectivity. This paradigm of consciousness tells us that intersubjectivity is primary, and our sense of individual subjectivity is a transient pattern in a much vaster ocean of reality. We are fleeting vortices, dancing whorls of consciousness and energy, in the Great Play of Being. In a very literal sense: We are the world. We are the way the world shows up—uniquely and meaningfully here and now, at *this* time and place where we experience ourselves to be. That's why each and every one of us is precious. The world could not be complete without us.

So, instead of being lone subjects in our own life's drama, we are "intersubjects" created by the original worldwide web—the web of intersubjectivity woven in the Great Cosmic Drama, in the Great Unfolding of Being.

■

By this time, I trust that I have made the "gist" of my two-part message clear enough: first, that *consciousness is fundamentally relational* (the nature of consciousness is, ultimately, *communion);* and, second, that to explore and understand consciousness we need to be open to *radically different ways of knowing* beyond reason and the senses. That's my central thesis.

We are now about to enter the deeper philosophical core of this book, where I discuss the finer details of my thesis. As I cautioned at a similar point in *Radical Nature,* if you happen to feel uncomfortable (or impatient) delving into philosophical subtleties, you may want to skip lightly through the next couple of chapters. I have tried to ease the flow of the text by placing the more technical parts of the discussion in appendix 2: "Subjectivity and Intersubjectivity." Reading that appendix now will give you key distinctions that will allow you to track my argument closely. However, you can still get the main points by reading straight through the text from this point onward.

I start by distinguishing between different meanings of "subjectivity" and "intersubjectivity," which I will summarize:

Subjectivity-1. The first and most basic meaning of subjectivity is *"experienced interiority"*—it *feels like* something to be an experiencing being, having a first-person perspective.

Subjectivity-2. The second, and more restricted, meaning is "a *private, experiencing self* or ego." This, too, has a first-person perspective, a sense of "I-ness," but here the emphasis is on the *independence* and *individuality* of the private "I." The first refers to a generalized feeling or experience of being, while the second is the private Cartesian ego.

The second-person perspective has three distinct meanings:

Intersubjectivity-1. *We connect by communicating.* This starts by assuming the Cartesian notion of self-encapsulated subjects, individual "I"s who connect with each other by *exchanging physical signals* (for example, by speaking or writing). Individuals form relationships through communication. We could call this *"linguistic"* intersubjectivity—and this is the weakest meaning of the three.

Intersubjectivity-2. *We condition each other.* Individual subjects don't merely exchange signals; we change each other's sense of self. By engaging and participating in communication, we *condition* each other's experience. This is *"mutual-conditioning"* intersubjectivity—and is "medium-strength."

Intersubjectivity-3. *We co-create each other.* This is the most radical of all the types of intersubjectivity because it means that individuals don't merely influence and change each other by communicating and participating in relationships, but literally *co-create* each other's very existence. Rather than connecting by exchanging signals and informing each other ("linguistic"), or coming together in relationships and changing each other ("mutual-conditioning"), this strongest meaning implies that *relationships are primary* and that our sense of individuality is secondary, arising from a larger network of relationships.

WHICH CAME FIRST: SUBJECTIVITY OR INTERSUBJECTIVITY?

Given these distinct meanings of intersubjectivity, we are faced with five questions:

1. *Is the basic distinction between "linguistic," "mutual-conditioning," and "co-creating" intersubjectivity valid?*

If we accept the first meaning of subjectivity ("experienced interiority" —and what else could subjectivity mean if we excluded this?), we still need a way to account for experiences such as rapport, empathy, and love between interacting subjects—and these cannot be wholly explained in terms of exchanges of linguistic or other signals. Something else besides an exchange of linguistic "tokens" (words or other signals) seems to be happening. People at least *seem* to connect with each other beyond physical modes of communication—through, for example, shared meaning or engaged presence. Therefore, we need some other term or terms to indicate more than a change in knowledge (linguistic) but also a change in the *being* (mutual-conditioning), and the possibility that we actually *create* each other in relationship (co-creation).

2. *Do interacting subjects actively shape the form and content of each other's experience?*

Volumes of data from social psychology, communications theory, psychoanalysis, anthropology, not to mention much commonsense folk psychology—plus the answer to (1) above—hardly leave us any doubt: Interacting people *do* influence and condition each other's experience and contents of consciousness (how else could communication occur?). So clearly, yes—intersubjectivity-2 occurs beyond intersubjectivity-1.

If this were the full extent of the expanded meaning of intersubjectivity-2, the point would be trivial. Questions (3), (4), and (5) go on to raise controversial and profound issues for philosophy of mind and consciousness studies.

3. *Can one subject have direct access—not mediated by signals— to knowledge of how the other experiences this change?*

If we can answer yes to this, then the epistemological tradition we have inherited from Descartes, Kant, and the Enlightenment would be radically undermined. The hoary problem of other minds would finally have a solution.

4. *Through knowledge of how "I" show up in "your" experience, can I come to know something about my own consciousness?*

If the answer to this as well as to (3) is affirmative, then the implications for a second-person methodology in consciousness studies would indeed be radical and far-reaching. But it's the next question that, if answered in the affirmative, poses the greatest challenge to philosophy and science.

5. *Does intersubjectivity actually create individual subjects, and is it ontologically primary?*

If yes, then pretty much the entire edifice of conventional philosophy and science, based on metaphysical assumptions of fundamental substance and individual units (both of matter and mind), would be seriously undermined. How could intersubjectivity exist without prior, already-existing subjects? How could there be relations without pre-existing relata? Commonsense, and even logic, may seem to demand that for there to be relationship there *have* to be things to relate in the first place.

Given an ontology of substance (whether of physical energy or of Cartesian minds), the primacy of discrete units or relata seems compelling. However, we have examples of alternative ontologies from, for instance, Alfred North Whitehead and Buddhism where *process* is ontologically fundamental.[1] These highly developed and robust philosophies explain why relationships are primary, and how individuals are *constituted* by their relationships. In such cosmologies, intersubjectivity precedes subjectivity-2 (Cartesian sense). Of course, even in these alternative ontologies, intersubjectivity presupposes subjectivity-1 in the sense of "experienced interiority."

Whereas the *fact* of experienced interiority (subjectivity-1) is a precondition for intersubjectivity, the *forms* of any individual subject (i.e., how interiority is shaped and experienced in individual subjects) need not—and in the cases of Whitehead and Buddhism do not—require preexistent Cartesian subjects (subjectivity-2). Such "forms," co-created as perishable centers of experience in the interplay and flux of intersubjective fact, *are* the individual subjects.

Whether we go all out and try to make a case for this strong version of intersubjectivity (with its profound philosophical implications) or keep our sights on a closer horizon by focusing on the "milder" second sense of intersubjectivity (with its implications for psychology and studies of the contents of consciousness), we still need to go beyond both first- and third-person perspectives when trying to understand the mind. We need to introduce and acknowledge the validity of the *second-person perspective* in order to complement our investigations of consciousness in philosophy of mind, cognitive science, psychology, the neurosciences, and the emerging field of consciousness studies itself. One way or another, the study of consciousness will be comprehensive only if we engage in second-person intersubjective, as well as first-person subjective, and third-person objective explorations.

The *idea* of intersubjectivity, as dialogic communication, is not particularly new, as noted earlier. However, despite an impressive list of dialogic-oriented thinkers, the philosophical understanding of consciousness from the second-person perspective *as a felt quality of mutual engagement*—a mutual participation, even co-creation, of subjectivities—has had nothing like the attention given to both first- and third-person perspectives.

In the next chapter, "Steps Along the Way," we will trace the historical roots of dialogic consciousness in a variety of disciplines. Common to all of them is an investigation into the relationship between the individual and society, between self and other.

16

Intersubjectivity-2

Steps Along the Way

Picture this: It's a thousand years from now, and scientific technology has evolved to the point that, finally, we have succeeded in mapping every single neuron and synapse in the brain, along with thoroughly understanding all their complex electrochemical interactions, right down to a complete understanding of how the quantum microtubules work in every brain cell. Everything anyone would ever want to know about the brain or nervous system is now available; we have cracked the "neural code."

Even so, we would still know nothing about the mind.

Now imagine that society has evolved to the point where the perennial separation between science and spirituality has long-since vanished and all neuroscientists are, as a matter of course, skilled practicing meditators. These same people who cracked the "brain's code" have also mastered contemplative self-inquiry to the point of having a profound insight into the subtle dynamics of personal consciousness. They have cracked the "mind code."

Even so—even with complete knowledge of both brain and mind—we would still be missing out on understanding the fundamental nature of consciousness.

We will never understand the mind by merely examining the brain. And we will not understand consciousness merely through mastery of our own minds. We also need to learn about consciousness through the direct lived experience of being in relationship.

Brain. Mind. Relationship. Knowledge of all three is essential if we are ever to have a complete and comprehensive study of consciousness. Such a science would include second-person investigations through dialogue and engaged presence alongside first-person contemplative studies and third-person observation and measurement of objective correlates in nervous systems and brains.

In Anglo-American philosophy of mind, the debate on how to study consciousness has been almost exclusively between objectivists and subjectivists—between analytically oriented and phenomenologically oriented scholars. On the one hand, the analytical-objectivists (in the tradition of Wittgenstein and Chomsky) tend to reduce mind to linguistic propositions, or, as materialists, to reduce consciousness to objective, functionalist computer-inspired models (Dennett), objective biological correlates (Searle), or, more extremely, aim to eliminate consciousness completely from philosophy and psychology (Churchland).[1]

On the other hand, the phenomenologists (in the tradition of Husserl) have been soaked in the subjectivist legacy of the Cartesian isolated *ego*. (Edmund Husserl's phenomenological *epoché* takes place in the private domain of the individual subject.) His student, Maurice Merleau-Ponty began to break out of this isolated subjectivism with his body-oriented and world-situated phenomenology. Mention of Husserl also raises the question of how Martin Heidegger's *Dasein* from *Being and Time* relates to intersubjectivity and consciousness. Heidegger, of course, made a deliberate effort to avoid issues about consciousness. His "Being" was an attempt to finally transcend the old Cartesian dichotomy of subject-object, consciousness-matter, and did not explicitly address intersubjectivity.[2]

It's worth noting in passing that in some ways Heidegger's position is radically third-person: His ultimate Being of all beings is neither first-person "I" nor second-person "you." As George Steiner noted about Heidegger's *Introduction to Metaphysics:* "In the grammar of essence, with its triple roots and areas of overlap, 'is' does occupy a privileged rank. It is not in respect of 'I am' that we most readily and most assuredly seize on the nature of being. . . . Nor is it in respect of 'you' (as certain schools of dialectical phenomenology would have it). The grammatical category that dominates our apprehension of being is the third-person singular of the present indicative—'is.'"[3]

Even from this cursory sampling, we see that contemporary philosophical literature echoes a long-standing debate on whether consciousness should be studied from the third-person (objective) or first-person (subjective) perspective.[4] And, as we saw in the previous chapter, very few philosophers (scientists or mystics) have paid attention to the *second-person* perspective—though the history of Western thought has some remarkable exceptions, as we will now see.

HISTORICAL ROOTS OF INTERSUBJECTIVITY

Despite philosophy's distance from Socrates, engaged interpersonal relationship continues to run through European philosophy as a backdrop, or hidden tributary, to the individualism that has dominated Western thought since Descartes, Kant, and the Enlightenment.

An interest in interpersonal relations can be found, for example, in the philosophy of Søren Kierkegaard, in Husserlian phenomenology, and in existentialists such as Jean-Paul Sartre and Ludwig Binswanger. Sartre believed that consciousness is a dialectical relationship between self-affirmation through choice and self-nihilation through interactions with others beyond the self, and that pre-reflective subjectivity necessarily precedes reflective intersubjectivity—for Sartre, consciousness is a pre-reflective experience of *presence*.[5] Binswanger believed that subjectivity, objectivity, and intersubjectivity were related through a dialectical "trichotomy," where subjective experience (thesis) is reduced to "total surrender" and "dissolution of the individual life by the objective principle of 'otherness'" (antithesis) and subsequently reemerges by a "reclaiming of objectivity in subjectivity" (synthesis).[6] And for Binswanger, the shared experience of love is determined by the "corresponding and equal togetherness of me and Thou," and the "dual mode of love [is] more than the sum of two separate, personal entities."[7]

The philosophical-social psychology of George Herbert Mead explains how knowledge of "me" is a result of internalizing some external "you." Humanistic psychologist Carl Rogers developed "person-centered" psychotherapy where the relationship between client and therapist was central; in radical psychiatry, R. D. Laing addressed the topic of "self and other." More recently, psychoanalysts Roger Stolorow and George Atwood have reinterpreted the transference-countertrans-ference phenomenon in therapy in terms of intersubjectivity. In sociolin-guistics and linguistic philosophy, Jürgen Habermas has developed a detailed account of the intersubjective-social basis for consciousness in his "theory of communicative action" (which we will examine more closely below).

In the Soviet Union during the 1920s and 1930s, social philosophers Mikhail Bakhtin and Valentin N. Voloshinov focused on "dialogue" as a linguistic-based alternative to mechanistic Marxist dialectical materi-alism. For Bakhtin, individual consciousness was fundamentally a social process—not autonomous cognition. The self is constructed through "simultaneous differentiation from, yet fusion with, another": "I achieve self-consciousness, I become myself only by revealing myself to another, through another, and with another's help. . . ."[8] For Voloshinov, indi-vidualistic subjectivism as the source of inner experience was replaced by the idea that experience arises out of social expression through commu-nication within a "sign community."[9]

In France, a major voice in linguistics, Sorbonne professor Francis Jacques, has developed a masterful and original philosophical analysis and critique of subjectivity, a development of the work of Emile Benveniste and Emmanuel Levinas, which proclaims the primacy of intersubjectivity and interpersonal relationship. The notion of inter-subjectivity also plays a central role in the reflexive model of percep-tion by psychologist Max Velmans—although in Velmans' work, the term "intersubjectivity" refers to consensual agreement (sharing of lin-guistic tokens) between independent observers, rather than the direct mutual engagement of subjectivities that I am focusing on here. And, more recently, the intersubjective domain of communal interiority is included in transpersonal theorist Ken Wilber's "four-quadrants" model (see below, pages 205–8).

In addition, the German school of "dialogue philosophers"—including Franz Rozenzweig, Eugen Rosenstock-Huessy—and Americans John Dewey and Charles Taylor have contributed to the wider debate on intersubjectivity.[10]

In a chapter of this length, I do not have the space to examine all of these scholars in detail. Instead, the thinkers I have selected (Kant,

Fichte, Kierkegaard, Humboldt, Mead, Buber, Jacques, Habermas, and Wilber) represent either key precursors to, or key exemplars or critics of, the intersubjective approach. In one way or another, each writer offers a new set of directions that could help us find our way back to an understanding of *relationship* as the essence of who we are. Instead of Descartes' focus on the lone subject, and the long detour in Western philosophy he inspired, we may once again have a relational philosophy inspired by Socrates and his method of engaging the hearts and minds of his students in transformational dialogue.

CONCEPTS OF SELF:
BEYOND SUBJECT-OBJECT MODELS

As we know, the key characteristic of consciousness is subjectivity—the experienced interiority of what it feels like to have or *be* a point of view[11]—and one of the key conundrums in philosophy of mind is how, through constant change, a sense of continuity and identity is felt by an experiencing subject. This is the classical problem of self-identity, first systematically addressed by British philosopher John Locke in *An Essay Concerning Human Understanding*.[12] How do we come to have a sense of self-identity? Following Locke, most discussions about self in Western philosophy focus on the individual Cartesian ego.

Even if we move beyond the primacy of the individual ego and embrace intersubjectivity, the capacity for interiority—for feeling from *within* what it's like to be (i.e., subjectivity-1)—remains the key characteristic of consciousness. The difference is that in this case, subjectivity need not be the unique privilege of a particular, individual subject (subjectivity-2) but could be the shared experience of co-creating mutual intersubjects. Such an approach to consciousness would radically reconfigure the perennial problem of other minds, assumed to be insoluble since Kant. Along with the problem of self-identity, this "problem of other minds" is another area in philosophy of mind where intersubjectivity could have a decisive impact and finally offer a solution.

Cartesian Individualism and the Enlightenment

Our story begins with Descartes and his profound and enduring influence on Western metaphysics. The original impulse driving the rationalist philosophies of the Enlightenment in the eighteenth century was a desire for greater autonomy of individuals—an urge traceable to the philosophical revolution in the seventeenth century centered on Descartes' declaration of independence: *Cogito ergo sum*—"I think, therefore I am." With this emphasis on the self-contained, spontaneous independent ego-subject, the Enlightenment plowed forward, valorizing the individualized subject, and generating a deep and chronic split between mind and body, between consciousness and the physical world.

The Cartesian primacy of the individualized subject led to a decisive split between subject and world. The world, as object, was "out there," while the ego, the subject, was "in here." Epistemologically, the subject came to know the separated, external world, by mirroring, or representing, objects within the private subjectivity of individualized consciousness. Given the Cartesian subject, there could be no *direct* knowledge or experience of another subject or object. All knowledge must be mediated by *representations* in the mind, and this epistemological model, adopted by Locke, Hume, and their followers, led to insurmountable difficulties in understanding how we could ever have true and certain knowledge of the world—an epistemological impasse that Kant heroically attempted to overcome.

Kant's Transcendental Ego

This same Cartesian subject-object dualism, which made knowledge of the external world problematic, also became the model for the modernist epistemology of consciousness. To know itself, the subject would reflect or represent itself to itself—the so-called "mirror model" of self-consciousness. But this approach failed, and continues to fail, to deliver up the elusive spontaneous self, the "I" that does the knowing.

As I mentioned earlier, Kant recognized this, and in his *Critique of Pure Reason* demonstrated that the Cartesian ego, as subject, could never be directly available to itself as an introspective object. As an object, the "I" becomes "me," and the spontaneity of the "I" is obliterated. In short the subject can never become an object to itself. At best, the first-person "I" recedes, and in its place an objectified third-person "me" appears. But this me-as-object lacks the very autonomy and spontaneity that is the characteristic essence of the I-as-subject. The "I" is autonomous, creative, and *now*; the "me" is reflected, and therefore *past* (a habitual construct in memory, built up throughout a lifetime).

In this Cartesian mirror-model of self-consciousness there is no way to bridge the gap between the autonomous first-person (subject of experience) "I" and the objectified third-person (object of memory) "me." The subject encounters itself only via the mediation of itself as object. For Kant, then, the spontaneous "I" remains "behind the scenes," invisible and unknown to itself (and, of course, to others). The spontaneous "I" is *transcendental*. The phenomenal "me," the aspect of self that appears as an object of knowledge, is merely the empirical ego that lacks autonomy and spontaneity.[13]

However, the Kantian critique of the Cartesian "mirror-model" of self-consciousness depends on a particular, and limited, notion of self-inquiry: epistemology through rational introspection. We could call it *rational empiricism,* where reason attempts to view or reflect the witnessing "I" by objectifying it as "me," the phenomenal self. And while the witnessing "I" remains forever inaccessible, a transcendental observer beyond the reach of reason and the senses, paradoxically this witnessing "I" is the ground of all our consciousness. Without it, we could know nothing.

Kant's method of self-inquiry, though a form of introspection (reason), analytically objectifies the ego and thus qualifies as a third-person perspective.

But there are other modes of self-inquiry that do not rely wholly on reason. Meditative and contemplative disciplines, for instance, can transcend reason and logic to arrive at deep intuitive, or noetic, knowledge—a knowing that transcends the duality of "I" and "me."[14] Kant's dichotomy, therefore, of the transcendental ego and the phenomenal ego—which posits an insurmountable divide between the objectively known self and the unknowable transcendental "I"-in-itself—is a result of his limited empiricism and epistemology. By engaging in contemplative practices, or *inner empiricism,*[15] the duality of "I" and "me" can be transcended.

Such inner empiricism penetrates the essence of subjectivity and thus qualifies as first-person perspective *par excellence.*

Our third approach to self-inquiry, *intersubjective empiricism,* also avoids the Kantian impossibility of the "I" reflecting itself without objectifying itself as "me."

By encountering others as centers of experiencing selves, just like our own self, we can, indeed, come to know ourselves reflected in the other. Unlike the failed Cartesian one-way mirror-model of self-consciousness, the intersubjective approach involves a kind of "two-way mirror," where not only can we "see through" to the other self, we can also learn to see our own spontaneous self reflected back through them—and this experience is itself *constitutive* of the experiencing "I." In other words, part of who I am, who I experience myself to be, is formed, perhaps even created, by engaging with "you."

This was Fichte's approach, modified by Humboldt and Kierkegaard, and taken up later by Habermas.

Fichte's Self-Positing Self

Johann Gottlieb Fichte attempted to augment Kant's transcendental ego by the notion of the "self-positing self."[16] For Fichte, the ego creates itself through an existential act of self-choice and achieves individuality through intersubjective encounters with other egos. Our uniqueness is shaped by these encounters. Thus Fichte's existential self-positing-intersubjective ego has both transcendental and immanent aspects. It also presupposes a pre-existing self that engages other pre-existing selves. His approach opens the way to account for what happens to the self-positing-self, to its forms or contents, but it does not advance our knowledge of consciousness or self as an ontological *context.*

Both Søren Kierkegaard and Wilhelm von Humboldt (see page 195) argued that Fichte's transcendental-immanent ego led to contradictions and paradoxes and did not resolve the paralogisms of self identified by Kant. The problem, they believed, resulted from the notion of the transcendental ego. They rejected the transcendental ego altogether and instead proposed a notion of a wholly immanent self, situated in the concrete world of life events and life histories (a view developed later, and along very different lines in John Dewey and Martin Heidegger).[17]

Kierkegaard's Existential Self-Choice

Kierkegaard retained and reworked Fichte's notion of self-positing into an existential theory of self-choice—a self that authentically *chooses* its own particular life history, and thereby establishes its unique individuality. Kierkegaard's "self-choice" involves a *performative* rather than a descriptive concept of individuality, an idea later taken up by Jürgen Habermas.[18]

In other words, when I *choose* myself as *this* person with *this* particular life history, and simultaneously *assert* and project myself into the world, what matters is not any third-person (or first-person) description of this self, but my claim to radical authenticity. Self, then, becomes not something to be described, but something to *perform*. The self is a *claim:* "I am who I am." But as a claim, the self must then be recognized or acknowledged, accepted, or rejected by other selves—by Other. For Kierkegaard, this Other was God.[19]

Humboldt's Linguistic Community

Wilhelm von Humboldt took a different approach. For him, the "other" became a community of other selves, united in a linguistic system. Instead of describing the self as an individual subject, he described encounters between speakers and hearers in a linguistic community—an exchange or meeting of perspectives, acknowledging, without objectifying, each other. Instead of Kant's transcendental subject, the locus of consciousness for Humboldt was a plurality of linguistic participants and perspectives. Unity in the participating community was achieved through "unforced agreement in conversation" without canceling diversity.[20]

Humboldt, thus, emphasized three elements that would later be essential to Habermas's theory of communicative action: the notions of "linguistic community," "intersubjectivity," and "unforced agreement in dialogue."

Mead's Intersubjectivity Alter Egos

From Kant, through Fichte, Kierkegaard, and Humboldt, the philosophy of consciousness progressively moved away from its moorings in the Cartesian subject-object dualism and the one-way mirror-model of self-reflective consciousness. However, even with Kant's transcendental ego, Fichte's self-positing ego, Kierkegaard's existential self-choice, and Humboldt's intersubjective linguistic community, no clear path had yet emerged by which the gap between first-person "I"-subjects and third-person "it"-objects could be bridged.

George Herbert Mead, social psychologist and social philosopher, introduced the crucial missing element: the *second-person perspective*.[21]

With this innovation, Mead made it possible for the self to know itself by mirroring itself in an "object." But this was no ordinary third-person object; in fact, it was not an "object" at all. It was another self—a second-person *alter ego*. Instead of the epistemological contortions of a first-person "I" attempting to adopt the third-person perspective of an external observer of itself, the self becomes known through the interactions of first-person and second-person perspectives of participants in active linguistic communication.

The self is no longer mirrored as an object from a third-person perspective, but as communicating egos mutually reflecting each other. My self, then, is perceived as the alter ego to your alter ego. I am "other," *as a self*, to you as another self: an encounter of mutually acknowledging selves. I perceive you as a subject in the second person, and "me" as *your* alter ego in the second person. From the second-person view, *who I am*—the self I experience myself to be—is shaped, or informed, by being with you.

Given this circle of intersubjectivity, of mutually participant subjects engaged in linguistic communication, how do we account for individual subjects? Underlying the "intersubjective project"—common to theorists from Mead and Buber to Habermas—is a motivation to not only counteract the exaggerated subjectivist bias in philosophy of consciousness, but also to avoid swamping the individual in overwhelming social norms of the collective, thereby depriving the individualized person of his or her autonomy and spontaneity. Intersubjectivity aims to create a middle course between the extremes of Cartesian subjectivism and Marxist collectivism.[22]

But if, as Mead argues, the self shows up only in the linguistic circle of intersubjectivity, how do we account for the individual subjects that intersubjectivity would seem to presuppose? How can there be a circle of intersubjectivity unless there are *subjects* already present to start with?

Mead recognized this problem and proposed as a solution that, in the same moment the self encounters an alter ego—the moment "I" encounter "you"—the concrete organism establishes a relationship to itself. "The self, as that which can be an object to itself, is essentially a social structure, and it arises in social experience."[23] The self, therefore, is "first encountered as a subject in the moment when communicative relations are established between organisms."[24]

The self, thus, has two components: the theoretical "me," my consciousness of myself, and the practical "me," the agency through which I monitor my behavior (such as speaking). "The 'I' is the response of the organism to the attitudes of the others; the 'me' is the organized set of attitudes of others which one himself assumes."[25] Hohengarten explains:

> This practical "me" comes into existence when the subject establishes a practical relation to herself by adopting the normative attitude of an alter ego toward her own behavior . . . such a conventionally constituted self is nonetheless a precondition for the emergence of a nonconventional aspect of the practical self: the practical "I," which *opposes* the "me" with both presocial drives and innovative fantasy. . . . Yet the *self is intersubjectively constituted through and through;* the relationship to a community is what makes the practical relation-to-self possible. (Italics added).[26]

Mead's emphasis on the intersubjective constitution of the self, of the subject's sense of continuity and identity, accounts for self as an "individualized context" for the contents of experience. But it still does not account for the "metacontext"—the non-individualized ontological context that underlies all contents of consciousness. Mead's "self," although a context for contents of individual experience, is itself a content within the ontological metacontext of consciousness-as-such.

Mead's intersubjectivity still leaves ontological subjectivity unexplained—the fact that at least some nodes in the universal matrix have a capacity for interiority, for a what-it-feels-like from within. It would still be possible, in Mead's theory, for a universe consisting wholly of objects to produce, via linguistic and social relations, what he calls "intersubjectivity." But this could be logically an "intersubjectivity" without any interiority, without any true subjectivity—and therefore not truly intersubjectivity (as defined here) at all.

Buber's "I and Thou"

Probably the theorist most readily associated with the notion of intersubjectivity (as a mutual engagement of interior presences) is the philosopher-anthropologist and theologian Martin Buber (1878–1965). As he himself acknowledged, he picked up the germ of the idea from the philosopher of religion Ludwig Feuerbach: "The individual man does not contain in himself the essence of man either in so far as he is a moral being or in so far as he is a thinking being. The essence of man is contained only in the community, in the unity of man and man—a unity which rests upon the reality of the difference between 'I' and 'Thou.'"[27] Feuerbach, however, did not pursue the idea, and Buber's priority, rightly, rests on the fact that he devoted his professional career, and a long list of works, to developing the implications of Feuerbach's revolutionary insight.

For Buber, Feuerbach's insight was comparable to the Copernican revolution, opening up new vistas in understanding about the nature of human beings, and not only with profound epistemological relevance but also ontologically revealing. In Buber's hands, these implications were worked out in great detail.[28] Specifically, the essence of human being was *relationship,* and Buber gave ontological status to the "between"—a mysterious force, "presence," or creative milieu, in which the experience of being a self arises. Relations, then, not the relata, were primordial, if not actually primary. "Spirit is not in the I but between I and You," he famously said.[29]

Only when "I" respond to "you," a fellow locus of presence or spirit, does my own being transcend the "oppressive force that emanates from objects."[30] According to Buber, human beings have two responses available to the world: to relate to what is present either as an object ("I–it" relationship) or as another responsible being ("I-thou" relationship). When we engage with the "other" as I-thou, relationship is mutually co-creating. The ontological status of the relationship, the "between," is emphasized by Buber when he refers to I-thou as "one word," representing a fundamental human reality of mutuality.

Buber's claim that a concrete reality may be related to as either an "it" or a "thou" raises some profound implications for philosophy of mind—particularly the issue of "other minds." As Whiteheadian philosopher Charles Hartshorne observed, there are at least three options available if we choose to relate to some creature as a "thou": (1) animistically, as a sentient and perhaps conscious individual, with a "soul" of its own (animistic-panpsychism); (2) as part of, or a manifestation of such an individual, perhaps as a member of a "cosmic organism" (e.g., Plotinian emanationist idealism, or Spinozistic monism); or (3) as a collection, or unity, of sentient, experiencing individuals (panpsychism).[31]

Science is incapable of determining whether any of these options is valid (we lack a "consciousness meter" to objectively observe or measure mind); and Buber's "I-thou" relationship may well extend beyond human interactions. Epistemologically, empirical validation of consciousness would require a major shift to the kind of radical empiricism discussed in previous chapters, and advocated by William James[32]—where *all* contents of experience (and *only* those), not just sense-mediated data, are legitimate data for a science of consciousness.

It would require also a radical ontology that allows for the intrinsic reality of consciousness or experience all the way down. The *process* philosophies of both Hartshorne and Whitehead, advocating a panpsychist ontology, are deeply compatible with this aspect of Buber's vision—replacing the notion of substance with dynamic relations.

However, Buber is not always consistent about whether the relationship, the "betweenness," is fundamental, or whether, as logic seems to require, any relationship must always be between some preexisting entities. Philip Wheelwright sums up Buber's position in *Between Man and Man,* which appears to support this latter view: "By nature each person is a single being, finding himself in company with other single beings; to be single is not to be isolated, however, and by vocation each one is to find and realize his proper focus by entering into relationship with others."[33]

Jacques' Tripartite Intersubjectivity

The primacy of relations, of intersubjectivity, becomes most explicit in the more recent work of Francis Jacques—perhaps the leading dialogue philosopher and linguist in France. His self-proclaimed project is to "found the conception of subjectivity on relations between persons . . . treating the relation as a primordial reality, a reality which constitutes one of the very conditions of possibility of meaning and which is prior even to *I* and *you.*" For Jacques, as for Habermas, "the *self* is a function of the communicative interaction which occurs in dialogue."[34]

Jacques has developed a theory of "being-as-speaking" and of the "being-who-speaks." He parts company with most other intersubjectivists, by presenting a tripartite schema of the subject—not just "I" and "thou," but one that includes also "he/she." Self-identity, he says, results from integration of the three poles of any communication: "by speaking to others and saying *I*, by being spoken to by others as *you,* or by being spoken of by others as a *he/she* that the subject would accept as appropriate."[35]

He takes issue with Buber who claimed that human beings become *I* and derive their interiority only when they encounter a *you.* Jacques argues that a human being becomes a personal self only when, in addition to *I-thou,* the "otherness" of an absent third-party, *he/she,* is acknowledged. Besides the *I* and *you,* self-identity requires "taking account of the third person and integrating it into the identificational process. . . . For when one speaks of someone else, *he/she* is not the same as *it*—a point that neither Buber nor Gabriel Marcel, nor Levinas appreciated."[36]

Jacques' main point may be encapsulated in the paradoxical notion of "presence of absence"—the felt presence of the departed other as an indispensable constituent of the sense of self. The absent third-party (not to be confused with third-person *it)* does not stand outside the intersubjective or interlocutive process. The other person is simply not present in the moment of dialogue but has a decisive influence nonetheless. Just think, for instance, how it is that an absent spouse or boss hovers in the background of many conversations. In a paradoxical way, their absence is a felt presence.

Jacques, with his tripartite interlocutive model of self-identity, has addressed head-on the subject-object "impasse" characteristic of modern philosophy of consciousness. In a comparable way, though from a different angle, Jürgen Habermas has developed a thoroughgoing intersubjectivity based on the centrality of language to consciousness.

JÜRGEN HABERMAS: LANGUAGE AND CONSCIOUSNESS

Building on Mead's view of the subject in *Mind, Self & Society,* and incorporating developmental ideas from psychologists Piaget and Kohlberg, Jürgen Habermas emphasizes that the process of individuation of the self depends on the development of a postconventional identity—a subject that simultaneously is shaped in intersubjective communicative action *and* that transcends the otherwise binding norms of his or her linguistic society.

Although the claim of radical authenticity depends on the recognition (though not necessarily the acceptance) of others, by the imaginative act of projecting a "universal community of all possible alter egos," the subject authentically retains autonomy—remaining a true subject within a creative web of intersubjectivities: "The idealizing supposition of a universalistic form of life, in which everyone can take up the perspective of everyone else and can count on reciprocal recognition by everybody, makes it possible for individuated beings to exist within a community—individualism as the flip side of universalism."[37]

Habermas is preeminently concerned with the role of language in shaping who we are as human beings. But his concern is not limited to an analysis of the structure or grammar of language, to its propositional content—he is not a linguistic analyst. Habermas is concerned with the real-world *speaking* of language, its impact on who we take ourselves to be, and on how we act in the world. He is hardly interested in the *theory* of language, but is emphatically concerned with the *practice* of language—with its *performative* function. Language engages speakers and hearers in such a way that both participate and *risk* themselves in communication. In the process, consciousness intersubjectively creates and reveals itself.

We can identify three central elements of Habermas's work—the three "P"s: (1) emphasis on *practice* away from theory; (2) the *public* or *intersubjective* origin and role of language and meaning; and (3) the *performative* function of language.

From Theory to Practice

Habermas is concerned to show that philosophy, to have any value and meaning, must engage with the world. Abstractions without the meat and muscle of practical action are little more than intellectual self-indulgence; such philosophy can do nothing for us. In this earlier phase of his work, Habermas displays the deep influence of Western Marxism in his thought and political engagement. (Habermas was active in German student political action in the Sixties.)

The Public Sphere

Later, Habermas reveals what has become a consistent theme throughout all his work: that language is first and foremost a *public* or social enterprise. At this stage, Habermas's central concern is political rather than philosophical (although in his work the two are never far apart). His focus is on working out an intellectual and practical basis for public discourse so that everyone, not just the bourgeois elite, would participate in effective control of public policy.

Communicative Action

Implicit in his political stance of discourse in the public sphere is a philosophical insight that he later made far more explicit: Meaning is not dependent on the grammatical structures or private "monological" subjective intentions of a speaker's language; meaning is derived from interaction through intersubjective communication. Language and meaning unfold from the "dialogical" reciprocity of "I-speakers" and "you-listeners." The two most dominant influences on Habermas in this regard are pioneer linguist-philosopher Wilhelm von Humboldt and philosopher-psychologist George Herbert Mead.

Language and meaning are products of the "public sphere," not the creation of individual, lone-operating subjects. Habermas's central concern is to argue that all language involves a *performative* function. That is, language does not merely describe the world but *engages the subject with the world through the listener.*

Intersubjective Meaning

While Habermas agrees that meaning cannot be understood independently of the conditions of its occurrence, he denies that these conditions are determined exclusively by structures of power and dominance, as claimed by deconstructive postmodernists. Instead, Habermas argues, the conditions for "interpretant relations" (that is, meaning) are dependent on conditions of *intersubjective communication* oriented toward *mutual understanding*. This view of language relations, and the consequent role of reason, is very different from that of postmodernists such as Derrida and Foucault.[38] Instead of individual and separate subjects engaged in interminable power struggles, Habermas's theory of communicative action refers to communities of subjects who partially create each other, and therefore strive for mutual understanding. Reasoning, thus, becomes a public enterprise.

In *Postmetaphysical Thinking*, Habermas observes that language performs three distinct, but intimately and invariably interconnected, functions: (1) a *speaker* comes to an understanding with (2) *another person* about (3) *something in the world*. In turn, these three functions of language correspond to three types of *validity claims*.

In Habermas's theory, meaning is not a product of any "picture theory of language" (as early Wittgenstein believed in the *Tractatus*); it is not a description of correspondences between words and facts or states of affairs. There is no independent subject unilaterally turning out "word pictures" that match some objective reality. And meaning is not a matter of Humpty-Dumptyesque arbitrary choosing what words mean. Nor is meaning an indefinite and indeterminate deferral of *différance*, forever sliding beyond reach, so that nothing really has any meaning at all (as Derrida and his deconstructionist followers would have it). Rather, says Habermas, meaning is constituted in the shared speech-acts of a communicating community of mutual-determining, uncoerced subjects.

Language, then, on this view, is a pragmatic, holistic act. Its smallest unit is not some disembodied or abstract sign, word, or phoneme, but an *utterance*, which involves three mutually interacting components—the speaker, the hearer, and the world in which they are situated. Each language utterance, or speech act, is like a token that the speaker offers to a listener (or community of listeners). This "token" *expresses* an experience of the world claimed to be true, right, and sincere by the speaker, and it may be either rejected or accepted by the hearer. In either case, the *validity claims* of "true," "right," and "sincere" can be tested by the community of speakers and hearers. It is here, in Habermas, where "intersubjective agreement" (through linguistic tokens) and "intersubjective co-creativity" (through shared experience) come together. The first is a foundation for consensual scientific knowledge established between communicating individual subjects. The second is true intersubjective mutual *beholding*—where the experience of self, of consciousness, arises as a felt experience from the encounter.

A final quote from Habermas sums up his intersubjective position:

> The ego, which seems to me to be given in my self-consciousness as what is purely my own, cannot be maintained by me solely through my own power, as it were for me alone—it does not "belong" to me. Rather, this ego always retains an intersubjective core because the process of individuation from which it emerges runs through the network of linguistically mediated interactions.[39]

Clearly, Habermas's philosophy offers a novel and intriguing second-person perspective. However, whereas he restricts the "other" to what can be communicated through human language—i.e., "you" would have to be another human being—I prefer to remain open to the Whiteheadian possibility that all organisms are centers of subjectivity and therefore available to me as "I-thou" partners, not only as objective "its." Even so, I am sure that the quality and character of human-human intersubjectivity is significantly different from interspecies intersubjectivity (see Epilogue).

Nevertheless, Habermas's emphasis on the intersubjective nature of language and consciousness is a major step forward. It may, more than Wittgenstein's or Heidegger's linguistic or phenomenological moves, lead Western philosophy, finally, beyond the perennial dualisms of subject-object, and mind-matter, thereby providing a philosophical agenda for a science of consciousness that includes a second-person perspective to complement third- and first-person perspectives.

KEN WILBER'S LOWER-LEFT QUADRANT

As we've just seen, a small, but growing, number of researchers and theorists are now beginning to pay attention to the second-person perspective in the field of consciousness studies. Ken Wilber, widely considered to be one of the most significant new-paradigm thinkers, has also been a recent contributor to the debate.

In a remarkable outpouring of books and articles—his *Collected Works* already fill eight thick volumes—he makes one of the strongest rational cases for opening up the modern worldview to include not only consciousness, but Spirit, too. With a characteristic combination of verve, wit, intelligence, humor, and provocation he takes his readers beyond the narrow confines of mere materialism and objectivity without sacrificing the many undoubted benefits of the rationalist-empiricist tradition, *and* without falling prey to the world-denying tendencies of various forms of idealism.

Wilber's great contribution to modern intellectual debate is to have made a provocative case for not only extending modern science—a model of evolution reaching beyond rational creatures all the way to Spirit—but for *integrating* it with premodern spiritual wisdom to produce a truly postmodern, all-encompassing spectrum of consciousness.

In Wilber's grand intellectual edifice, the world, including human beings, consists of exteriors and interiors, the two great domains of his Four Quadrants (see fig. 16.1).

Why, then, *four* quadrants, not just two domains? You will see from the figure that both exteriors and interiors come in two forms: individual and communal. So, in the Upper Left (UL) quadrant, we see individual-interiors (the domain of individual subjects). In the Lower Left (LL), we find communal-interiors (the domain of mutual intersubjectivities). In the Upper Right (UR), we see individual-exteriors (the domain of atomistic objects). In the Lower Right (LR) quadrant, we find communal-exteriors (the domain of systems or networks of objects).

This is Wilber's map of reality, his ontological mandala.

But that is only part of the map. Each quadrant is co-evolving, from the lowest, least complex forms to the highest, or *deepest*, most complex realities. This means, simply, that individual-interiors (subjects) evolve, communal-interiors (cultures) evolve, individual-exteriors (individual

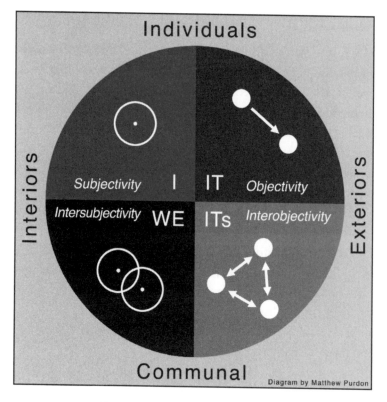

Fig. 16.1. Wilber's Four Quadrants

physical objects) evolve, and communal-exteriors (objective, physical systems) evolve. Further, nothing evolves in any single quadrant without a concomitant evolution in all the other quadrants.

A Placemarker for Intersubjectivity

One aspect of Wilber's work I particularly endorse is his emphasis on including intersubjectivity in any comprehensive understanding of consciousness. Not only is it essential, it is *fundamental*. Wilber and I agree on this: "Failing to see that subjective experiences *arise in the space created by intersubjective structures* is one of the main liabilities of many forms of spiritual and transpersonal psychology."[40]

And, I would add, of contemporary philosophy of mind.

While Wilber and I are in basic agreement about the importance of intersubjectivity, there are some finer points of the discussion where we are not. The most important difference is that Wilber's lower-left quadrant, according to his own declarations, tends to be restricted to intersubjectivity-1, as previously discussed. In other words, Wilber's "intersubjectivity," following Habermas, is a matter of *linguistic* exchanges. And this, as I have explained, is the weakest meaning of the term. It doesn't account for experiences of shared *presence*—of true, unmediated *subject to subject* engagement—or, indeed, for familiar experiences such as empathy, compassion, and love.

Wilber and I have disagreed—sometimes passionately—about his version of intersubjectivity, and for the record I should acknowledge that he now does entertain the other two meanings (and has added a few more of his own). Readers interested in this debate can turn to appendix 3: "Wilber and de Quincey: I-to-I," where I have included a thorough discussion.

A Map for Integral Science

Notwithstanding our differences, we both agree that science, at the very least, needs to acknowledge the reality of the interior depth of the world—of subjectivity, the domain of experience. As Wilber says, it is beyond ludicrous to believe that only exteriors exist. Such a view is utterly nonsensical. Exteriors can exist only in the presence of interiors. To claim otherwise would be like saying the world consists only of "ups," and that "downs" are just figments, or, to use a favorite phrase of eliminative materialists, just "folk fictions." Exteriors (objective realities) without interiors (subjective realities) are meaningless. The "fiction" is to believe that one could exist without the other. Of course, Wilber's logic here applies only to the semantic distinction between "exteriors" and "interiors."*

Despite this logical slip, Wilber's point that science needs to acknowledge the "interior" or experiential aspect of reality remains valid. It is clear *as an empirical fact* (not a logical necessity) that consciousness

---

*When these refer, respectively, to physical and experiential existence—as, indeed, intended by Wilber—the logic is no longer valid. It is *logically* possible that reality could ultimately consist of purely physical things or events (the position of materialism), or of purely spiritual beings (the position of idealism). The existence of physical reality and spiritual reality, therefore, is not analogous to the logical distinction between "ups" and "downs."

("interior") exists amidst the multiplicity of physical forms in the universe. We know this for absolutely certain in our own case, as Descartes showed when he discovered the starting point for his new philosophy.

The paradox facing science (the central topic of volume three in this trilogy) is that for science to exist at all it requires experiencing beings who can *know*. Yet the subjective experience of *any knower* is precisely what modern science cannot account for. If science is ever to become a *comprehensive* exploration of the cosmos, then, clearly, it must find a way to study consciousness. To overcome this glaring omission, science must begin by acknowledging that the cosmos possesses the *consciousness that knows* and gives rise to science in the first place. Otherwise, by default, science will remain incomplete, confining itself to exploring only the exterior "objects" of the cosmos that show up in consciousness—but not the subjective fact, nature, or dynamics of consciousness itself.

Intentionally or not, science may remain a collection of disciplines that restrict inquiry exclusively to *phenomena* (to what "shows up" in consciousness) but not inquire into the fact that it is possible for *anything* to "show up" at all. In such a case, we could never have a science of consciousness. Science would forever remain focused on objects, and leave the investigation of subjects to other disciplines such as philosophy and spiritual practice.

Wilber's integral quadrants model offers a very useful roadmap for a comprehensive science—a "map" that not only includes consciousness but, more to the point, also has a placemarker for intersubjectivity. I applaud Wilber's intention to put the second-person perspective on the consciousness studies map—this has been my own intention for many years.

If we do include intersubjectivity in our studies of consciousness, how then might we fit it into an evolutionary model? Earlier in this book, we learned that "consciousness slides from our grasp like a slippery fish" whenever we try to catch it in the net of language. Next, we will try one more time to coax it out of its lair with a strange incantation—intended to reveal its origins, to place it in evolution, and to reveal its fundamental and intrinsic intersubjective nature.

17

Origins

Evolution of Consciousness

"Pssssst. Do you want to know a secret?" Usually when we hear this there's some kind of conspiracy afoot. Let's say, for instance, I wanted to share with you the original meaning of "consciousness," and I wanted us to keep the secret within our own private group. Why would I do that? Surely as a teacher of consciousness studies I would want many people to know this "secret"? Well one good reason is that by telling you and inviting you into our select group of initiates, we'd actually be demonstrating the original meaning of consciousness. As we will see below, "consciousness" originally implied a "shared secret" or "knowledge of a privileged few." So, keep it to yourself—for now.

THE ORIGINAL MEANING OF CONSCIOUSNESS

The *Oxford English Dictionary* identifies seven varieties of consciousness:[1] (1) sentience, (2) awake/awareness, (3) interpersonal, (4) personal, (5) reflective, (6) unitive, and (7) dissociative.

All varieties reveal a common characteristic, *subjectivity*—they are known from "within." And, with one notable exception, all are private—the privileged domain of the individual knower. The exception is *interpersonal* because it means, "knowing or sharing the knowledge of something together with another."[2]

What is interesting about this is that it is actually the form of consciousness that originally gave rise to the very concept itself—*conscientia,* meaning "knowing with" others.[3] It reveals that, originally, the word "consciousness" implied a *dialogic* process—an interaction or communication between two or more knowing beings. To be conscious meant that two or more people were privy to some item of knowledge not available to others outside the privileged circle. In this sense, "consciousness" is similar to "conspire" (to "breath with" others). "Consciousness" meant that the privileged circle of knowers *knew that each of their conspirators knew, too.*

Consciousness, in other words, was originally *communal,* a property of the group. This sense remains today in forms of consciousness referred to, for example, as "social consciousness," "political consciousness," "feminist consciousness," "racial consciousness," and is manifested in such diverse groups as church congregations, religious movements, political parties, sports teams and fans, and religious and political cults. "Social consciousness" essentially refers to the *contents* of consciousness—only this time on a large scale within a community, rather than in one person. However, since it still deals with contents— with changes in consciousness at the level of groups—it is still a form of "psychological" consciousness (we might call it "psycho-social" consciousness). "Social consciousness," ironically, often masks the deeper, metaphysical, intersubjective nature of consciousness—the very condition that allows for any individual or social form of consciousness to emerge in the first place.

We have many examples of "expanding or changing social consciousness"—e.g., in feminism, new age movements, alternative health practices, ethnic diversity, human rights, animal rights, and ecological awareness. But these are not the most interesting cases facing a science of consciousness. These kinds of changes or shifts in consciousness have happened throughout human history. What has never happened (at least not in modern, Western society) is the development of a true *science of consciousness* that can explore the world of mind with the same degree of rigor we have so far used to explore the world of matter.

CONSCIOUSNESS AS CONTENTS AND CONTEXT

An important aspect of interpersonal consciousness is that it offers explorers of mind a third alternative mode of inquiry. It is important to distinguish here between (1) *forms* or *manifestations* or *contents* of consciousness—which already presuppose consciousness-as-such as a context; and (2) the ontological *fact* or suchness of consciousness, the raw reality of consciousness as a *substratum* or "canvas" that underlies the multiplicity of forms or contents of consciousness that show up within the context.

As we saw in chapter six, the first meaning, contents, tends to be the domain of psychology; the second is more the focus of philosophy, particularly philosophy of mind. One of the most intriguing—and philosophically most important—questions about interpersonal consciousness is whether it provides us only with epistemological accounts of the contents of consciousness or whether it can advance our understanding of the context, or nature, of consciousness itself.

Related to this is the ontological question raised earlier: "Which came first: individual subjectivity or intersubjectivity?" Which is primary: the relations or the relata? If individual consciousness or subjectivity preexists interpersonal, intersubjective consciousness, then a study of interpersonal consciousness would reveal only what happens to the mental *contents* of two or more individual subjects when they experientially engage each other. If, however, intersubjective *relations* are primary, then so-called individual subjectivity would arise only through the dynamics of dialogic relations, and the study of intersubjectivity would inform us about consciousness as an ontological *context*—we would gain insight into the essential nature of consciousness itself.

INTERSUBJECTIVITY AND INTERPERSONAL CONSCIOUSNESS

I noted above that "consciousness" originally meant to "know with" others—it was interpersonal or intersubjective. However, I now want to unpack this claim and propose some further subtle distinctions that may help clarify why we may now have an opportunity to explore intersubjectivity in a way that was not available to our predecessors. These distinctions will borrow a concept central to Ken Wilber's critique of the evolution of consciousness.[4]

Wilber argues that it is a fallacy to equate "pre-egoic" consciousness (or self)—as in the so-called *participation mystique* of animistic worldviews—with "trans-egoic" consciousness of nondual, mystical experience. There is an evolutionary progression, Wilber argues, from pre-egoic, through various stages of egoic, to trans-egoic consciousness. And it is a serious category mistake to equate (confuse or conflate) the "pre" with the "trans."

Similarly, the seven varieties of consciousness listed in the dictionary may be viewed as an evolutionary sequence—from consciousness as Sentience, Awake, Interpersonal, Personal, Reflexive, to Unitive. To help me remember this sequence, I devised the mnemonic "SAIPRUD." (Since "D" represents *dissociative* consciousness—a pathology that may occur at any stage in the process—it may be better to write "SAIPRU[D].") Yes, it is a clumsy mnemonic. Nevertheless, it may serve as a kind of "incantation" to help us lure the slippery fish of consciousness out into the open where we can get a closer look at it.

In this model, it is clear that interpersonal consciousness (C_i) precedes personal consciousness (C_p)—intersubjectivity is prior to subjectivity, it is "pre." This accords with the position implicit in Buber and explicit in Jacques and Habermas. However, taking a cue from Wilber's "pre/trans" distinction, I want now to distinguish between "intersubjective" and "interpersonal."

If, as claimed here, subjectivity (i.e., experienced interiority) is the essential, key characteristic of consciousness, then it is present throughout the entire spectrum of consciousness, from raw sentience (C_s) to mystical unity (C_u). And if, following Buber, Mead, Jacques, and Habermas, we take *relations* as ontologically primary, then subjectivity is *always* embedded within a matrix or context of mutually cocreating intersubjectivities. Thus, even at the level of raw sentience (C_s), (be it a newborn baby, a worm, bacterium, atom, or electron), intersubjective interiority (what-it-feels-like to be that entity) is ontologically fundamental.

Similarly, this is true all the way up, through consciousness-as-awake (C_a) to unitive consciousness (C_u). Thus, if C_i is present throughout, it no longer serves as a useful distinction—or indeed, a valid stage—in the evolutionary progression. In fact, it is not a stage; it is a *condition* of all stages. So, our mnemonic, minus C_i, would now read: "SAPRU(D)." However, this model is incomplete: It does not account for interpersonal dialogic consciousness.

Now let's revisit the "pre/trans" distinction from the perspective of the evolution of "individual self." Historically, the notion of the "individual" as an autonomous self—one that could separate from the collective or community—is itself an evolutionary phenomenon. Prior to the time of Alexander the Great, from Homer down to Aristotle, the "individual" was identified with the group or city-state.[5] At this stage, consciousness was *pre-personal* (Wilber's "pre-egoic"), a pre-individualized collective "self." Thus, although intersubjectivity was present, its character was still "pre." Consciousness, "knowing with," was group consciousness, where members of the group had no sense of individual self-identity. Their identity was with the tribe or group.[6]

But following the great unification of the Hellenistic world during and after Alexander's time, the uniformity of the empire made it possible and practicable for individual members to leave their city-state, for example to travel from Athens to Alexandria. Individual citizens could move from city-state to city-state, and still feel "at home" because many of their familiar cultural trappings surrounded them as they traveled. Their collective identity moved with them, and the way opened up for a *detachable individual* self that could move around the empire. Result: the birth of the individual. Only then could consciousness evolve to the stage of C_p, personal consciousness.

I now want to propose a similar model (or extension of this same model) for the emergence of *trans*-personal intersubjective consciousness. Just as it was almost impossible for the average citizen prior to Alexander's empire to experience individual self-identity (pre-personal)—they just didn't *notice* the personal quality of consciousness embedded in the group—it has been almost impossible for the average individual in contemporary society to experience intersubjectivity at the level of transpersonal consciousness. Until now (and perhaps even still), we have been too embedded in our personal consciousness, in our Cartesian-Enlightenment "lone ranger" individualism, to *notice* that the deeper reality or grounding of our consciousness is the intersubjective matrix of interdependent relationships.

I'm proposing that a crucial aspect of the widely anticipated "new paradigm"—a worldview of nonlocal interdependence—may be the emergence of *transpersonal* awareness of our deep intersubjective nature. Elements or facets of this emerging worldview would include, for example, the discovery of nonlocality in quantum physics;[7] accumulating documentation of evidence for nonlocal psi phenomena;[8] increased globalization of economies;[9] awareness of ecological interdependence;[10] and, perhaps, even the globalization and interconnectedness of communications technologies such as satellite TV, telephones, and the Internet.[11] It is becoming less and less easy to deny our deep interconnectedness. We might also include in this list a growing awareness of the central doctrine of co-dependent arising in Buddhism, as it continues to spread into modern, Western societies and worldviews.[12]

Given this perspective, the evolutionary mnemonic might now be written as "I-SAPRIU(D)":

- **Intersubjective** (primordial condition and foundation for consciousness shared between all intersubjects—what many traditions refer to as "spirit");
- **Sentience** (primitive capacity for feeling and self-motion in any individual organism);
- **Awake/awareness** (higher form of sentience where organism can be either conscious or unconscious, awake or asleep);
- **Personal** (individualized awareness with a sense of self-identity);
- **Reflective** (capacity for self to be "aware that I am aware"— gateway to altered states of consciousness: "aware that I am aware that I am aware . . .");
- **Interpersonal** (gateway to transpersonal consciousness, involving awareness not only of personal identity, but also of deep intersubjective foundation of all consciousness);
- **Unitive** (integrates all prior forms of consciousness into experienced unity);

- **Dissociative** (pathological failure to integrate prior forms of consciousness).

According to this view, C-sentience and C-awake are pre-personal, C-personal and C-reflexive are personal, with C-interpersonal evolving out of C-personal, emerging as the first stage in transpersonal consciousness. The integration of all stages from C_S to C_i is unitive consciousness (C_u). ("D," as before, represents the potential for dissociation at any stage, the pathological shadow side of intersubjective consciousness that prevents development toward unitive consciousness.)

Let's now look more closely at these different levels or varieties of consciousness.

EVOLUTIONARY MODEL OF CONSCIOUSNESS

0. C-intersubjective: *Primordial Relatedness*

The prefix "I" in I-SAPRIU(D) signifies intersubjectivity permeating the entire evolutionary spectrum. I repeat: If C-intersubjective is present throughout, it no longer serves as a useful distinction in the evolution of consciousness. It is not, strictly speaking, a variety, or a state or level of consciousness like the other seven. It is the context or condition for all varieties of consciousness and permeates the entire evolutionary spectrum.

1. C-sentience: *What It Feels Like to Be*

Consciousness as sentience has two distinct aspects—"raw feel" and intentionality. To be sentient, first and foremost, means, as philosopher Thomas Nagel pointed out, there is something it is like—something it *feels like* from within—to be a particular sentient organism. To be a human being, a bat, a worm, or a bacterium, there is some experience characteristic of that organism.[13]

Another way to say this is that a sentient being has a point of view—its subjectivity—from which it surveys or receives input from the rest of the world. By contrast, non-sentient things do *not* have a point of view—there is nothing it feels like to be a rock, a chair, or a computer (to use standard examples). Without feeling or subjectivity, the world cannot be experienced from the point of view of a rock. (This may not be true of its constituent molecules and atoms, however. See appendix 5, "The Philosopher's Stone," for a discussion on the question of "rock consciousness.")

Sentience may be *un*conscious, but it cannot be *non*-conscious. To be non-conscious is to be wholly insentient, without the possibility of felt responsiveness. A worm, a bacterium (and a human being) may be unconscious, but (to continue with our paradigm example) a rock is non-conscious. A rock is never alert to its surroundings. It just is—an object among other objects. The intrinsic being of a rock is objective "raw exis-tence," "raw isness." By contrast, the intrinsic being of a sentient organ-ism is subjective "raw feeling"—a felt responsiveness to its surroundings.

This brings us to the second aspect of consciousness as sentience: intentionality. To be sentient also means to have experience *of* something, or consciousness *about* something (either in the external surroundings or internally within the organism's own system). Psychologist-philosopher Franz Brentano (1838–1917) said that the fundamental distinguishing mark of consciousness is intentionality.

According to this view, all consciousness is always of or about some-thing; it refers to something beyond itself. Only sentient beings can be intentional; only sentient beings can refer, or point, beyond themselves.

(Some non-sentient things, such as road signs, labels, and so on, of course, do refer to things beyond themselves. But they are not inten-tional because the significance of the reference—the meaning of the relationship between the signifier and the signified—does not reside in the sign itself. The significance, the meaning, is the creation of the con-sciousness that constructed (or reads) the sign and established the rela-tionship between the sign and the thing pointed at. The sign means something only because some sentient being chose or decided on that relationship.)

2. C-awake: Normal Waking Consciousness

I've already noted that sentience may be unconscious (but not non-conscious). This implies that it may also be conscious, in the (psy-chological) sense of being awake, aroused, or alert. In addition to the intentionality of basic sentient consciousness, awake-consciousness is characterized by an "orientation response"—a state of awareness or arousal, a readiness potential to respond to contingent stimuli from the environment.

C-awake is associated with an organism's preparedness to act, whereas C-sentience is receptive or passive awareness. "Raw feel" is simply moment-to-moment experience; and intentionality, as distinct from orientation-response, points or indicates without necessarily prompting any action on the part of the organism.

Nevertheless, the difference between C-sentience and C-awake is essentially a matter of degree. Both have in common the "aboutness" of intentionality or orientation (what some philosophers call "transitive" consciousness), and both are characterized by "raw feel," the what-it-feels-like to be the subject of experience ("intransitive" consciousness).

3. C-personal: To Know "Me," I Need You

When you wake up in the morning you recognize that you are the same person who went to sleep the night before. You have a sense of personal identity that continues from day to day. Personal consciousness includes but goes beyond raw sentience and being merely awake, alert, aroused, and oriented to the world. It moves to the next level where consciousness becomes aware of itself as a continuing identity. It involves a sense of "self," an individual "I" (René Descartes called it the "ego").

As discussed earlier, following Descartes, Immanuel Kant showed that the "I" cannot know itself, just as the eye cannot see itself. As pure experience, sentience, or subjectivity, the "I" eludes the gaze or the grasp of consciousness. Much as the eye cannot see itself without its reflection in a mirror, to know itself, the "I," too, must have a way to reflect back on itself. But the reflection is not what is doing the reflecting. Consciousness-as-I is transparent to itself (American Transcendentalist Ralph Waldo Emerson called it the "transparent eyeball").

To illustrate the transparency of consciousness-as-I, philosopher Gilbert Ryle used the metaphor of the index finger that can point at anything but itself. Again, the only way a finger can point at itself is in a mirror. Even the sense of personal identity—the sense of self as "me"—depends on some "other," on some other consciousness or subjectivity in which it is reflected. Therefore, even personal consciousness arises from intersubjectivity.

To know myself as "me," I first need you (another conscious being) to know and "reflect" me. (In developmental psychology, an adequate mirroring relationship between infant and mother has been recognized as essential for a child to develop a healthy sense of self. The mother's empathic gaze serves as a mirror for the emerging self to internalize the "mirror" and to recognize itself as "me.") For self-consciousness (C-personal), the mirroring-other is indispensable. It is this realization that seems to lie at the root meaning of "consciousness"—*knowing with others*.

We can know ourselves as "me" only when reflected in another. Without the mirroring-other, without the "you" or the "we," there could be no "me." Individual personal consciousness (C-personal) depends on an "internalizing" of the other, so that the "I" can become conscious of "me." Without an internalized mirroring-other there is simply a transparent "I," but no self-reflective consciousness of "me." To be self-*reflective* is to be self-*reflected*. We can never know ourselves as "I"—except, as we shall see, in paradoxical transpersonal intersubjective states of "I-to-I" where the sense of individuality is dissolved into the community of shared consciousness.

4. C-reflexive: Gateway to Altered States

One step beyond self-reflecting, personal consciousness is the ability for consciousness to *reflect on itself reflecting,* to move deeper into other layers or levels of itself. It becomes self-reflexive rather than simply self-reflected. C-reflexive refers to consciousness of being conscious. It is what allows us, for example, to experience the self-consciousness of embarrassment, or the angst of existential knowledge that we will surely die. At the level of C-reflexive, we can ask questions such as "What is the meaning of my life?" or "Who am I?"

By pursuing such questioning in an authentic way, by experiencing the movement of consciousness as it reflects back on itself (not merely engaging in intellectual concept-games), C-reflexive can guide consciousness through its own experiential labyrinths and lead to altered states of consciousness. This is "self-witnessing" consciousness, sometimes arrived at during the practice of meditation or contemplation, where the "I" witnesses the multiple subtle layers of egoic mind, each time believing that "This is it! This is the real, ultimate self," only to discover that each "true self" turns out to be yet another content showing up for the witnessing Mind.

Although the "I" forever remains elusive, reflexive consciousness can lead to a progressive refinement of awareness between illusion and the true self—even though the self forever retreats or hides from inspection. It is a *via negativa*, what Buddhists refer to as *"neti-neti"*—"not this, not that." At some point, in an altered state of non-ordinary consciousness, we come to glimpse that we can *never* inspect or witness the true self because *it is the inspector or witness.*

5. C-interpersonal: Original Meaning of "Consciousness"

As we noted earlier, subjectivity is a characteristic common to all seven varieties of consciousness in the I-SAPRIU(D) model; all are known from within. And with one exception, all are the private experience of each individual knower. The one exception, we saw, is C-interpersonal, because it means *conscientia*, "knowing or sharing the knowledge of something together with an other." It is closest to the original meaning of "consciousness." It is the root of both "conscience" and "consciousness."

As the term implies, C-interpersonal transcends personal consciousness. It is not confined to the isolated egos of individual persons. As a form of shared consciousness, C-interpersonal extends beyond the boundaries of our "skin-encapsulated egos," and thus is the first stage in transpersonal awareness. This mode or level of consciousness marks a decisive transition from monologic, self-focused, mind to dialogic, group consciousness. It is the form of consciousness experienced, for example, in effective Bohmian dialogue and, as we shall see in the next chapter, it may be the dominant form of consciousness among dolphins and whales.

6. C-unitive: Highest State of Consciousness

The integration of all stages from C-sentience to C-interpersonal is unitive consciousness. Beyond C-reflexive (gateway to altered states) and C-interpersonal (first stage of transpersonal consciousness), C-unitive transcends the differences between the five previous levels or varieties of consciousness and, by integrating them, can break through to mystical experience.

As mystics and sages throughout history and across cultures have commonly pointed out, at this stage we eventually move completely beyond the reach of reason and the power of language. It is here where words and concepts give way to silent knowing or "no-knowledge"—to enlightenment that "passeth all understanding."

7. C-dissociative: Fragmented Consciousness

Finally, C-dissociative is the flipside of C-unitive: Instead of *break-through* to the harmony and order of integration, consciousness can *break down* into the fragmentation of self-deception, or more extremely, multiple personality disorder. C-dissociative represents the potential for dissociation at any stage, the pathological shadow side of intersubjective consciousness that prevents unitive consciousness.

In Bohmian dialogue we learn that fragmentation in consciousness arises from the mistaken assumption that our thoughts (concepts, ideas, beliefs) are accurate reflections of reality. All thoughts and beliefs are static, abstract products of consciousness, and by nature are fragmentary. They are mental "deposits" and tend to clog up the experiential "arteries" of consciousness connecting our embodied selves with the wider environmental body of planet and cosmos. This fragmentation in our thoughts is then projected back onto the world and shows up in our social, economic, political, scientific, and religious institutions. According to Bohm, the contents of our consciousness always, necessarily, distort our perception of reality.

Instead of being mesmerized by the contents of our minds (no matter how fine and elaborate they may be), we would do better to develop awareness of the *context* of consciousness, the natural arising of our "thinking"—the process of consciousness itself "flowing" in and through our bodies. Only then (as we discover in a community of dialogue) . . . only by shifting awareness from "thoughts" to "thinking," from belief to experience, can we begin to find a path back to wholeness.

As we fish for consciousness, coaxing it with our strange incantation "I-SAPRIU(D)," it begins to emerge from the shadows, revealing its innermost secret: The ultimate nature of consciousness, we discover, is *communion*.

In the next chapter, we'll look more closely at four different ways of knowing required to integrate these different evolutionary levels of consciousness. I have mentioned these "four gifts" from time to time throughout this book. Having come this far, we can now use philosophy to move beyond philosophy, guiding us into other ways of knowing.

18

Radical Knowing

The Four Gifts

Have you ever noticed that knowledge gained during one state of consciousness sometimes seems to contradict knowledge gained while in some other state? You may see deeper into the nature of things during meditation, for example, or you may experience a profound insight in a dream; but then, back in the ordinary state of "daylight" consciousness, you may begin to question the accuracy, wisdom, or validity of what came to you in your non-ordinary state. Many of us are familiar with this form of epistemological doubt—but, as we will see, we need not invalidate any way of knowing.

My way of dealing with seemingly contradictory or incompatible domains of knowledge is to cultivate and use what I call the "four gifts of knowing." I believe that we come into the world with different innate capacities or potentials for learning about ourselves and how we fit into nature. These capacities, or "gifts," are: The Philosopher's Gift of *reason*, the Scientist's Gift of the *senses* (and empirical *methodology*), the Shaman's Gift of participatory *feeling*, and the Mystic's Gift of "transcendental" *direct experience*, unmediated by the senses or conceptual processing, and often accessed via sacred silence.

The following pages are a kind of "Owner's Guide to Consciousness"—designed to help sort out the tangles and knots philosophers and scientists (and the rest of us) often get into when trying to explore the mind and how it relates to the body.

First, we will learn how the Philosopher's Gift of *clear thinking* opens the way to talk about *why* we can know (or not know) what consciousness is, and why we can (or cannot) talk about it. The Philosopher's Gift gives us *reasons* and explanations.

Next, we will look at the Scientist's Gift of *observation and method,* and how this opens the way for investigating *what* the brain is, how it works, and how it correlates with mind. It gives us data and descriptions.

Then we will shift focus to look at the Shaman's Gift of *embodied feeling* and *altered states of consciousness.* It is seeing and knowing *where* consciousness can take us, and trusting in the wisdom of the body (our own body, the Earth's body, and the great body of the Cosmos itself). The Shaman's Gift gives us deeper vision into subtle realms.

Finally, we will explore the Mystic's Gift of *sacred silence,* source of intuition and transcendence, gateway to the clearing of consciousness and the unspeakable domain of spirit. The Mystic's Gift brings us closer to knowing *who* guides the mind.

THE PHILOSOPHER'S GIFT:
REASON AND CLEAR THINKING

Philosophers are interested in *why* it is meaningful to talk about consciousness. Everybody has a mind, yet few of us really know how to talk about it. If asked about its nature, we quickly discover the limitations of language. If asked how it works, we are tempted to either talk about the brain, about behavior—or we are left scratching our heads. If we wonder how to develop this ghostly faculty, launching ourselves to new spiritual heights, again we are often at a loss for words.

So, first things first: In any conversation—but particularly about consciousness—clarity depends most of all on getting our meanings straight. As we learned in chapter 6, so much talk about consciousness is confusing because our words can mean many different things. For now, we will approach the question of consciousness *philosophically*— because philosophers are the professionals when it comes to meaning.

It may be helpful here to recall the two different kinds of meaning we explored in chapter 6—*symbolic* meaning and *experienced* meaning—and also how they relate to each other. Both kinds of meaning have something in common: They both refer to what is beyond themselves. In the case of language, words have meaning because they refer to things beyond the words themselves. In the case of a person's life, the life itself gets its meaning within the larger context of the world or cosmos as a whole. Our life—as it is actually, concretely lived and experienced (not just as an abstract word, idea, image, or symbol)—gets its meaning from participating as part of a greater whole, whether in time or space, or beyond.

Thus, although it may be true to say that your life has *intrinsic* meaning—that is, it is meaningful in and of itself—such meaning gets its richness from its interconnectedness and interdependence with the whole. For instance, if we feel disconnected from the whole (whether life as a whole, the universe as a whole, or existence as a whole) we feel that our life has lost its meaning. The more we feel connected with the whole, the more we experience life to be rich with meaning and possibilities.

The first kind of meaning is philosophical, where meaning depends on *symbolic* connections grasped by reason. The second kind of meaning is psychological, mystical, or spiritual, where meaning depends on *experienced* connections revealed through intuition or mystical insight. This is not to say that philosophers never concern themselves with the deeper kind of meaning—many of them do, especially those who follow in the tradition of Socrates and Plato. But when writing or talking about the deeper kind of meaning, they recognize the great value of paying attention to *symbolic* meaning.

It is one thing to *experience* meaning, it is something else to *talk* about it. When we feel moved to talk or write about our experience, it helps a lot if we make use of the philosopher's gift of reason.

The tools of the philosopher's trade are logic and analysis, sharpened by the rigor of precision. And we can take advantage of the work philosophers have done through the centuries—particularly some of the magnificent discoveries they have revealed about the mind. Unfortunately, sometimes philosophers probe so deeply into the fine structure of language that it takes a trained and diligent mind to follow the twists and turns of their arguments. Often in the process, simple clarity and meaning get lost in a fog of conceptual gymnastics that leave ordinary folk more confused than enlightened. It's not so surprising, then, that many people show no interest in what philosophy has to say—it all seems so unrelated to real life.

But good philosophers not only dive deep, they also return to the surface with polished nuggets of insight, pried loose from the bedrock of language and reason, sparkling with the wisdom of intuition and lived experience. These philosophers still speak to us because they take care to talk our language. They know the power of metaphor and have the ability to balance rational precision with the evocative ring of poetic language.

But they are a rare breed. Many—perhaps even most—books on consciousness by philosophers are by-specialists-for-specialists trained in the remote language of analysis. Meaning and clarity suffer, leaving non-specialist readers blinded and bewildered in dust storms of dry logic. But it would be a mistake to dismiss and ignore the contribution that philosophy can make to our understanding of consciousness.

In the discipline called "philosophy of mind" philosophers have applied the gift of reason to uncover key problems and have proposed ways to tackle them. These problems include, *other minds* (how can you tell if a zombie, a robot, a computer, a dog, a chimpanzee, an amoeba—or even another human being—is conscious?); the *mind-body relation* (how does consciousness happen in brains? can minds exist apart from bodies?); and *free will* (do we really exercise choice, or are all our actions determined by biology and environment?).

Such questions puzzle many of us at one time or another. And you don't need to be a philosopher to explore them. But philosophers can help, with their gift of reason—a gift that we all share. This gift of reason comes as part of the package of who we are as conscious beings capable of abstract thought. We don't need to have *things* immediately in front of us, detected by our senses, in order to explore them. We can, instead, abstract *images* and *ideas* from things, and carry them away in our heads where we can explore them at our leisure. We can use words and ideas as symbols to point to things that we no longer perceive, and that we know about only through memory and thought. Imagination frees us from the confines of matter, space, and our senses—and launches us into the realms of symbols and speculation. Reason is our guide in this wild land.

With this gift of reason comes the ability to recognize, not only its own limitations, but also to point to what is beyond. Once reason takes us as far as it can, *true* reason has the wisdom to say "This far, no further. Beyond this point lie paradox and mystery."

But, as we have seen throughout this book, reason also knows that the limits of reason are not the limits of *knowledge*—and certainly not the limits of *reality*. Beyond reason, lie other ways of knowing. From below, it is grounded in preverbal feelings and intuitions; and above, it projects imagination toward experiences that language and concepts cannot grasp.*

The wise philosopher teaches us to balance head and heart, reason and intuition, precision and mystery. But such balance stands or falls on our ability to think clearly—to see the distinctions that make up the nuanced shadows, shades, and contours of the reality presented to our minds. In chapter 6, we began to do just that. Remember, we paid close attention to distinctions between different meanings of the words "consciousness" and "energy." That was an example of using the philosopher's gift for clear thinking.

THE SCIENTIST'S GIFT:
SENSES, OBSERVATION, AND METHOD

We all share another special gift—a gift we sometimes take for granted, a gift that reveals the world to us in all its naked glory. It is the gift of *sensing*—the ability we have to observe: to see and touch, to hear and smell and taste the beauty, the vastness, the complexity, the diversity, the ordered systems, and sometimes the chaos, of the world around us. We can call it the "Scientist's Gift"—a method of organizing what our senses reveal to us—but this, too, is not unique to scientists, and not even unique to our species.

Scientists are interested in *what* the brain is and how it works with

---

*The domain of the philosopher is also vast. Long before we can approach the uncertain shores of the magical or the mystical, there is much ground to cover in the territory of reason itself—guided by philosophers, the guardians of linguistic meaning. Philosophers can teach us the power of precision, using the laser of logic to get our concepts and words in order. But such rigor and coherence are only part of the way to truth. Good philosophers also teach us that truth can sometimes be fuzzy, elusive, ineffable— but through imagination and intuition, approachable nonetheless.

consciousness. The Scientist's Gift is ultimately a method for gaining knowledge by *observing* the world using some or all of our senses (and their extension or amplification through instruments such as microscopes, telescopes, computers, and data recorders).

Sensing Energies

We live in a world of energy—we are surrounded by it, we consume it, we transform it, and, in a way, *we are it*. As Einstein showed, all matter is a form of energy ($E = Mc^2$). The entire world around us—the land, mountains, forests, deserts, oceans, cities, sky, and the vast, perhaps infinite, cosmos of innumerable stars and galaxies—is a world of energy vortices, fluxes, flows, currents, and vibrations. As embodied creatures, we are thoroughly embedded in this vast energy matrix as it streams in, through, and around us.

And one of the greatest miracles of all is that not only are we part of this magnificent, eternal, infinite flux—but *we can know our part in it*. According to the best understanding of physics, there are four known forms of energy. Two of them operate at the level of the very small, the micro domain of subatomic particles: called the *"strong"* and *"weak" nuclear forces*. A third operates most noticeably on the scale of the very large, the macro domain of massive bodies, such as planets, stars, and galaxies: familiar to us as *gravitation*. And the fourth operates along the vast spectrum in between, the domain of cosmic rays, light, and radio waves: familiar to us as the *electromagnetic spectrum*.

From this vast pool of energy and information, our species is able to pick up only a very, very thin slice of the electromagnetic spectrum through our most dominant sense, *vision*—from red to violet light. Our other senses, too, even our sense of gravity, are channeled through our nervous system that operates on electrochemical energy transmissions—all reducible to electromagnetism. In fact, everything we know about the world around us, many scientists and philosophers believe, is completely funneled through our detectors of electromagnetic radiation and energy pulses.

Our five senses—sight, hearing, touch, smell, taste—rely on electromagnetic exchanges detected by, or occurring in, the body. Although the slice of the electromagnetic spectrum available to our senses is relatively tiny compared to the whole span of energies, nevertheless that slice serves as a window on a vast and seemingly infinite expanse and variety of objects in the universe.

Our senses serve us well. They have helped us survive through millions of years of evolution. They have helped us observe the patterns of climate and weather, the growth of plants, and the movement of animals, resulting in the invention of agriculture. They have helped us locate minerals and other materials for use in building civilizations. They have helped us experiment with nature, to discover and invent an impressive array of food sources and medicines. They have helped us create sophisticated technologies for information acquisition, storage, and transmission.

Without our senses, we would never have created the network of technologies that not only connect us around the globe, but also extend our senses themselves so that now we can reach out beyond the spectrum of visible stars and galaxies, to the deepest depths of space and time, almost back to the very moment of creation itself. That is a truly magnificent achievement.

Our senses connect our bodies to the vast network of energies and information that constantly swirl through us. In a very real sense, our senses have given us the universe. But of course that is not the whole story. Not only have our senses been aided in all this by other gifts, such as reason, imagination, and intuition, they have not by any means revealed (or ever can reveal) one entire domain of reality. They have given us the *physical universe*, but not the dimension of our interior, experiential lives—the inner cosmos of consciousness.

And perhaps the greatest irony facing every materialist is that the senses alone, without this interior cosmos, would be no more than windows opening onto a vast unseen, silent, unfelt, odorless, and tasteless universe. By themselves, without the added spark of consciousness to *experience* the world, our eyes, ears, flesh, noses, and taste buds would be no more than shuttered windows. At the end of the chain of events beginning at the sensory receptors, moving along activated nerve fibers, jumping across quantum synaptic gaps in the brain's enchanted network of neurons, nothing would be *sensed* without the mysterious presence of consciousness. To get from the senses to *sensation* the miracle of consciousness is required.

But the senses play their part—an immensely important part. The senses act in concert with our other gifts—of reason, feeling, and spiritual insight—not only to put us in touch with the whole panorama of the physical world, but also to connect us with, and guide our participation in, the majestic symphony of all-being.

The mysterious connection between our senses and consciousness, between perception and *sensation,* lies at the heart of the mind-body mystery. How do the senses inform our experience of what is happening in the world? How do physical impulses of electromagnetic energy get transformed into the colorful, lively, sensational qualities of felt ideas, images, thoughts, and emotions? How does experience connect with raw data?

Brain and Consciousness

Clearly, in our own case, our nervous system and brain play an immensely significant role in this process. We may never be able to tell what's going on in consciousness by simply looking at what's going on in a brain; but by exploring and discovering more and more about how the brain works, and how these operations correlate with what is experienced in consciousness, we may come to learn quite a lot about which *contents* of consciousness are affected by what happens in the brain. As holistic organisms—that is, creatures with intimately related brains and minds, creatures of energy and consciousness—there is a world of discovery awaiting us in the brain.

Science can lead us in exploring the fine details and connections within the brain, within its astronomically complex network of cells, and within the cells themselves, and their microneuronal structures, down to the quantum level—by a rigorous combination of acute observation, recording, analysis, and evaluation of data, reporting results, proposing hypotheses and theories, and testing and retesting findings. It is a slow and meticulous process—but it often works to advance the frontiers of human knowledge.

A Method for Questing Knowledge

The Scientist's Gift, then, is not just that of the senses, but that of a disciplined perception and attention to detail in a search for truth. It is, above all, uniquely a gift of *method*—the empirical method—a procedure for observing some specific thing or event in the world, register-ing the data observed, and testing them to see if they fit (confirm or refute) our expectations. In this way, science helps us move step-by-painstaking-step toward expanding our knowledge.

It is a rigorous discipline, as worthy and as capable of advancing toward truth as any spiritual practice. In fact, this method is the essence of spiritual practice, too. Although it is "empirical," this does not mean that the method is confined only to sensory observations of physical phenomena. The same procedure can be successfully applied to *any* quest for truth or knowledge—as long as it employs the three-step *radically* empirical "POR" method we looked at in chapter 10, "*Knowing-2: Radical Science*":

1. *Procedure* for following a disciplined set of protocols—by engaging in actual practices; then
2. *Observe* the experiences (data) generated by that practice; and then
3. *Report* and compare the data of these experiences with those reported by a *community of peers.*

If we do this—and we get results that match those of others—then we know we have gained *intersubjective* or consensual knowledge as distinct from mere subjective personal opinion.

This, in a nutshell, is the method followed by science—although since Western science is focused on the physical universe it relies greatly on knowledge gained through the physiological senses. This is a habit of science, not a necessity. Science doesn't have to confine its quest to the physical universe, nor to sensory knowledge.

But due to force of habit lasting nearly four centuries, many scien-tists interested in the new field of consciousness studies still think they need to look for mind in the "nuts and bolts" of the physical universe—more specifically, in a highly localized region of it found in the brain (and for many, this means the *human* brain).

As we've seen, consciousness is not to be found in the physical universe. Physical things are made of energy and they occupy space; consciousness is nonphysical, is not a form of energy, and does not occupy space. Scientists won't find mind by looking in matter, but they will, and do, find it *associated* with matter—particularly the brain. So by exploring the fine details of the brain, and paying attention to how these are *correlated* with experiences in consciousness, scientists can learn quite a lot about the "mechanisms of the mind"—or, more accurately, they can teach us a lot about how the brain works.

But exploring the mechanisms of the brain and nervous system is not the only option open to scientists who want to study consciousness. There are other ways that do not involve looking for mind in the complex machinery of matter.

In the early days of psychology, about one hundred years ago, the most popular method was through introspection—by reflecting on the processes of consciousness and observing the way the mind works first hand. Austrian philosopher Edmund Husserl developed another similar method called "phenomenology." He attempted to explore the mind by paying rigorous attention to what shows up in consciousness when we block out, or "bracket," opinions, beliefs, and theories. And, more recently, taking advantage of ancient spiritual traditions, often from the East, a growing number of consciousness explorers are engaging in meditation and other contemplative practices.

Science does not have to (in fact cannot) confine its quest for consciousness to observations of *objective* processes in the brain, to third-person objects. By using the three-step empirical method described above, science can also approach consciousness *subjectively* through introspection, phenomenology, and meditation. It can investigate consciousness from the first-person perspective.

And, as emphasized in this book, a third approach is open to science: a *second-person* perspective that explores consciousness intersubjectively, as a phenomenon created in intimate encounters between two or more experiencing subjects.

Now let's turn to some of these other ways of knowing—to what I call *"radical science"*—found in shamanism and mysticism.

THE SHAMAN'S GIFT: PARTICIPATORY FEELING

Where does consciousness take us? A few years ago, a Stanford University anthropologist, Jeremy Narby, wrote a wonderful book, *The*

Cosmic Serpent, where he described Amazonian shamans who possessed knowledge of DNA in plants. He had learned from friends who had visited the rainforest that these shamans claimed to have gained knowledge about the essence of life *from the plants themselves.* They said the plants *spoke* to them.[1]

At first, Narby was sure they couldn't have meant this literally. Even if plants do possess intelligence or information, they don't have vocal chords, lips, tongues, or teeth and therefore could not speak. But perhaps they could communicate in a silent language—something like telepathy? Perhaps they could communicate through exchanges of photons? And photons, as we know from quantum physics, are nonlocal: they transcend time and space.

Life Is *Light*

All life begins with light. We know from basic biology that life on Earth is fueled by the Sun in the process known as photosynthesis. Green chlorophyll molecules in the leaves of plants literally capture the Sun's energy in the form of photons. That's what "photo-synthesis" means: "making whole by light"—"building by light."

The role of light in life goes far beyond chlorophyll molecules—however immensely important they may be. Below the level of the living cell lie the complex building blocks of life we know as DNA and proteins. Within the cell itself, and between various networks of cells, life is sustained moment to moment by vastly complex and rapidly changing networks of biochemical reactions. Something like ten million cells die in your body every second. These must be replaced at precisely the same rate in exactly the right locations for integrity or health of your body to be maintained. How do the individual cells know when and where to grow? How does the body as a whole coordinate and orchestrate this vast symphony of the chemistry of life? Where does the living body's intelligence come from?

According to philosopher Arthur Young, it is all a question of quantum *timing.*[2] All chemical reactions involve sharing or exchanging of electrons between molecules. These *electromagnetic* interactions are, in fact, exchanges of photons, quanta of action. The spinning or rotating quantum of action "snatches" energy from the environment, *stores* it, and builds up order and organization in the form of DNA and living cells. And so the first steps of life begin. The spinning photons "hook up" with ambient energy by coordinating with the movement of electrons and atoms around it—kind of like an ice skater gathering up angular momentum by pulling in her arms as she spins. The tighter, or smaller she makes herself, the faster she spins, and the more energy she stores. Photons or quanta, similarly, build up energy and carry or store it as angular momentum.

Quantum *timing*, therefore, lies behind the amazing varieties of living forms that populate our oceans, marshlands, forests, mountains, lakes, rivers, plains, prairies—every crack and crevice on our planet where life has taken hold. Light, or photons—exchanged between DNA and cells—forms the ultimate basis of the entire global economy of life. Life, quite literally, *is* light.

That is the key message for biology from Arthur Young. His insight matches the visionary wisdom common to the world's shamanic traditions about the interrelatedness of life and light, so well documented by Narby.[3]

The Cosmic Economy of Light

In a very real sense, life on Earth (and, no doubt, beyond) is *"borrowed light,"* forming the world's most fundamental living economic system—the economy of light. All life shares in an interdependent network of exchanges of light. Instead of "food chains," indigenous wisdom prefers to talk in terms we might translate as "light economies," "energy circulations," or "spirit exchanges." The shamanic perspective recognizes that all life forms are integral parts of a tightly knit system. For the shaman, true photosynthesis occurs at all levels of life—literally "making whole by sharing or bringing together of light."

Arthur Young points out that the photons involved in life are the very same quanta that began the long evolutionary descent through the levels of nuclear forces into the atoms and molecules of matter.[4] Frozen in matter, the quantum still retains a minute degree of freedom, which science recognizes as the "quantum of uncertainty." This shows up as spontaneous action, for example, in "quantum jumps." From Young's perspective, this uncertainty is the final residue of quantum choice or purpose. It's what frees spirit from the frozen grip of dense matter to begin the process of life, and open the way for an evolutionary ascent toward Spirit.

Jeremy Narby studied anthropology at Stanford University and among the Quirishari people in the Amazon rainforests of Peru. His central message is that shamanic knowledge, gained from direct communication with certain hallucinogenic plants, predates by centuries if not millennia modern scientific data about the basis of life. He notes that shamanic visions of entwined or double serpents, recorded throughout history and across the world, foreshadowed in remarkable detail the twentieth-century discovery of the double-helix or "twisted ladder" structure of DNA, the fundamental molecule of life.

Many shamans use special plant "guides"—such as *ayahuasca, peyote,* or psilocybin mushrooms, along with special chants, whistles, drumming, or dancing—to prepare the mind for receiving altered states of consciousness capable of penetrating alternative realities.

How had Narby hooked together his understanding of Western molecular biology—particularly knowledge of DNA—and the visionary insights of the shamans? After some shrewd detective work, he discovered that the key had to be photons. He came to believe that the visionary dreams the shamans had told him about were actually conversations with "spirits" contained in the hallucinogenic plants—and these conveyed accurate knowledge about DNA and the role of light in all living systems.

Under normal circumstances, we cannot see DNA. It took the invention of powerful electron microscopes before Western science could focus in on the structure of these esoteric molecules. But whether or not we can see them, their presence throughout our bodies is fundamental. And their quantity is staggering, as Narby points out: "There are approximately 125 billion miles of DNA in a human body. . . . Your personal DNA is long enough to wrap around the Earth five million times."[5]

How could we access this incredible database of life—without the aid of modern science and immensely complex technology? How do shamans do so? This was the puzzle Narby attempted to solve, and, like a true scientific sleuth, he tracked down evidence from different sources in science, mythology, anthropology, and shamanism, paying attention to the most unlikely clues.

Then, using a technique called *"defocalizing"* learned from his shaman guide, he started putting the pieces together. He began to see common *"forms"* in the teachings of the various disciplines. Most dramatic of all the clues was the form common to both the scientific description of DNA as a twisted ladder, or double helix, and the shamanic description of the essence of life as entwined cosmic serpents.

Narby also learned that DNA is actually a kind of crystal that emits photons. *All living things emit light.* This could account for a wide variety of phenomena associated with shamanic and other "non-ordinary" realities—such as dream visions, auras, subtle bodies, near-death experiences of light bodies (we might call them "angels"). Narby had written: "In their visions, shamans take their consciousness down to the molecular level and gain access to information related to DNA, which they call 'animate essences' or 'spirits.'"[6]

One of his indigenous informants, comparing shamanic spirits to radio waves, had said: "Once you turn on the radio, you can pick them up. It's like that with souls; with ayahuasca . . . you can see them and hear them." When a shaman ingests ayahuasca, peyote, or some other "hallucinogen," Narby concluded, certain molecules in those substances activate receptors in brain cells, which in turn trigger a cascade of electrochemical reactions inside the neurons. This stimulates the cells' DNA and the emission of visible photons. Result: Shamans literally *see* three-dimensional images—such as cosmic serpents.

However, to account for the accurate information shamans ostensibly possessed of DNA and medicinal plants and animals, it would not be sufficient for DNA to merely emit photons, it would have to be capable of *receiving* them, too, to complete the circle of communication. Narby had to find a suitable mechanism for human brain DNA to receive information in the form of photons from the sacred plants. Otherwise, the shamanic visions could be dismissed by Western minds as "mere hallucinations."

He found it in crystals. He discovered that almost all experiments that measure biophotons (i.e., photons associated with living tissue) make use of quartz—a crystal whose atoms vibrate at very stable frequencies. This makes quartz crystals excellent receptors and emitters of photons. Narby noted that not only is quartz used abundantly in electronic technologies such as radios and watches, it is also widely used by shamans around the world. He speculated:

"What if [shamanic] spirits were none other than the biophotons emitted by all the cells of the world and were picked up, amplified, and transmitted by shamans' quartz crystals? This would mean that spirits are beings of pure light—as has always been claimed."[7]

For Narby, the clincher was the realization that large sections of DNA form *periodic* crystals—just like quartz. And just like quartz, they could also *pick up photons*. This is not "junk DNA," Narby noted, despite what many biologists claim. Based on solid evidence from science, and backed by thousands of years of shamanic wisdom, Narby came to a revolutionary conclusion: When the shaman's DNA is stimulated by the psychoactive chemicals in "sacred" plants such as ayahuasca or peyote, it not only emits biophotons but also increases its capacity to "tune into" and receive photons emitted *anywhere* in the world.

The whole planet (and perhaps the entire cosmos?) is permeated by a complex network of DNA-based life forms, all emitting photons, carrying information about their host organisms. Any suitably sensitized DNA, such as the DNA in a shaman's brain cells, could pick up images and information from any living being anywhere in the global network.

Since photons are nonlocal, that "global" network of messages could extend to the entire universe. Shamans may be picking up coded information not only from the plants and animals of the Earth, but also from the heavens. If photons are messengers of the gods, shamans may be their emissaries on Earth.

What if cosmic intelligence—the mind in the cosmos that shamans and mystics alike have reported in all cultures down through the centuries—is carried by photons from stars and galaxies throughout the universe? As *manifest* photons in the domain of space and time, they would travel at the speed of light, and by that reckoning would take millions or billions of years to reach our solar system. And, of course, that is precisely what we do see when we look into the night sky: the universe as it was many millions or billions of years ago.

But for *unmanifest* photons enfolded in the implicate order of the universal zero-point energy field—that is, photons *as they experience themselves*, not as seen by some observer—there is no time or space. They are thoroughly nonlocal. True, they cannot communicate information or energy—no *physical* signals—but as messengers of meaning, of presence, of consciousness, they could be truly universal. The "why" of consciousness, then—its purpose—could be to serve as a "messenger of the gods" helping to unite the cosmos across time and space through a universal sharing of meaning and presence: One Mind.

Which takes us to . . .

THE MYSTIC'S GIFT: DIRECT EXPERIENCE

Who guides consciousness? To receive the Mystic's Gift, we have to develop or evolve our consciousness to what Arthur Young calls Level 1 or Stage 7—the domain of Spirit (see fig. 18.1 on page 240). And for that, we have to move into the realms of silence, into those spaces between words and between breaths, into the mysterious nothingness that gives birth to Being itself. It is the wordless paradoxical domain of no-knowledge, beyond even the reach of intuition.

Of course, I cannot tell you about it—even if I have been "there" myself. But I can tell you a little about some of the final steps mystics have reported after crossing the threshold—and having returned.

I'll focus on a form of thinking, and a kind of mysticism, almost alien to modern Western minds. I could have chosen almost any culture (Indian, Australian, African, Native American, Celtic, Nordic, Polynesian . . .) to make the same points. But I have a particular affinity with Taoist wisdom—rooted in a shamanic sensitivity to nature, and therefore a fine example of a transition from shamanism to mysticism. So let's turn again to the ancient wisdom of China.

As we saw in chapter 9, "*Knowing-1*: Shafts of Wisdom," from ancient times, the Chinese distinguished two types of knowledge that correspond, roughly, to what Westerners call "objective" and "subjective." Westerners tend to rely heavily on the first kind because it is amenable to reason. Subjective knowledge is so often out of bounds to reason that our culture tends to dismiss it as knowledge.

From early childhood, our thinking patterns are mapped out along this "groove of objectivity." For the most part, it has served us well in dealing with the material world, though it has now brought us—and the rest of nature—into a global crisis.

Western society is now finding out that thinking dominated by reason does not work well when dealing with the far more subtle problems of human relations and consciousness. By confining knowledge to objective events, Western scientific thinking can find no place for thinking itself. Modern knowledge of material things is undoubtedly great, but modern Western knowledge of the spirit world is almost nil—and of how the two worlds come together Western culture seems to know nothing at all.

Things developed very differently in China. The Taoists came from an old tradition with roots stretching back to the twilight days of tribal sorcerers, adept at working with nature. Often, they were solitary hermits who lived in inaccessible places on the sides of mountains and in hidden valleys. They were not organized into any system or collective, but they had in common a refusal to be tied to any conventions, preferring to develop a feel for the "natural way" by living close to the Earth.

The readiness of Taoists to "touch the Earth," and their mystical rather than rational approach to nature was very different from the way of scientific knowledge in the West. Taoist shamans were experts at divination, using as oracles fire and smoke, bones, tortoise shells, and sticks. Always, their way was to return to "original nature," a *returning* to the source.

A famous Taoist saying from the sage Lao Tzu advises: "Learning consists in adding to our original stock piece by piece. The sage returns to Tao by subtracting from his knowledge day by day, until he has reached inactivity."[8]

"Doing nothing, everything happens," expresses the essence of Taoist wisdom. They called it *wu-wei*—which means "action-through-nonaction." *Wu-wei* does not simply mean "doing nothing." There is no easy translation in English but it definitely means "action that is not contrary to nature," action that is not forced in any way—hence *wu-wei* is sometimes called "actionless activity"—like water following the path of least resistance, or light filling all space by not using any energy at all, as Arthur Young described the photon and quantum of action.

"Non-action" carries an ethical tone, as well. It implies not doing anything violent or aggressive—though it refers more to the attitude behind the action than to the nature of the action itself. It is non-motivated action; action performed not as a means to a desired end, but as its own reward. *Wu-wei* is spontaneous—action that simply lets things be.

Lao Tzu's advice applies not only to how we deal with nature, it is also good for individuals who wish to control or purify their minds (and sound advice for healthy relationships, too). For ordinary folk, actions normally spring from the incessant buzzing and never-ending internal chattering of the monkey mind. Therefore, in order to have our actions flow in the spirit of *wu-wei,* we need to apply it to the mind as well. Unless we silence the internal dialogue by leaving the mind alone, our actions will reflect the mind's confusion.

The more you try to silence your mind, the more you disturb it and the faster it buzzes like a restless bee. The only way to stop the mind is to stop thinking about it, otherwise we make matters worse. Picture the mind as a muddy pool: The more you try to clear it, the more you agitate it, making the water even murkier. If you want clear water, leave it alone to settle by itself.

When thinking about what we should *do*, or what we should *be*, we block the natural spontaneous awareness of life. Yet thinking is part of our natural way, too. It would be false and unnatural to force ourselves to stop thinking. All we need to do is realize that our thoughts are "happenings" along the way as much as anything outside our heads. What matters is paying close attention to whatever is unfolding here and now.

The central idea of this tradition is the "Tao"—which means the Way. It refers to the stream of change, the flow of time, the course of life, the path to perfection, the current of consciousness, the source of everything and nothing. To look for Tao in the mind, or to look for Tao using the mind, is a bit like looking for electricity in an electric current—it is there, we see its effects, but we don't know what it is. The more we try to grasp it with the mind, the more it eludes us. Tao achieves everything by doing nothing, and the mind can "achieve" awareness *of* Tao only by *following the way* of Tao. Thoughts or words cannot capture this experience any more than a search light can capture darkness. This is not at all surprising, for as Lao Tzu said: "The Tao that can be spoken of, is not the real Tao."

Experience in itself is wordless. The more we get involved in trying to figure things out, the less room there is for the simple but beautiful everyday experiences that Taoists and Zen masters tell us are the basis of *satori* or enlightenment. Intuition serves us by continually filling in the gaps between bits of knowledge produced by reason. Our ability to enrich intellect with intuitive understanding allows us to make advances in knowledge. It is intuition, with its spontaneous grasp of wholeness, that gives us knowledge of the interrelatedness and continuity of nature.

And, as we saw in chapter 9, "*Knowing-1:* Shafts of Wisdom," beyond even intuition lies the paradoxical mode of consciousness Taoists call *wu* or no-knowledge—the ever-changing communion of knowing and being that we cannot know in words or ideas, but only experience. This is the realm of sage-knowledge.

To appreciate *wu*, one must forget all distinctions and definitions, and be open to receiving the silent spontaneity of no-knowledge. All true mental creativity springs from the shafts of wisdom connecting this ineffable region with some rational or artistic expression. And just as there is no method for translating intuitive knowledge successfully into rational language, the ineffability of no-knowledge makes it even less translatable. We must rely on our own ineffable awareness of the ineffable.

THE FOUR LEVELS OF BEING

I will conclude this chapter on different ways of knowing by summarizing Arthur Young's four-level model of the evolution of consciousness. According to Young, the cosmos is structured in four levels of being, each with its own "ways of knowing." (See fig. 18.1 on the following page.)

Level One: *Spirit.* The Ultimate. This is the domain of pure potential—inhabited by the completely unconstrained photon or quantum of action. It is dimensionless, pointlike, and beyond time and space.

Level Two: *Soul.* The domain of time, forces, feelings, and emotions. Spirit has given up one degree of freedom and generated the single dimension of time. It is linear, projective.

Level Three: *Mind.* The domain of space, concepts, and analysis. Spirit has given up two degrees of freedom and generated the dimensions of extension. It is planar, the realm of surfaces.

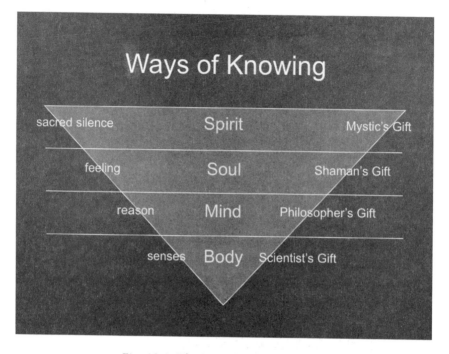

Fig. 18.1. The Four Ways of Knowing

Level Four: *Matter*. The domain of time-space, of solid objects. Spirit has given up all its degrees of freedom—except for the final quantum of uncertainty. Just enough wiggle room is left to choose to turn, and to begin the homeward journey toward Spirit.

These are *ontological* levels—levels of being. However, Young's model also reminds us that there are different *epistemologies*—different ways of knowing—associated with each level. Let's take them in reverse order:

Level Four: *Matter*. To know objects in space-time, we need to perceive them with our senses. At this level, we need to employ the Scientist's Gift and method of sensory empiricism. This is the realm of *sensory intelligence*.

Level Three: *Mind*. To know objects in the abstract domain of conceptual space, we need to use the Philosopher's Gift of language and reason. We need to be able to juxtapose and compare different words and ideas. This is the realm of *intellectual intelligence*.

Level Two: *Soul*. To know entities in the domain of soul, forces, and the flow of time, we need to open up to the Shaman's Gift of feeling and emotions. We need to engage and participate in intersubjective shared feelings. This is the realm of *emotional intelligence*.

Level One: *Spirit*. To "know" the domain of Spirit, the dimensionless domain of the ground of all being, we need to let go of all separation between knower and known, between subject and object, between knowing and being. Here we must open up to the Mystic's Gift of transcendence—beyond all distinctions, beyond thought, even beyond knowledge and experience itself. This is the silent realm of *spiritual wisdom*.

One of my students, Matthew Purdon, an MFA candidate in the Arts and Consciousness program at John F. Kennedy University, designed an alternative way to illustrate the Four Gifts of Knowing to include "Artist," "Poet," and "Warrior" as well as "Scientist," "Philosopher," "Shaman," and "Mystic" (see fig. 18.2 on page 242).

I particularly like how his overlapping-circles model reveals the way these various "archetypes" use the different gifts of knowing (sensing, thinking, and feeling) in different combinations. He noted: "I prefer the interconnected circles over the triangle or reflexive arc, because they emphasize relatedness between the ways of knowing. Two things to note about the diagram: First, the archetype of 'The Poet' refers to the use of language, spoken or written, to communicate clearly and powerfully. Second, based on my own experience, opposite archetypes are shadows of one another, providing clues for personal and cultural healing. We can see this in action when a Western 'Scientist' or 'Philosopher' dismisses an indigenous 'Shaman' as a superstitious witchdoctor."[9]

Note that by "sensing," Purdon means here *sensory perception*—i.e., perceiving with the five physiological senses of sight, hearing, touch, taste, and smell. As primarily the Scientist's Gift (and Purdon's "Warrior's Gift"), sensing is *physical knowing*, involving the body's detection, reception, and processing of electromagnetic, chemical, or acoustic signals. Sensing primarily directs attention outward onto the external world of objects.

On the other hand, the Shaman's Gift of feeling is different

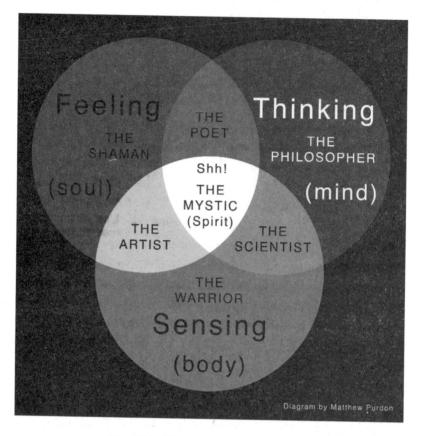

Fig. 18.2. The Four Gifts of Knowing

because it is primarily nonphysical shared presence. It is *soul knowing*. Unlike the sense of touch, for example, feeling can be nonlocal (indeed, it is nonlocated), not requiring physical contact or transmission of signals between knower and what is known. Feeling begins by directing attention inward in a way that opens and sensitizes the soul and grounds the body—what David Bohm referred to as "proprioception," a key practice in Bohmian dialogue. The more open and grounded the subject is, the more the soul responds to the nonphysical presence of other subjects—to intersubjectivity.

In Purdon's model, the gift of thinking, though primarily the domain of the Philosopher, is shared with poets, scientists, and mystics alike. It is *mental knowing*, involving two different kinds of reason. The first kind is intellectual analysis, which focuses attention on concepts and abstractions—mind engaging with mind (philosophers), or mind attending to sensory data (scientists). The second kind is grounded or embodied reason, where attention is directed to information coming in through the soul—mind and language giving voice to the soul (poets).

Finally, in the circles-model, the Mystic's Gift, though central, is not indicated as the fourth way of knowing *per se*. Instead, in this model, mystical or spiritual wisdom fully integrates and balances all of the other ways of knowing (sensing, feeling, thinking). Of course, all the "archetypes" (Warrior, Shaman, Philosopher, Poet, Artist, Scientist, as well as Mystic) use all of the gifts of knowing to some degree.

Except for the Mystic, all the others use the gifts of knowing in different combinations, with different emphasis. For the Shaman, feeling is dominant; for the Philosopher, thinking is dominant; for the Warrior, sensing is dominant; for the Artist, feeling/sensing is dominant; for the Poet, feeling/thinking is dominant; for the Scientist, sensing/thinking is dominant.

In the Mystic, the three gifts of sensing, thinking, and feeling are integrated to create an opening for the fourth gift. Although included in sage-knowledge, the three other gifts are transcended in the sacred silence of what we referred to earlier as "no-knowledge"—the silent spontaneity of the pure presence of being. This is *wu* or *"no-knowing"*—the paradoxical consciousness of knowing-without-knowing, of knowing simply by being.

The Mystic's Gift, then, is ultimately utterly beyond expression in thought or language because it is not an object of knowledge. It is the nondual integration of all objects and subjects—even beyond the union of intersubjects in universal *communion*.

And, as the diagram suggests, perhaps the wisest advice for accessing and cultivating this gift is to simply let go and pay attention to the divine, eternal "shhhh"—the zero-point of sacred silence forever open to us *now*.

Cosmos and Communion

Millions of sane, intelligent people today seem to live in a world that modern scientific cosmology tells us just doesn't exist. Either they are deluded, or science is wrong. At the very least, what they have to say about the nature of reality calls into question the worldview of science—specifically its underlying cosmological myth of materialism.

Judging by a steady stream of media reports and a growing body of respectable scientific literature, a great many people are having experiences that don't fit into our civilization's dominant cosmological map or philosophical paradigm. You may be one of them: someone who has experienced, for example, precognitive dreams, remarkable synchronicities, undeniable psychic events, convincing mystical experiences, or shamanic altered states of consciousness.

But, according our culture's cosmology, none of these experiences is supposed to be possible or meaningful.

In a deeply insightful book, *Dark Night, Early Dawn,* transpersonal scholar Chris Bache opens up a different way of approaching this conundrum—by exploring the full spectrum of human consciousness and what it implies for a much wider and comprehensive cosmology. The personal and social consequences of such an expanded worldview are profound.

Cosmology orients us in the universe. It tells us where we came from, where we are, and where we are going. Implicitly or explicitly, it defines what is possible for us as human beings, and thus it channels, or limits, our highest ambitions.

Modern Western culture lives entirely within the confines of what

Bache identifies as "daytime" consciousness (see excerpt below)—that is, it takes into account only what we can perceive through our outer, physical senses, and of those perceptions it takes seriously only what we can measure. These data are then organized according to the rules of logic and reason (mostly mathematical).

"Nighttime" consciousness—what we can learn about the world through, for example, dreams, intuition, psychic or mystical experiences, and other non-ordinary states—plays no part in designing modern cosmology. As a result, we are moving into a kind of cultural dislocation, in which the official cosmology fails to map many of the experiences that matter most to many of us.

Bache presents one of the most persuasive accounts—based on many years of personal spiritual exploration and incisive scholarly work—of why our culture needs to take seriously the spectrum of non-ordinary states of consciousness experienced by so many people.

> Imagine for a moment, [he writes] a civilization that denied itself the vision of the night sky, a society where by custom no one dared leave their homes after sundown. Trapped within the sun-drenched world, they would have intimate knowledge of the things that lie near at hand but be unaware of distant realities. Without knowledge of the night sky, they would have a deeply incomplete understanding of the larger cosmos within which they lived. They would not be able to answer the question, 'Where did we come from?' with any accuracy. Cut off from the vision of the stars, they would be restricted to the relative immediacy of here and now, stranded in near-time and near-space. They would never discover our celestial lineage, never place our solar system in the Milky Way or the Milky Way in a cosmos almost too large to be imagined.
>
> We are this civilization, of course. Taken as a whole, Western thought has committed itself to a vision of reality that is based almost entirely on the daylight world of ordinary states of consciousness while systematically ignoring the knowledge that can be gained from the nighttime sky of non-ordinary states. As the anthropologist Michael Harner puts it, we are 'cogni-centric.' Trapped within the horizon of the near-at-hand mind, our culture

creates myths about the unreliability and irrelevance of non-ordinary states.

Meanwhile, our social fragmentation continues to deepen, reflecting in part our inability to answer the most basic questions about meaning or value, because neither meaning nor value exist in mere sensation nor in the compounds of sensation. Similarly, we will not be able to explain where we came from or why our lives have the shape they do as long as we systematically avoid contact with the deeper dimensions of mind that contain the larger patterns that structure our existence.

Though of enormous importance, the victories of the age of Enlightenment were purchased at the terrible cost of systematically disparaging the depths of human experience and of prematurely dismissing our ability to penetrate these depths. In the modern university, being 'rational' or 'logical' includes the rider of not straying too far from sensate experience and its derivatives, and 'critical thinking' is marked by its epistemological commitment to ordinary states of consciousness.

Meanwhile, non-ordinary states are little explored or understood, and their relevance to basic questions being raised in epistemology, philosophy of mind, or even ethics is seldom acknowledged. But this is changing. As the twenty-first century opens, new evidence is challenging old assumptions in practically every department. Seldom have so many axioms been questioned on so many fronts at the same time. The historian of ideas can barely keep up with the revolutions brewing, and one of these revolutions, a major one I believe, centers on non-ordinary states of consciousness.[1]

I began this book with my personal story of transformation—waking up as a philosopher to the central importance of relationship in the exploration of consciousness. I saw that "truth" without feeling or compassion cannot lead to *wisdom,* and that as a philosopher and a human being my ultimate concern is what the ancients called *"sophia."* To be a true philosopher, worthy of that name, I saw that I needed to balance head and heart, to open up my ways of knowing beyond the dry abstractions of rational thought and to embrace, also, those extra-rational shafts of wisdom we sometimes refer to as intuition and what the ancient Chinese called *wu,* a kind of paradoxical knowing translated as "no-knowledge."

You won't, of course, as Bache observes, find that kind of knowledge or wisdom in a typical college or university. It is a way of knowledge that anthropologist Carlos Castaneda called "a path with a heart," an approach that requires a courageous willingness to let go of our beliefs and self-important egos, to engage in the deep work of the psyche, work that frequently takes us into the "dark night" of long-buried emotional and psychospiritual demons, and through the purifying fires of transformation—a way of knowledge pursued by countless mystics and shamans throughout the millennia.

For some years now, I have realized that to be the kind of philosopher I originally intended to be, I needed to find ways or techniques that helped me to bypass the ingrained habits of the rational mind. Simply reading the great philosophers and thinking about consciousness or pondering the experiences and insights of spiritual masters would never get me there. I needed to experience these other ways of knowing for myself, and so I have sought out and found teachers to guide me into these other realms. I am no longer a philosopher crusading for truth "at any cost." I am also a student and practitioner of various psychospiritual disciplines.

My consciousness studies involve multiple ways of knowing: In addition to my regular "third-person" work analyzing language and dissecting philosophical abstractions, I meditate regularly for direct first-person access to the wondrous (and sometimes bizarre) operations of my mind. I have worked, too, with experienced guides who have taken me on what are sometimes called "shamanic journeys." These involve techniques for achieving altered or non-ordinary states of consciousness—second-person, intersubjective experiences that often involve interpersonal or transpersonal, non-linguistic communication, not only with other people, but also sometimes with other animals and even with plants (see sidebar "Alternative States of Consciousness").

As well as moving through the halls of academia, then, I also spend time walking, running, sitting, and lying in nature, communing with the Earth and its great variety of plants and animals, with the winds and the

Alternative States of Consciousness

Transpersonal psychologist Stanislav Grof (author of books such as *Beyond the Brain*, *The Adventure of Self-Discovery*, and *LSD Psychotherapy*) prefers the term "non-ordinary states of consciousness" because he feels that "altered states" privileges ordinary consciousness and implies a subtle pejorative that diminishes the value and meaning of non-ordinary states.

I've oscillated on this one over the years. It seems to me that the same kind of objection could be directed at the distinction between "ordinary" and "non-ordinary" states. I know what Grof (and others, such as Chris Bache) mean: Calling them "altered" states implies that there is some baseline "unaltered" state that should serve as our guide to the "proper" or "right" state of consciousness. But, as I see it, the same implication applies to "non-ordinary" versus "ordinary" or to "normal" versus "non-normal" (obviously, anyone who takes these states seriously wouldn't want to contrast "normal" states with "abnormal" states). That's why I like Bache's poetic-metaphoric use of the distinction between "daylight" and "nighttime" consciousness.

What we're really trying to get at is a distinction between Western-post-Enlightenment culturally-conditioned or accepted states of consciousness (yes, there are more than one) and alternatives to these. My own preference, therefore, is to refer to them as *alternative* states of consciousness"—indicating that we have different, optional modes or states of consciousness, and that we have some choice about which state to be in. For shorthand convenience, I sometimes use "alter-states" to refer to alternative states of consciousness.

oceans, its deserts and mountains—but lately especially with the oceans.

I realize that what I have to say in this chapter may well put me beyond the pale as far as many of my mainstream colleagues in philosophy are concerned, but that is a risk I am willing to take. In the past few years, my greatest teachers have included non-human animals—

such as the cats and dogs I live with, and especially the dolphins and whales I swim with in the wild ocean.

I have learned from these teachers and companions a great deal about the nature of consciousness, and the relationship between humans and the rest of the natural world. I have had many direct and profound experiences of what "communion" means. And although much of this knowledge has been gained through an epistemology of feeling and is therefore transverbal, these experiences have been invaluable in elucidating for me my philosophical explorations into the nature and meaning of intersubjectivity.

POD CONSCIOUSNESS

For example, not too long ago I spent a week swimming with dolphins off the Kona coast in Hawaii. From the very first day, my companions and I were blessed with the presence of a large pod of two hundred or more spinner dolphins. I am not a particularly experienced or skilled swimmer, but with snorkel and fins and the surprising buoyancy of the warm Pacific, I felt comfortable and confident enough to slip overboard from our boat into what seemed to be the infinite depths of the ocean near Kealakekua Bay.

Face down, eyes wide open, all I could see was translucent blue receding to a depth of almost twenty thousand feet. The Big Island's Mauna Kea volcano is actually the world's tallest mountain, even surpassing Mount Everest. Above the ocean, it rises to a height of nearly 14,000 feet, while below it reaches down to the submerged volcanic crust another 18,000 or so feet. Because the angle of descent is acute, the land falls away sharply and the offshore waters are very deep. You do not have to sail out far from land to find yourself in some of the deepest ocean on Earth. Floating there in that vivid azure world was the closest I will ever come, I suppose, to knowing what it feels like to be suspended in the dark infinities of space. It was my first opportunity to encounter an "alien" civilization. And I was not disappointed.

At first I couldn't see anything, except for a few tiny speckles of organic debris flowing past me like miniature stars (including occasional and mysteriously glinting burnt-orange flakes that I supposed were scales liberated from some exotic species of fish). All around me, the water sparkled and was remarkably clear. For a novice snorkeler, the view was exhilarating, and only a little disconcerting if I thought about the vast depths below. It is hard to gauge distances in water, so most of the time I could fool myself that I was swimming in a large pool in someone's backyard.

The first signs of life appeared way down below me, a handful of small fish, so far beneath that I couldn't judge their actual size. From my perspective they could have been goldfish, except for their off-white color. Gradually, they rose up closer, and I gasped, swallowing a mouthful of sea through my submerged snorkel. When I recovered, I realized these were no fish, but a pod of about a dozen dolphins, directly below me. I could now recognize their distinctive shapes, close enough to make out their blowholes and, when the angle was right, see their eyes. I was mesmerized by their beauty, their grace, the silky smoothness of their bodies, and the way they moved in formation, as though dancing to the orchestration of an invisible choreographer.

I was mostly struck by their silence. It was immense, broken only by the rhythmic sound of my own breathing. Then I heard a ripping noise next to my right ear, like Velcro tearing open. I reached up to adjust the strap holding my mask in place. But it was secure, just as I had fixed it before leaving the boat. The sound persisted, and only when I turned my head did I realize what it was: Three dolphins were right there beside me, within arms length—*talking to me*. The most distinctive experience (shared by my fellow divers) was the unmistakable intelligence of these impressive beings.

I looked to my left and saw more dolphins just a few feet away. Up close, they were much bigger than I had thought—powerful, swift, and undoubtedly masters of their realm. I was surrounded by them. The pod below had by now begun to fade off into the distant aquamarine haze, but to my left and right two families of dolphins were escorting me through their world. We were eye to eye, and I had no doubt whatsoever they were checking me out, sizing me up, letting me know I was welcome.

It is hard to describe the encounters because so much of what I experienced during those days in the ocean rippled through my body as feelings that have no clear counterparts in words. Yet the experiences were rich with meaning. The best I can do is to say that, surrounded by a couple of hundred dolphins—some hanging out beside me, others going about their business far below, while yet others near and distant to my right and left, apparently ignoring my presence, were caught up in their own daily occupations—I felt I was witnessing, participating in, an alien "terrestrial" civilization.

I had been invited to the "Wisdom of the Dolphin" workshop by my friend Peter Russell (author of books such as *The Global Brain, Waking Up In Time,* and *From Science to God*) who was co-facilitating the event with long-time dolphin aficionado Joan Ocean (yes, that's her real name). The purpose of the seminar was to see what, if anything, we might learn about ourselves, about human consciousness, and our relations with cetaceans through connecting with dolphin consciousness, from immersing ourselves in their world. We swam with the dolphins in the mornings, and in the afternoons and evenings our group of about fifteen men and women would meet to hear a talk from either Pete or Joan and to dialogue about our experiences.

On paper, the combination of Peter Russell and Joan Ocean at first seemed a little odd: a Cambridge-trained scientist (he studied with Stephen Hawking) and a quintessential "new-age" therapist who matter-of-factly talks about her telepathic (or, to use her word, "telempathic") channeling of whales and dolphins, not to mention her communications with beings from distant galaxies and stars such as the Pleiades. How could a scientist, committed to exploring verifiable empirical knowledge, work with an unabashed new-age channeler without a clash of cultures or paradigms?

And how could I, a philosopher committed to critical thinking, participate without either, on the one hand, falling back into my "postconquest" mode of incisive questioning—thereby closing down any possibility of "preconquest" consciousness revealing itself to me—or, on the other, risk falling into mushy new-age credulity by suspending my critical faculties?

Actually, it worked out just fine. A simple little thing, not always found in science or philosophy, made the complementarity of worldviews possible and enjoyable: *mutual respect.* We openly listened to each other, as much or more to *the feelings behind the words* as to the words themselves. I listened intently for *meaning,* for sincerity of expression. I wanted more to feel the bond of shared experience and community as a *fact of consciousness itself* than to gain verifiable objective knowledge (knowing full well that such knowledge of consciousness is unattainable). Yet I also wanted to avoid the dangers of illusion born of excess enthusiasm, wishful thinking, or lack of critical discernment.

Pete cautioned us to pay attention to the common, if not habitual, tendency we all seem to have to project out own thinking onto other creatures (sometimes we even do it to our cars and computers). Such anthropomorphism can be the bane of interspecies research, and ethologists are trained to guard against such naïve, sentimental, and unprofessional distortions—so as not to miss the subject of their study by overlaying and obscuring the animals' true nature with human projections. This is particularly the case if the intent is not merely to study animal behavior but to engage in true intersubjective, or mind-to-mind, interspecies communication. And that's what I was there for—at least to explore its possibility.

But how would I know? How could I tell the difference between my projections and "tuning into" the dolphins' consciousness? There's just no way to get third-person confirmation that there's "anybody home"—that mind is present in the "other," or, more subtly, to learn what its particular characteristics might be. It's easy enough in our own personal case, of course: All we have to do is break the usual cultural trance of fixating on objects in the world around us, and instead pay attention to the *subject* that's doing the observing—our own consciousness. That's first-person access, and a "no-brainer" (so to speak) for confirming "I think (or feel), therefore, I am." It is immediate and irrefutable evidence that our own minds exist.

But gaining access to another's mind, well that's a different story. Standard Western philosophy—still playing out the consequences of Descartes' insight about the isolated, self-contained, individual ego—has yet to find a solution to the "problem of other minds." Consciousness is private and privileged, we are told, and there's no way for one person to know about another's mind unless that person speaks to us or gives us some other confirming signal. The plain fact (unfortunate for consciousness science) is that we have no "consciousness meter." No technology exists (or conceivably *could* exist) to give us direct access to anyone else's consciousness—be it man, woman, dolphin, dog, cat, bird, or bacteria (not to mention rocks, molecules, atoms, quarks, or quanta).

Let's take a moment here to look at the issue of whether any technology *could* give us access to consciousness, and how this relates to the problem of other minds and intersubjectivity. Commenting on a draft of this chapter, Chris Bache observed: "I think psychedelics would test this assertion and possibly overthrow it." His implication, as I understand it, is that psychedelics (for example, LSD or *ayahuasca*) could be considered "technology," and these *can* be used to facilitate access to (or "communion with") the consciousness of another being. I appreciate Bache's comment: He is drawing attention to the fact that we can use something physical (some "psychedelic technology") to enhance the possibility of accessing the consciousness of some "other."

My point, however, is that *no* technology can give us an objective indication of the presence of consciousness or can measure it. I should clarify that by "technology" I mean any physical, objective, manufactured "machine." In this sense, all technology (including any psychedelic agent) is exterior, objective, and physical and therefore could *never* give direct access to another mind (which is interior, subjective, and nonphysical).

Consciousness can be detected only by consciousness.

Consciousness does not show up in the psychedelic agent (a drop of LSD or an *ayahuasca* brew) in any way analogous to, for example, an electric current registering in a voltmeter or the presence of radioactivity registering in a Geiger counter. Unless a subject ingests the psychedelic agent, the "technology" would have absolutely no epistemological use. And once ingested, it alters the state of the subject's brain, which is accompanied by a changed state of consciousness. Without this "alteration," the psychedelic would yield no information about consciousness (either of the subject or of the "other").

Psychedelics are physical (objective) substances and therefore may be considered a *kind* of "technology"—but their epistemological relevance for consciousness is precisely because they "alter" or "enhance" the sensitivity of the *subjectivity* of the experiencing subject(s). It is the *intersubjectivity* of participating subjects, and not the objective physical psychedelic agent, that opens direct access to other minds.

By "direct," I mean unmediated by physical signals, information, or energy. Yes, in psychedelic work some physical substance is involved (and from a panpsychist view this is inevitably always the case). But the physical aspect of the psychedelic agent does not "mediate" (in the sense of creating a link) between one subject and another. Rather, what happens is that the physical properties of the psy-agent enhance or alter the physical properties of the subject's brain and nervous system, and (from the panpsychist view), because all matter is "ensouled," changes in the matter are accompanied by changes in the mind. It is *changes in the mind*, and not changes in the brain per se, that open direct, unmediated access to another's mind.

Thus, no conceivable physical system by itself—no matter how complex, sensitive, or psychoactive—could ever detect or register the presence of consciousness.

The following "formulae" simplify the point:

Subject-1 → Object → Subject-2 ≠ Direct access to other consciousness

(here, "object" represents any mediating signal or energy)

Subject-1 → Subject-2 = Direct access to other consciousness

(here, no object/signal/energy intervenes)

One further clarification: When I said above that "in psychedelic work some physical substance is involved" I am not ignoring other ways of achieving psychedelic states—for example, Stanislav Grof's holotropic breathwork, or other means such as trance-inducing dancing, drumming, or chanting. But, of course, even here there is always something physical involved, too (the body).

The point is that it is not merely changes in body chemistry resulting from such activities that open the possibility of direct intersubjective communion. Again, it's the fact that the body is "ensouled." It has a subjective component along with its objective physical component—and it is this *subjective* component that allows for direct subject-to-subject communion. No object-to-subject coupling will, on its own, yield information about consciousness. Even in the first-person case where our own objective bodies can serve as a medium for knowing consciousness, it is the *subjectivity* inherent in the body (and not the objective body per se) that yields us knowledge of our own consciousness. This, of course, was Descartes' core insight in his famous "*cogito*"—although he entirely disconnected the body, as if mind could float free in some imagined disembodied state.

In my own work (particularly in this book), I have attempted to make a case for a different way of accessing consciousness—second-person intersubjectivity—where one person can know the mind of another by "engaging his or her presence" beyond any mediating signals.

So I believe it is possible to gain access to another's consciousness, and not just see our own projections reflected back to us. (Of course, anyone who's ever been in love and had it reciprocated knows this. We don't need philosophy or science to validate our intimate relationships.) Because intersubjectivity involves a mutual co-creation of experiencing subjects (as described in chapter 15, "*Intersubjectivity-1: We Are the World*"), we *can* know the presence of "other minds." We are partly created by the "other," and vice versa, and that's how we know there's "somebody home."

This works for *any* sentient being—not just humans. Even when the "other" is a member of another species, we can still know without a doubt that we are in the presence of another mind. (If you've ever taken time to be with a dog, cat, or horse—or looked into the doleful eyes of a gorilla, chimpanzee, or elephant at the zoo—you are aware of this.) It's not just anthropomorphic projection.

I knew this swimming with the dolphins, and I knew it afterward when we returned to our hotel conference room to dialogue about the day's events. I knew, too, however, that even though it is possible to engage the consciousness of a non-human animal, it was still possible—even likely—that we might "contaminate" such knowledge with unnecessary, though automatic, projections of human qualities onto other species.

So back to my question: How could we sort out the "chaff" of our own projections from the "wheat" of real dolphin consciousness? That's what I came to find out. When others in our group reported, for example, that dolphins have "pod consciousness"—that their primary locus of identity is the pod and only secondarily the individual dolphin—and, further, that members of our group had learned this from messages the dolphins themselves had communicated, how was I to take it? How was I to remain intellectually honest without falling prey to postconquest consciousness?

My dilemma was how to balance my philosopher's mind with the process of opening up my heart, trusting in my feelings and intuition. How could I evaluate the reports from my fellow swimmers? How could I tell if they had some genuine knowledge about the sheer fact and distinctive form or qualities of dolphin consciousness?

I had learned by now not to always impose my desire for conceptual clarity and logical coherence on colleagues who were operating from within a different set of experiences and beliefs. Yes, certainly, I could have easily spent my time challenging everyone who seemed to me to be using loose or contradictory language while reporting his or her experiences—"Hey, just a minute! Can you please explain how you arrived at *that* conclusion?"—but that would have been both impolite and unproductive. I chose instead to be as open-minded as I could, keeping my skepticism to myself, and simply listened to what the others had to say about their experiences. Then I checked in to see how or if their accounts fitted my own experiences.

After all, as we saw in chapter 10, *"Knowing-2:* Radical Science," this is the essence of the scientific method: Someone follows a certain *procedure* (called "experiment"—in our case, getting into the ocean with dolphins), *observes* whatever shows up in their experience (called "data"—in our case, whatever interactions or communications we had with the dolphins), and then *reports* and *compares* the results of their experiment with those of colleagues or peers who have followed the same or similar procedure (called "confirmation" or "disconfirmation"—in our case, reporting to each other afterward whatever we had experienced).

As noted earlier, Ken Wilber has summed up this three-part approach to knowledge as *injunction, illumination, communal confirmation*—in other words, procedure, observation, communication. And it's as applicable to spiritual experiences as it is to the sensory experiences that provide the raw data for science.

The difficulty—as Peter Russell and I were aware—was to be able to filter out the inevitable overlay of speculation, wishful thinking, and other interpretations or beliefs that would have distorted the purity and clarity of the original experience. Did someone *actually* have a telempathic connection with a dolphin or have a conversation with an ET on the Pleiades? For me, that was not the issue. Honestly, how could I tell one way or the other? Yes, if I operate fully within the dominant Western paradigm it would seem unlikely at best, and probably impossible, for someone on Earth in the early years of the twenty-first century to be in dialogue with a being many millions of light years away. For one thing, we have no "scientific" evidence that any such beings exist. But do you or I know *as a certainty* there are no ETs? No, of course not.

In fact, even within our own dominant physicalist paradigm, given what we know about the size and density of the universe and the conditions for life and evolution, it is highly probable that life does exist beyond our solar system; and, given the age of the universe, it is possible that elsewhere intelligent beings have evolved far beyond human capacities.

Furthermore, operating from within a different paradigm, and given what we know about consciousness (not only is it *nonlocated*, unaffected by distances in space, but also that its deepest nature seems to be *communion*) then we can at least be open to the possibility that something like intergalactic communication *could* happen. I couldn't rule that out, even if my silent skepticism urged me to probe the claim with forensic questioning. Rather than search for a way to establish the objective truth or falsity of dolphin or ET communications, I had decided to trust in the intersubjective process.

By paying close attention to the *meaning* and *wisdom* being communicated, and not getting distracted by wondering about the "true" source of the communication, and then comparing what I was hearing with my own experiences, I did indeed learn much about my own consciousness, that of my colleagues, and about the dolphins that opened up their world to us during that remarkable week in Hawaii.

Independently, all of us experienced the undeniable and powerful *presence* of the dolphins—not just their visible proximity, but also their *intersubjective* communion with us. Not only were we aware of them as they swam and danced around us, we also knew that they were aware of us. And each one of us reported (as best we could put it into words) the experience of being welcomed, not just by individual dolphins but also by their community. Watching their remarkably synchronized acrobatics it was easy to understand the notion of "group mind," of telepathic "pod consciousness." But we didn't just *understand* this phenomenon, we *felt* it. Each of us was part of it. *That's* how we knew.

Being immersed in this profoundly nonverbal intersubjective experience with the dolphins opened us up to experience "pod" consciousness among our own group. The sense of empathic bonding was unmistakable. We quickly learned how to be with each other—both in the close and intimate quarters onboard the boat and back in the seminar room—without the usual need for verbal or visual clues to enhance our communication. Of course, we spoke with and could see each other; but beyond that, we all sensed a high degree of harmony and mutual support that deepened as the days passed, and that seemed to emanate not so much from each of us as individuals but from our collective presence. Our group took on a distinctive identity of its own— just as we had experienced with the dolphins.

And this sense of shared harmony gave us insight into the nature of cetacean communication. As well as the dolphins, we were fortunate to also be accompanied by some humpback whales in the deep waters off the Big Island. Hearing their penetratingly mournful songs yielded an insight from the collective consciousness of our group. We agreed that the function of cetacean language differs radically from human communication. For the most part, humans speak to share information and details about ourselves and our environment—more often than not to enhance our ability to *do* something, to manipulate some part of our world. It is *instrumental* communication. By contrast, we learned that the cetaceans communicate primarily to restore, enhance, or create an experience of harmony and well-being both within the pod and between the pod and the ocean around them.

Some in our group went further. They said that the purpose of cetacean songs is to bring harmony to all life on our planet—and perhaps even beyond. I don't know if this was merely speculation or whether it was based on their own intersubjective experience with the whales and dolphins. But I do know that when a group of humans sings together (or dances together), often the effect is to induce a sense of harmonious well-being among the group. I can well imagine the same effect resulting from the songs of the humpbacks.

Singing is a form of *intuitive* communication. To do it well in a group, you have to let go of your own individual identity as the central unit of consciousness, and, instead, get into the "flow" of the chorus. If you try to think self-consciously about your singing, it can throw you off rhythm or off-key. Singers and musicians know you have to *feel* the music—it's called "soul."

That week with the dolphins and whales reinforced a key insight for me about the difference between instrumental and intuitive modes of consciousness—reflected in the difference between postconquest and preconquest consciousness. As the word implies, "instrumental" mind is about *manipulation* (not necessarily a bad thing, especially if you want to create technology). "Intuitive" mind, however, is about *flow* (about merging with a greater wisdom or intelligence that transcends individual egos).

THUMB CONSCIOUSNESS, FLIPPER CONSCIOUSNESS

Peter Russell offered a compelling speculation that could highlight a fundamental difference between human and cetacean consciousness. He proposed that perhaps it is just a fact of nature and evolution that when an animal combines a high level of intelligence with an ability to skillfully manipulate its surroundings the end result is environmental degradation and devastation. The combination intelligence-plus-hand may turn out to be pathological. And it's not the hand as such that makes the crucial difference, but the possession of an *opposable thumb*. We might call it the difference between "thumb" consciousness and "flipper "or "fluke" consciousness.

Having spent an extended time with the dolphins—basking in the peacefulness and sense of harmony they emanate—it was easy enough for me to develop this line of speculation and imagine that, on one hand, "thumb consciousness" leads to a civilization where things and information about *things* are prized above all else. It is what gives us technology, science, and a particular kind of philosophy. On the other hand, intelligence-without-thumbs leads to a radically different kind of consciousness, focused not on things but on *experiences*. "Thumb consciousness" by its nature draws our attention *outward* onto the world. Conversely, thumbless intelligence draws attention *inward*, to value and explore experiences within consciousness itself, to what, for want of a better term, we might call "wisdom."

Almost by definition, a "wisdom society" is one that values optimizing experiences of well-being among its community, including the sustainability and health of its environment—*and* develops ways of knowing that enhance and help actualize this goal.

Human "thumb consciousness" and cetacean "thumbless consciousness" impact evolution and environment in radically different ways. The human animal is small, slow, and weak. Without intelligence and thumbs to compensate for our comparative lack of speed, strength, and size, our species, almost certainly, would have long ago joined the list of extinct animals that could not make it in the evolutionary stakes. Larger, faster, and stronger creatures either would have caught and consumed us as prey or would have out-competed us for food. We survived because we developed large and complex brains that came with a high-level of intelligence linked to an opposable thumb.

Whereas dolphins and whales have evolved over many millions of years to be optimally adapted to aquatic habitats, by comparison humans are a poor environmental fit. Without big brains and opposable thumbs to help us hunt, make clothes, grow food, build houses, and create a vast array of technologies, our species would have been confined to a much narrower ecological niche. "Thumb intelligence" enabled us to manipulate the environment to suit our needs. As a result, our species has spread all over the planet, occupying habitats as diverse as hot deserts, steamy jungles, and icy tundra. *Cetaceans fit their environments; we adapt environments to fit us.*

Together, neocortex and thumb compensated for humans' otherwise poor evolutionary fit. But our success may also be our failure. We have now so massively overcompensated that the survival strategy of "thumb intelligence" may yet be our undoing. Having come this far, we are now precariously at the point of severely damaging the long-term viability of the environment that supports us.

The purpose of cetacean communication, then, would be not to relate ideas or abstractions, but to enhance the experience of harmony and balance in the pod, and in the ocean around it. This is not to say they do not also use language for practical purposes—for example, telling each other where to locate a school of fish for dinner. I can hear the objection: "How can a pod of dolphins chasing and feeding on a school of fish 'enhance the harmony' of the ocean around them? Surely, it scares the daylights out of the unfortunate fish?" Well, yes, I'm sure it does.

Similarly, I'm sure when Native Americans hunted bison those great mammals were also running scared. But over time and multiple generations, the *species* of humans (represented in our case by Native Americans) and the bison did achieve a sustainable and harmonious relationship. Same with the *species* of dolphins and fish (or whales and krill): Cetaceans do not hunt their prey to the point of extinction.

If there is any truth to this "thumbless intelligence" speculation (and I suspect there is), we should be aware of the effect that the U.S. Navy's low-frequency active sonar (LFAS) may have on cetaceans. Research shows that the volume, intensity, and range of the LFA can interfere with whale and dolphin communication, damage their hearing, and even kill them many miles away. Polluting the oceans with such noise and drowning out the songs of the whales would be like pulling the plug on our Internet, telephone, radio, TV, and satellite communications systems. Our ability to share information would be drastically degraded, and without a functioning communications infrastructure our society would be "blasted" into information chaos. A similar fate awaits the whales, dolphins, and other marine mammals if the U.S. Navy gets its way: LFAS would literally acoustically blast into chaos the communications systems that cetaceans rely on for the well-being of their species and their oceanic habitat.

The following is adapted from an article "When Sound Is Dangerous" by whale researcher Linda Weilgart, in *The Christian Science Monitor*:

Some technologies simply should never be used. The Navy's Low Frequency Active Sonar (LFAS) program is one. It's a device the Navy has been developing since the late 1980s, which would allow it to detect newly quiet enemy submarines over great distances. Speakers send out pulses of low frequency sonar that creates a powerful sound and pressure wave through the water. A similar LFAS system already has caused havoc underwater. A March 5, 1998, article in the journal *Nature* conclusively linked the operation of a LFAS system to a stranding of 13 Cuvier's beaked whales, which beached themselves and died, apparently as a panic reaction to the sound. The Navy wants to deploy four LFAS-equipped ships around the world.

Sound travels very efficiently in water, and the lives of fish and whales revolve around sound. They use sound to feed, mate, navigate, detect predators, and communicate with one another. Use of LFAS could well alter hearing ability in whales and other marine animals over a 15-mile radius, and could cause profound behavioral disturbance over an area bigger than Texas.

There are far too many critical issues to address before the Navy should go forward with use of this sonar technology. No one has even studied the ecological impact of using LFAS. I am concerned that the sounds will interfere with whales' ability to: find mates over long distances (which would affect reproduction); listen to the quiet sounds emitted by predators and prey; detect beaches and avoid stranding themselves or getting tangled in fishing gear; stay with members of the group; stay in contact with their calves; and avoid the reaction (probably of panic) that has already been demonstrated with the Cuvier's beaked whales.

As a scientist—and as a mother and fellow inhabitant of this fragile planet—I am alarmed at this new threat to our oceans. I cannot imagine why we would subject marine inhabitants, the majority of which are highly sensitive to sound, to yet another source of pollution.[2]

We can learn a lot from our marine cousins—provided we let them survive. As a philosopher, I have learned from direct experience what it means to be engaged in intersubjective interspecies communication. I have learned (and continue to learn), beyond books and seminars, the deep value of opening up to other ways of knowing that transcend the fine distinctions in language so typical of modern philosophy. I have learned that true philo-*sophia*—true love of wisdom—requires developing an ability to "feel our thinking," to honor what Stanford anthropologist E. Richard Sorensen called "preconquest" feeling-based consciousness; to honor what amateur anthropologist Jean Liedloff called our "innate evolved expectations"; to honor what the great philosopher-psychologist William James called "radical empiricism"; to honor intuition and feeling, and what the ancient Chinese called *wu* and sinologist R. G. H. Siu called "no-knowledge"; to honor the immense body of knowledge and epistemologies that still survive in the few and rapidly diminishing indigenous and shamanic cultures; and to honor what are sometimes called "non-ordinary states of consciousness."

I agree with transpersonal theorist and practitioner Chris Bache that if we are ever to have a comprehensive cosmology, one that includes explorations of the inner cosmos of mind as well as the outer cosmos of galaxies and stars, we will need to become a society that encourages, enables, and teaches its citizens how to enter altered, or *alternative*, states of consciousness, and how to develop an epistemology and a new kind of science based on what we discover from such deep explorations.

STATE-SPECIFIC KNOWING

The more I open up to non-ordinary experiences, expanding my epistemological horizons, the more I am drawn to a distinction made by transpersonal psychologist Charles Tart back in the 1970s. In a landmark book *Transpersonal Psychologies,* he introduced the novel idea of "state-specific sciences" to describe different realms of knowledge accessed via different states of consciousness.[3] Similar to a point made earlier in this book (chapter 9, "*Knowing-1:* Shafts of Wisdom"), Tart noted that it is both epistemologically irresponsible and inappropriate to attempt to judge one set of data, accessed in one state of consciousness, by criteria that apply to data gathered in some other state of consciousness.

A guiding rule for any such radical epistemology is that no one state of consciousness is privileged over the others. Each state (and data derived in that state) reveals some aspect of reality not available in other states. For example, as a philosopher I am trained to apply the rules of logic and reason to the ideas and words we use to describe our experiences of the world around us. In this mode or state of consciousness, for something to count as "knowledge" it has to meet minimum requirements of conceptual coherence—it cannot, for instance, violate the rule of non-contradiction: Something cannot be both itself and its opposite at the same time. But this may not be the case in some other state of consciousness.

On a particularly profound and intense shamanic journey, for example, I experienced with great clarity not just the possibility but also the *fact* that not only can something be both itself and its opposite at the same time but that everything and its opposite is true—*always*. The clarity and impact of this "revelation" came with a degree of certainty I rarely experience in my "ordinary" rational state of mind. It definitely came with the sense of a profound truth and highlighted the narrowness and limitations of my usual modes of thought.

In *that state,* I knew without a doubt that time is not confined to any simple linear flow from past to present to future. Somehow, at a deeper level, time can curl back on itself, interpenetrate itself, so that events judged by clock time, which would normally follow a particular sequence, in that state did not need to. Something that was due to happen the next day had already happened and was interwoven like a pretzel with other events from different times in my life.

Back in my normal rational state, I cannot make sense of such experiences. And I notice a familiar tendency to downplay or even dismiss the significance of the experience from the alter-state. My rational mind looks for ways to explain away the experiences and is reluctant to count insights accessed during non-ordinary states as real knowledge.

So, in the non-ordinary state, the typical workings of my rational mind seem laughingly simplistic and myopic; yet back in my rational mind the products of my alter-state are judged to be questionable if not even delusional. Reason urges me to put it all down to a strange quirk of brain chemistry—something happened in my brain while in the alter-state that made it *seem* as if "pretzel time" was real and "pretzel logic" made sense.

But, if I'm consistent, even my rational mind will alert me to the epistemological dangers inherent in this way of thinking. Why should one set of chemical events in my brain count as "real" (those that happen while in my normal rational state), while other chemical events in my brain do not? How could we decide this? Why should we privilege reason and declare that whatever state the brain is in during those periods is the "right" or "real" state appropriate for knowledge? To believe so—as our Western culture has taught us to—is to fall victim to a dysfunctional cognocentrism. Furthermore, to doubt the epistemological validity of one neurochemical state is to cast doubt on the epistemological status of *all* brain events—including those associated with ordinary, rational "daylight" consciousness.

According to neuroscience, *every* experience we ever have must pass through the brain and nervous system. This is as true for an everyday experience such as seeing a tree outside your window as it is for a shamanic experience of engaging with plant or animal consciousness or a mystical experience of God. Now, we accept that the tree really exists "out there" and not only in our brains and minds. We *must* accept this otherwise all of our experiences, including the whole of science, would be nothing more than private illusion. But since there is no intrinsic neurological difference between an experience of a tree, communing with another animal, or an experience of God, we have no rational justification for believing the tree to have a reality independent of our brain while doubting the reality of human-to-animal intersubjective communion, or the independent existence of God.

The key word here is "intrinsic"—meaning an "essential" or "fundamental" difference. Of course, an experience of God may involve different neurochemical processes than those accompanying an experience of a tree. In fact, I'm sure this must be the case, otherwise how would the brain deal with such differences? But the point is that beneath any differences, all neurochemical processes involve the same underlying ("essential" or "intrinsic") physical events. They all involve electrochemical events firing across neuronal synapses, and up and down axons and dendrites; they all involve events at the quantum microtubule level; they all involve atomic and subatomic events. We have no reason or justification to privilege any differences in any of those events above any of the others as avenues to "true" or "real" knowledge about reality.

The fact is, whether we have an experience of God or of a tree, all such experiences are accompanied by events in the brain, and we have no way of determining that one group of events corresponds with "reality" while the others do not. How could we? Any attempt to decide the issue would itself involve events in the brain, and then we would have to find a way to evaluate the epistemological validity of *that* set of events . . . which would throw us into an infinite regress.

Of course, if we move beyond such a "brain-centric" view of consciousness, and open to the possibility of a panpsychist view where all matter tingles with experience, our epistemological horizons open up dramatically. In addition to rational knowledge based on events in the neocortex, we would honor, for example, knowledge based on the body's feelings, and other so-called non-ordinary or alter-states of consciousness—discussed in the previous chapter as the "four gifts of knowing." An integral philosophy or science will honor and include all four, and integral philosophers will learn to cultivate all ways of knowing, including the sensitivity and discernment to know when—and *how*—to move from one way of knowing to another appropriate to circumstances and objectives.

After many years now experiencing different states of consciousness, I am learning to become more comfortable with the notion of "state-specific knowing," switching between domains of experience, and not having to force data or insights from one domain into the rules of another. I am aware that experiences I may have as a result of either the Shaman's Gift of feeling or the Mystic's Gift of unitive knowing often do not have any clear translation into rational thought.

In the end, the focus of this book—intersubjectivity as an experience of engaged presence—is not wholly graspable by intellectual analysis. It is at least partially extra-rational, involving feeling and direct, shared, subject-to-subject experience. My experiences with the dolphins may not translate into words that hold up under rigorous philosophical analysis. Nevertheless, I am convinced that such experiences do provide a wider, richer context for my work in philosophy—allowing me to "feel my thinking," to move beyond captivating but lifeless abstractions and to ground my words and ideas in the body's natural knowing. Philosophy, true philosophy, is the mind giving voice to the wisdom of the body.

In this and the previous chapter, I have ventured far beyond accepted boundaries of "respectable" philosophy. I have turned to transrational ways of knowing to illuminate my path toward a deeper understanding of second-person, intersubjective consciousness. Although radical, I believe this is a necessary move if we are to open modern philosophy to the mystery of consciousness beyond the abstractions of third-person linguistic analyses that inevitably turn consciousness into an objective "it."

If we are to have a true philosophy of mind and a science of consciousness, we need to continue to develop ways of exploring consciousness as a subject, as an "I." And when we do, we discover that the "I"—our precious sense of ego or self—is actually a kind of illusion, an identity borrowed for a time from the wider, cosmic matrix of an intersubjective "we"—from a deeper *communion* of "I–I."

I mean "borrowed" in the sense that the ego is a *temporary* phenomenon. I do not mean that the ego pre-exists in the intersubjective "matrix," just hanging out in the realm of potential existence waiting for its moment to incarnate. No, the egoic mind is its own self-creation made up of the complex habits of thought and action we come to identify as "me." Another way to say this, echoing the great Indian sage Ramana Maharshi, is that the ego "springs up" or, like a wave, "arises from" the deeper, wider ocean of (intersubjective) consciousness.

I realize, of course, that any "standard" academic philosopher who reads this book and applies the usual analytical tools to critique my advocacy of intersubjectivity and "non-ordinary" ways of knowing is likely to find its meaning dissolving or evaporating before his or her eyes. This is to be expected. Since what I am proposing—and engaging in—here is a *trans*-rational method for exploring consciousness, any attempt to subject the meaning of what I am saying to the typical rules of reason and logic will inevitably miss the point.

We cannot enter transrational consciousness via the path of reason. We cannot grasp soul or spiritual levels of being with the tools of the rational mind. We need different modes of expression: Instead of attempting to restrict philosophy of mind to analyses and descriptions of mental dynamics, I am saying we also need to be willing to shift to different states and modes of consciousness and communication that can *evoke* the meaning we wish to communicate.

That is why I have included aspects of my own personal narrative in these pages. If done well, *story* is an effective way to evoke meaning because it engages both storyteller and listener in shared, common experiences. If you have responded with moments of recognition and insight while reading this book, it is because the words in these pages have connected with your own embodied knowing—with the innate wisdom you also carry as part of our common evolutionary birthright.

Afterword

By Linda Kohanov

When I picture Christian de Quincey swimming with wild dolphins, I can't help but feel optimistic about the next level of human evolution. Our intrepid philosopher was, after all, entering *their* territory, not taking notes from afar, creating a laboratory experiment, or cavorting with a captive pod that had been trained to respect two-legged land mammals. Those dolphins could have tossed him about like a plaything—or simply ignored him. Instead they chose to engage.

What impressed me most about this story was not the outcome but the intent. Dr. de Quincey wanted to explore how another species might affect *him*, how he might engage in consensual dialogue with a non-human intelligence while also maintaining a researcher's poise. In this act, he was expanding the postconquest mind's potential beyond its penchant for dominating, dissecting, and objectifying life.

Not so long ago, describing this cathartic intersubjective experience in print could have meant professional suicide for a respected scholar. In certain circles, it's still suspect, and I'm not just talking science. I'm a horse trainer and riding instructor, not a psychologist, biologist, or college professor, but I've been accused of similar acts of treason against a rigid, pseudo-scientific mentality that infiltrates our culture in countless ways. While equestrians find it perfectly acceptable to align with the horse's instincts and become the alpha member of an interspecies herd, anyone who discusses the animal's feelings, desires, or, heaven-forbid, *consciousness* is considered part of the lunatic fringe. We're encouraged to study and control these "beasts of burden," but we're not supposed to notice, let alone admit, how profoundly they affect us.

Some of the more innovative riders substitute words like "leadership" and "partnership" for milder forms of dominance, but a horse with an opinion is still a "problem" and the dreaded "L-word," namely "love," is still taboo. I've been called a "horse lover" on occasion, and it's *never* intended as a compliment. Then again, three hundred years ago I might have been burned at the stake for treating a horse as a colleague, confidant, and friend, so I'm counting my blessings. Luckily, I'm living in the right time and place to explore the human-animal bond, and Christian de Quincey's work has been crucial to my understanding of why animal-assisted therapy in general and equine-facilitated experiential learning in particular can be so powerful in helping people relate to other people.

In earlier writings, Dr. de Quincey acknowledged a rather disturbing phenomenon I had observed but didn't quite have the vocabulary to discuss with others: that unchecked rationality seemed to possess a destructive by-product, a downright carnivorous appetite for dominance. As Thomas Moore once wrote, "Logos without Eros becomes sadistic." I wasn't the only one horrified by what some of the most intelligent people on the planet were doing to other humans, and other species, in the name of science and progress. The adults who came to study riding with me suffered from a blatant mind-body disconnect, and they instinctively knew that, at least for them, horses held the key to some vague inner desire to learn a different way of being in the world.

Over time, through much research, trial, and error, I came to understand the root of this yearning. An article I read by Christian de Quincey, elaborating on the work of E. Richard Sorensen, was the turning point, and the book you're holding in your hands has since become required reading for the Epona Apprenticeship Program, my advanced training for professionals in the field of equine-facilitated therapy and experiential learning. With this book, my students and colleagues finally have a shared vocabulary for discussing some of the principles, mechanisms, and most certainly the *meaning* behind the "miracles" we witness at the barn.

Horses are remarkably effective in helping people reach that state of "radical knowing" de Quincey so brilliantly and accessibly outlines here, a state that integrates feeling, intuition, relationship, and preverbal body wisdom with the focus, will, inventiveness, and problem-solving abilities that are among the best qualities of the postconquest rational mind. Because horses operate from the preconquest state of consciousness, because of their size and non-predatory nature, and because so much of our work with them involves body-to-body contact, these animals are able to reactivate the sociosensual mind in their human handlers. And that's only the beginning.

Riding, working with a horse on the ground, or even standing quietly in the presence of one of these gentle giants sometimes gives rise to an unexpected harmony, a resonance that feels telepathic, although that word doesn't begin to do justice to the ecstatic communion experienced in those moments. It's as if the boundaries between both beings dissolve. Sensory and extrasensory information flows freely. If action is involved, a third entity seems to take over, directing both horse and human in synchronized movements that stretch well beyond the knowledge and skill of either individual. It always looks effortless, as if horse and rider are dancing to the beat of an unseen drummer. It always feels like a miracle. And like a miracle, it has transformative repercussions that linger long after the episode has passed.

Some competitive equestrians refer to this as being "in the zone," and they pretty much know they're going to win whenever they tap this elusive state. World-renowned trainer Dietrich von Hopffgarten calls it "the magical connection." It's possible, he says, "only if we *listen* to our partner the horse . . . only if we try to achieve with *feel* and not *force*." Von Hopffgarten is describing the potential of intersubjectivity in action. It works as well with other humans as it does with horses. And it can be *taught*.

It turns out that animals in general quite naturally do what de Quincey recommends we humans do: forge an unobstructed dialogue between the mind and the heart, and "*feel* our thinking." Yet without that most uniquely human gift—the power of speech—they cannot engage us in colorful discussions about how people misplaced this ability to begin with, and why it's an evolutionary imperative that we reclaim it. For that we need an eloquent, imaginative philosopher like

Dr. de Quincey, who outlines here a form of radical knowing capable of leading us all back to that paradise we lost when "higher thought" took over and became obsessed with dominating nature rather than collaborating with her.

As civilization promoted reason over feeling, and language over the nuances of silent, experiential knowledge, people systematically relinquished vast resources of inner wisdom. In the process, they sacrificed a vital connection to other people, other species, and ultimately to the universe at large. The resulting sense of existential loneliness is at the root of so much needless destruction in the world, but as de Quincey effectively shows, that loneliness is a trick of the mind.

We are not alone; we are part of an infinite web of relationships. The reasoning mind, cut off from the nonverbal nuances of the heart, however, is strangely autistic, unable to harmonize with others because it cannot *feel* the music of connection. In cultivating the art of relationship, we reunite mind and heart, becoming conscious collaborators with the mysteries that stir within us, around us, and beyond us.

We are in desperate need of developing what de Quincey calls "a communal science of the heart." Centuries of dominance-submission paradigms, and bloody revolts against those paradigms, have demonstrated that social conformity and rugged individualism are *both* dead ends. In *Radical Knowing,* Dr. de Quincey has shown us how it is ultimately through conscious, consensual relationships that we mine the depths of what it means to be a human tuner and receiver for a much vaster intelligence, ultimately fulfilling our destiny: that of "giving voice to the cosmos."

LINDA KOHANOV, AUTHOR OF *THE TAO OF EQUUS* AND
*RIDING BETWEEN THE WORLDS: EXPANDING OUR
POTENTIAL THROUGH THE WAY OF THE HORSE*

What Jung Meant by "Synchronicity"

In chapter 7, "*Synchronicity-1:* Beyond Energy," I explored the scientific status and philosophical coherence of the concept of synchronicity, and suggested a modification of Jung's own initial definition. But since the idea of synchronicity was developed by Jung over many years, it may help to be clear on how he used the term throughout his work. A close study of Jung's writings reveals that he, too, played with "weak" and "strong" versions of the principle, and he consciously left the way open for further exploration. With only minor comments, the following are twenty different ways Jung defined or explained his concept in *Synchronicity: An Acausal Connecting Principle*[1]. I head each definition with a concise summary of its key points:

1. Meaningful Coincidence of Causally Unrelated Events

Here I would like to call attention to a possible misunderstanding that may be occasioned by the term "synchronicity." I chose this term because the simultaneous occurrence of two meaningfully but not causally connected events seemed to me an essential criterion. I am therefore using the general concept of synchronicity in the special sense of a *coincidence in time of two or more causally unrelated events that have the same or similar meaning*, in contrast to "synchronism," which simply means the simultaneous occurrence of two events.[2] (Emphasis added.)

2. Coincidence of Psychic State with External Event(s)

Synchronicity therefore means the simultaneous occurrence of a certain psychic state with one or more external events that appear as meaningful parallels to the momentary subjective state—and, in certain cases, vice versa.[3]

3. Coincidence of "Present" Psychic State with "Future" Psychic State

Synchronistic events rest on the *simultaneous occurrence of two different psychic states* . . . we find a simultaneity of the normal or ordinary state with another state or experience that is not causally derivable from it, and whose objective existence can only be verified afterward. This definition must be borne in mind particularly when it is a question of future events. They are evidently not *synchronous* but are *synchronistic*, since they are experienced as psychic images *in the present*, as though the objective event already existed.[4]

4. Coincidence of Psychic States Connected with Objective Event

An unexpected [mental] content that is directly or indirectly connected with some objective external event coincides with the ordinary psychic state: This is what I call synchronicity.[5]

5. Acausal Phenomena, Not "Transcendental Cause"

Synchronistic phenomena cannot in principle be associated with any conception of causality. Hence the interconnection of meaningfully coincident factors must necessarily be thought of as acausal.

Here, for want of a demonstrable cause, we are all too likely to fall into the temptation of positing a *transcendental* one. But a "cause" can only be a demonstrable quantity. A "transcendental cause" is a contradiction in terms.[6]

6. Psychic Relativity of Space and Time

Space and time are constants in any given system only when they are measured without regard to psychic conditions. That is what regularly happens in scientific experiments. But when an event is observed without experimental restrictions, the observer can easily be influenced by an emotional state that alters space and time by "contraction."[7]

7. No Transmission of Energy Possible

How could an event remote in space and time produce a corresponding psychic image when the transmission of energy necessary for this is not even thinkable? However incomprehensible it may appear, we are finally compelled to assume that there is in the unconscious something like an *a priori* knowledge or an "immediacy" of events that lacks any causal basis.[8]

8. Coincidence of Unconscious Image and Objective Situation

There seems to be an *a priori*, causally inexplicable knowledge of a situation that at the time is unknowable. Synchronicity therefore consists of two factors: a) an unconscious image comes into consciousness either directly (i.e., literally) or indirectly (symbolizes or suggested) in the form of a dream, idea, or premonition; and b) an objective situation coincides with this content.[9]

9. Indispensable Criterion of Meaning

The synchronicity principle asserts that the terms of a meaningful coincidence are connected by *simultaneity* and *meaning*. . . . We must conclude that besides the connection between cause and effect there is another factor in nature that expresses itself in the arrangement of events and appears to us as meaning. Although meaning is an anthropomorphic interpretation it nevertheless forms the indispensable criterion of synchronicity.[10]

10. Meaning Beyond the Human Psyche

Synchronicity postulates a meaning that is *a priori* in relation to human consciousness and apparently exists outside man. Such an assumption is found above all in the philosophy of Plato.

In view of the possibility that synchronicity is not only a psychophysical phenomenon but might also occur without the participation of the human psyche, I should like to point out that in this case we should have to speak not of meaning but of equivalence or conformity.[11]

11. Synchronicity Is "Irrepresentable" and Fundamental

I am only too conscious that synchronicity is a highly abstract and "irrepresentable" quantity. It ascribes to the moving body a certain psychoid property that, like space, time, and causality, forms a criterion of its behavior.[12]

12. Synchronicity and Mind-Body Problem

The assumption of a casual relation between psyche and physis leads on the other hand to conclusions that are difficult to square with experience: Either there are physical processes that cause psychic happenings [materialism], or there is a pre-existent psyche that organizes matter [dualism]. In the first case it is hard to see how chemical processes can ever produce psychic processes [problem of emergence], and in the second case one wonders how an immaterial psyche could ever set matter in motion [interaction problem]. . . .

The synchronicity principle possesses properties that may help to clear up the body-soul problem. Above all it is the fact of causeless order, or rather, of meaningful orderedness, that may throw light on psychophysical parallelism.

The "absolute knowledge" that is characteristic of synchronistic phenomena, a knowledge not mediated by the sense organs, supports the hypothesis of a self-subsistent meaning, or even expresses its existence.

Such a form of existence can only be transcendental, since, as the knowledge of future or spatially distant events shows, it is contained in a psychically relative space and time, that is to say in an irrepresentable space-time continuum [transcendental idealism].[13]

13. Fourth Universal (Psychic) Factor

The synchronistic factor . . . stipulates the existence of an intellectually necessary principle that could be added as a fourth to the recognized triad of space, time, and causality. . . . Synchronicity is a phenomenon that seems to be primarily connected with psychic conditions, that is to say with processes in the unconscious.[14]

Synchronicity [is an] inconstant connection through contingence, equivalence, and meaning, the fourth component of the universal *quarternio* of "indestructible energy," "space-time continuum," and "causality," "constant connection through effect."[15]

14. An "Acasual Orderedness" of Psychic and Physical States

The meaningful coincidence or equivalence of a psychic and a physical state that have no causal relationship to one another means, in general terms, that it is a modality without a cause, an "acausal orderedness."[16]

15. Narrow and Wider Meanings of Synchronicity

The question now arises whether our definition of synchronicity [as] the equivalence of psychic and physical processes . . . requires expansion . . . [to] a wider conception of synchronicity as an "acausal orderedness."

Into this category come all "acts of creation," *a priori* factors such as the properties of natural numbers, the discontinuities of modern physics, etc. Consequently, we would have to include constant and experimentally reproducible phenomena within the scope of our expanded concept, though this does not seem to accord with the nature of the phenomena included in synchronicity narrowly understood. The latter are mostly individual cases that cannot be repeated experimentally. . . .

Our narrower conception of synchronicity is probably too narrow and really needs expanding. I incline in fact to the view that synchronicity in the narrow sense is only a particular instance of general acausal orderedness. . . . But as soon as [the observer] perceives the archetypal background he is tempted to trace the mutual assimilation of independent psychic and physical processes back to a (causal) effect of the archetype, and thus to overlook the fact that they are merely contingent. This danger is avoided if one regards synchronicity as a special instance of general acausal orderedness.

. . . The archetype *is* the introspectively recognizable form of *a priori* psychic orderedness.[17]

Note: Jung here defines "narrow" synchronicity as "equivalence of psychic and physical processes," and "wider" or "expanded" synchronicity as "general acausal orderedness," which is the objective (*a priori*) arrangement of deeper psychoid archetypes. Thus, "narrow synchronicity" (coincidence of psychic and physical events) is the explicit, detectable, unfolding of deeper, implicit, and unknowable, archetypal "acausal orderedness." Jung's archetypal domain of *acausal* orderedness differs, therefore, from Bohm's implicate order, which is *causal*.

16. Eternal Creative Pattern
We must regard [synchronicities] as *creative acts*, as the continuous creation of a pattern that exists from all eternity, repeats itself sporadically, and is not derivable from any known antecedents. We must of course guard against thinking of every event whose cause is unknown as "causeless."[18]

17. Simultaneous and "Future" Psychic-Physical Coincidences

1. The coincidence of a psychic state in the observer with a simultaneous, objective, external event that corresponds to the psychic state or content (e.g., the scarab), where there is no evidence of a causal connection between the psychic state and the external event, and where, considering the psychic relativity of space and time, such a connection is not even conceivable.

2. The coincidence of a psychic state with a corresponding (more or less simultaneous) external event taking place outside the observer's field of perception, i.e., at a distance, and only verifiable afterward.

3. The coincidence of a psychic state with a corresponding not yet existent future event that is distant in time and can likewise only be verified afterward.

In groups 2 and 3 the coinciding events are not yet present in the observer's field of perception but have been anticipated in time in so far as they can only be verified afterward. For this reason I call such events *synchronistic*, which is not to be confused with *synchronous*.[19]

18. Parallelism of Time and Meaning
Causality is the way we explain the link between two successive events. Synchronicity designates the parallelism of time and meaning, which scientific knowledge so far has been unable to reduce to a common principle.

The term explains nothing, it simply formulates the occurrence of meaningful coincidences, which, in themselves, are chance happenings, but are so improbable that we must assume them to be based on some kind of principle, or on some property of the empirical world. No reciprocal causal connection can be shown to obtain between parallel events, which is just what gives them their chance character. The only recognizable and demonstrable link between them is a common meaning, or equivalence.[20]

19. New Version of Old Theory of Correspondence
The old theory of correspondence was based on the experience of such connections—a theory that reached its culminating point and also its provisional end in Leibniz's idea of preestablished harmony, and was then replaced by causality.

Synchronicity is a modern differentiation of the obsolete concept of correspondence, sympathy, and harmony. It is based not on philosophical assumptions but on empirical experience and experimentation.[21]

20. Psychic Content Represented by External Event without Causal Link
Synchronistic phenomena prove the simultaneous occurrence of meaningful equivalences in heterogeneous, causally unrelated processes; in other words, they prove that a content perceived by an observer can, at the same time, be represented by an outside event, without any causal connection. From this it follows either that the psyche cannot be localized in space, or that space is relative to the psyche.[22]

Appendix 2

Subjectivity and Intersubjectivity

Like "consciousness," subjectivity has at least two critical meanings:

- Subjectivity-1: meaning "experienced interiority";
- Subjectivity-2: meaning "private, independent, isolated experience."

Subjectivity-1: In this first case, subjectivity means, essentially, an "intrinsic capacity for feeling" and "experiencing a point of view." Contrasted with external objects, subjectivity is "interior"—it's the familiar experience of "what-it-feels-like" to be you from within. The key notion here is "experienced interiority" as distinct from vacuous (i.e., without experience) external relations.

A subject is constituted by internal relations, and these are *felt* or experienced. Without experience there could be no subjectivity (and vice versa; in fact, the two words are virtually synonymous); and experience is always internal or intrinsic to the subject—that is to say, experience doesn't "happen to" a subject, it is *constitutive* of the subject.

Subjectivity has a point of view. It "takes account of," or feels, its own being. Its being is validated, felt, or known from within itself—hence it is *first-person*. It cannot be accounted for by external, physical processes, and it is inaccessible to objective investigation. A subject lives or endures through time, feeling its own continuity.

In subjectivity-1, experienced interiority is not automatically self-contained within its own private domain. It is interior, but not necessarily independent or isolated. Here, the question of whether it is self-contained or interdependent is left open: It is possible for subjectivity-1 to be either interior and *shared,* or interior and *private.*

Subjectivity-2: In this second, related through restricted, sense, subjectivity means an isolated, independent, self-sufficient locus of experience. Classically, this is the Cartesian ego, wholly private, and independent of all reality external to it. In this Cartesian meaning of subjectivity, the subject is not only interior, it is self-contained and private. Such independent egos, or subjects—Leibniz called them "monads"—can communicate only via mediating signals, whereas subjectivity-1 can communicate by participating in shared *presence.* With subjectivity-1, interiority or feeling can be "intersubjective" and precede individual subjects; in subjectivity-2, interiority is *always* private, and intersubjectivity, if it occurs, is always secondary.

I have used both forms of "subjectivity" in this book but have been careful to indicate, when not obvious from the context, which variety I mean. For now, I want to note that this distinction raises a crucial philosophical and existential question (addressed in chapter 15): *Which comes first, subjectivity or intersubjectivity—individuals or relationships?*

INTERSUBJECTIVITY

Again, we should make a crucial distinction between two basic meanings—standard and experiential—with a further subdistinction of the experiential meaning.

Intersubjectivity-1. *Linguistic* (consensual agreement). This standard meaning—"consensual validation between independent subjects via exchange of signals"—derives from Cartesian subjectivity (isolated, independent subjects). Here, individual subjectivity ontologically precedes intersubjectivity. Individual, isolated subjects come first, and then through communication of signals arrive at consensual agreement. Here, the "inter" in intersubjectivity refers to agreement between subjects about so-called objective facts—and the subjects don't even have to interact (their agreement could be validated by a third party, as indeed is often the case in science). Standard intersubjectivity relies on exchanges of physical signals (for example, through spoken words communicated via air vibrations and/or electronic signals, or written words or symbols printed on a page).

Intersubjectivity-2. *Mutual Conditioning* (participation). This is the weak-experiential meaning: "Mutual engagement and participation between independent subjects, which *conditions* their respective experience." Here, the sense of individual subjects remains, but now intersubjectivity refers to how the experience or consciousness of participating subjects is influenced and conditioned by their mutual interaction and engagement. The emphasis here is on the "experienced interiority" of the subjects (their shared presence) as they interact, not on their "objective" agreement about some item of knowledge.

Although this is a significant shift of emphasis from the standard meaning of intersubjectivity, nevertheless it is "weak" compared with the "strong" shift we will look at below. It is "weak," not because the participation or engagement involved is weak—indeed it could be intense—but because it refers to changes that happen to the *form* of consciousness of the participating subjects, not to the *fact* of such consciousness. It is "weak" insofar as it refers to the contents, not the context, of consciousness; "weak" because it addresses *psychological* rather than *ontological* issues; "weak" because it still posits subjectivity as ontologically prior to intersubjectivity. Here, the "inter" in intersubjectivity refers to the mutual "structural coupling" of experiencing subjects, where the *already existing* interiorities of the participating subjects are interdependently shaped by their interaction. Weak or "psychological" intersubjectivity relies on nonphysical presence and affects the contents of preexisting subjects.

Intersubjectivity-3. *Mutual Co-creation.* This is the strong-experiential meaning: "Mutual co-arising-and-engagement of interdependent subjects, or 'intersubjects,' that *creates* their respective experience." It is *ontological*, the most radical meaning, and the one that poses the greatest challenge to philosophy of mind. According to this "stronger" meaning, intersubjectivity is truly a process of co-creativity, where *relationship* is ontologically primary. All individuated subjects co-emerge, or co-arise, as a result of a holistic "field" of relationships. The being of any one subject is thoroughly dependent on the being of all other subjects with which it is in relationship.

Here, intersubjectivity precedes subjectivity (in the second, Cartesian, sense, but subjectivity in the first sense, of experienced interiority, is implicit throughout). The *fact*, not just the form, of subjectivity (Cartesian sense) is a consequence of intersubjectivity. In this case, the "inter" in intersubjectivity refers to an "interpenetrating" co-creation of various "centers" of subjectivity—a thoroughly holistic and organic mutuality. Strong, or ontological, intersubjectivity relies on co-creative nonphysical presence and brings distinct subjects into being out of a prior matrix of relationship.

The basic difference to note among these three meanings is that in (1) *intersubjective agreement* (I–I$_1$), my language about the world conforms to yours, through exchanges of conceptual and linguistic tokens. These are *physical* connections. However, in meanings (2) *intersubjective participation* (I–I$_2$) and (3) *intersubjective co-creativity* (I–I$_3$), the connections occur through non-physical *presence* and *meaning*. In I–I$_2$, my experience of myself shows up qualitatively differently when I engage with you (or others) as a reciprocating center of experience; and in I–I$_3$, my very experience of being—my "what-it-feels-like" to be—is a mutual co-creation, in every moment, among all reciprocating centers of experience.

The first kind, the standard meaning of intersubjectivity (I–I$_1$), is used to describe what otherwise goes by the name of "objectivity" in science[1] and is not what I am concerned with in this book. I am trying to get at something deeper, something with potentially profound implications for philosophy of mind and consciousness studies in general.

In the second (and third) sense, intersubjectivity happens through participation and mutuality, and we don't even have to agree. In fact, the vitality of this form of intersubjectivity is that it is often heightened by authentic disagreement and exploration of differences.

OBJECTIONS TO INTERSUBJECTIVITY

With so much controversy these days about whether consciousness should be studied from a first-person or from a third-person perspective, to propose including yet another perspective, as I am doing in this book, is likely to be even more controversial. And, indeed, this is the case. Objections from fellow philosophers fall into two, related, categories:

1. Whether the notion of intersubjectivity, or the second-person perspective, is logically, epistemologically, or ontologically meaningful.
2. If the second-person perspective is truly distinctive, in what ways would a methodology of intersubjectivity differ from either first-person subjective or third-person objective methodologies?

Clearly, these are valid and important questions, and I will address them by responding to comments and objections from anonymous referees who reviewed an earlier version of this work submitted to the *Journal of Consciousness Studies*.

One reviewer remarked that he/she didn't "feel" or introspect the difference between "intimate and non-intimate" relationships, referring to my suggestion that intersubjectivity involves "engaged presence." This is tricky. If someone doesn't "feel it"—and, remember, this mode of knowing involves the Shaman's Gift of feeling—then no amount of ostensive rational argument is going to win that person over. I can point all I like, but if the referent I'm pointing at just isn't available for that person within their own experience, then it will seem to be an "empty set" to them. I've pointed to what is probably the most likely element common to just about everyone's experiential set: namely the experience of love, of being in love. I think it is unlikely that any reader of this book has never felt the difference I'm pointing at between an intimate (love relationship) and a non-intimate one (say, a next-door neighbor, or the local shopkeeper). *That's* the kind of difference I'm pointing at when I speak of "engaged presence."

The difference, however, is not absolute; it is graded on a continuum. It is possible, of course, to have a second-person experience with your neighbor or shopkeeper. What matters is our willingness and ability to acknowledge and be open to the *presence of the other as a "locus" of experience that can reciprocate that acknowledgment.* We can interact with the shopkeeper (and, indeed, with a lover) mechanically and habitually without experiencing them as a reciprocating center of experience (many of us do this more than we'd care to admit)—or we can interact intersubjectively. The experiential difference is dramatic. Unfortunately, I can no more give a prescription for how to do this than I can for how to fall in love. But I trust that the ability is innate.

This does not mean, however, that there is no methodology we can use to facilitate second-person inquiry—we just cannot guarantee the methodology will work in every case, every time (which is true, of course, of any scientific or exploratory methodology). The procedure I have found to be most conducive to this kind of intersubjective experience is the form of dialogue developed by David Bohm (see chapter 13, *"Dialogue: Consciousness and Cosmology"*).

Numerous tapes, books, and articles are available, as well as practicum courses and meetings, where any interested inquirer can learn and practice this method of dialogue.[2] In chapter 13, I gave an outline of how dialogue works. A "recipe" is available, and anyone interested in this methodology must "bake the cake" for themselves. Fewer things are as dry and as uninspiring as a step-by-step procedure for how to attain a particular experience. If you want to experience the joys of sex—go do it. Similarly, if you are interested in researching intersubjectivity, follow the procedure for yourself.

REDUCTION OF INTERSUBJECTIVITY?

But, some researchers have objected, why should we take the time to investigate an alleged second-person methodology when there is a dispute about whether such a perspective is even logically and epistemologically meaningful? One reviewer thought it "plausible" that intersubjectivity could be explained as "a combination of subjectivity and objectivity," and that any description of intersubjectivity must rule out such a reduction. Another objected to the notion that a second-person "you" is a logically and ontologically distinct category between the self and the object. This reviewer dismissed the second-person as "logically incorrect" and "unnecessary."

I believe I have given a fairly extensive description and discriminating analysis of all three perspectives in this book, arguing why none can be reduced to either of the other two (even though intersubjectivity, in one sense, may be most fundamental). For the sake of brevity, I will summarize the essence of my argument here:

As I see it, we have three options: We could take an extreme eliminativist position and claim that the notion of a second-person "you" is semantically empty, without *any* referent. Alternatively, we could say that the second-person referent is ultimately reducible to either of the two other perspectives. I reject the first option for the same kinds of reasons I reject eliminative positions on first-person consciousness. It involves a performative contradiction: In this case, whom might the eliminativist be talking to? If there is no "you," no "others," why publish anything at all on this position?

If, then, we reject the hard eliminativist position, is a "softer" reductionist position more viable? On one hand, we have the first-person subject, and on the other, the third-person object as options for intertheoretic reduction. Now if the second-person "you" is both "logically incorrect and unnecessary," then it must either fall into the category of first-person subject or third-person object. Which is it?

Is another person wholly accounted for from the first-person perspective? This would be tantamount to solipsism and would deny any experiential reality to the "other"—again leading to performative contradictions. Failing this, is another person (a "you") wholly accounted for as a third-person object or collection of objects? Is there no difference between an entity that might be wholly objective (i.e., without any experiential interiority)—say a rock—and another human being? On experiential and logical grounds, I refuse to accept that "you" (meaning any other person) are nothing but a collection of objective physical things, lacking any sentience and experience with which I could engage in dialogue. (And if you are such a zombie, what on Earth are you doing reading a book on intersubjectivity?)

The "you" that the reductionist would like to ignore is any other "locus" of experience, which both logically and ontologically cannot be accounted for exclusively in terms of either first-person "I"s or third-person "its."

A THIRD KIND OF KNOWING?

In connection with this, however, one of the reviewers raised an interesting epistemological point by doubting that "there is a third kind of knowing." According to this objection, intersubjectivity would "correspond to introspection and inspection (first- and third-person forms of knowing)." But how can you "introspect" the presence of another person, or "inspect" consciousness in any form (first- or second-person)? The best that third-person inspection can offer is knowledge of *correlates* (neurological or behavioral) or computer-inspired flow-chart representations of the functions and schemata of mental events.

It is certainly possible that there may be first-person introspection going on simultaneously with second-person engagement—in fact, such introspection is an integral element in the methodology of Bohmian dialogue—where it is called "proprioception."[3] But the point is that both the quality and the content of such introspection is radically different when done in conjunction with another person (or a group of people) *similarly engaged*, from when done solo. As I say elsewhere in this book, "we show up differently" to ourselves when we engage intersubjectively. This kind of knowing is pertinent to exploring the "forms" or "contents" of consciousness (i.e., to a comprehensive *psychology* of consciousness). It is not so clear whether it would also enlighten us regarding the nature of experience (i.e., *philosophy* of consciousness)—nevertheless, it does raise the important question whether subjectivity or intersubjectivity is fundamental to the nature of consciousness.

I am not sure that a second-perspective alone (using, for example, the methodology of Bohmian dialogue) would be sufficient to enlighten us regarding this question. Likewise, I doubt that either the first-person or third-person perspective on its own would be sufficient. Part of the point of this book is to call for a comprehensive, integral approach that includes first-person introspection, second-person engagement, and third-person rational and empirical analysis. In my own work, as I follow this integral approach, I find the combination of subjective meditation, intersubjective participation, and third-person rational analysis leads me to suspect that consciousness is fundamentally a co-creative, intersubjective phenomenon.

Given the only ontology that seems to me to provide a coherent approach to understanding the perennial mind-body problem (as well as the problem of other minds)—namely panpsychism or radical naturalism—where all material entities are intrinsically experiential, and that all such entities are constituted by internal relations that *include* the actualities of others, intersubjectivity would be an ontological, as well as an epistemological, fact. But the reasons for siding with panpsychism (as opposed to materialism, idealism, or dualism) would take me far beyond the focus of this book. However, I have given my reasons in detail in *Radical Nature,* and A. N. Whitehead provides a highly detailed account of this ontology in *Process and Reality.*

A "DISTORTED MIRROR"?

This same reviewer raised another valid, and challenging, question: "If the second-person knowing is mirrorlike as de Quincey suggests, why should we trust it? I would think it would be more like a fun-house mirror than like a true mirror since human beings are notoriously flexible, fickle, and unstable. Such beings would seem likely to introduce so much distortion into the image that it would be very difficult to glean any information from it."

I can see no way of decisively eliminating all possibility of epistemological error—particularly regarding issues of consciousness. This is as true for first-person investigation of subjectivity, where we must confront the notorious biases and hidden motivations of the unconscious, as it is for intersubjectivity. It is also true, of course, for third-person investigation where the senses can be, likewise, notoriously deceptive. In the case of first-person subjectivity, many spiritual disciplines advocate working with an already-enlightened master to minimize illusion and self-delusion. In the case of third-person investigation, the unreliability of the senses is counteracted by the procedure of peer-review and repeated experiments, leading to what is usually called "objectivity" but which is really "intersubjectivity" in the sense of consensual agreement ("Intersubjectivity-1").

In both cases, the precautions against epistemological distortion involve, interestingly enough, some form of intersubjectivity. In the case of the student-master relationship in spiritual disciplines, that relationship is a quintessential example of second-person engagement. In the case of scientific experiments, researchers put a premium on peer review—on "standard intersubjectivity," as defined earlier. Similarly, the best way to guard against second-person distortion would be to engage with multiple dialogue partners—on the premise that if the reflection of the self in all others is liable to distortion, it is unlikely to be distorted in the same way in every case. A canceling-out effect, and/or repetition of common elements in the reflection from multiple partners, would be the best guarantee of epistemological accuracy.

FROM MECHANISM TO MEANING

Given these methodological considerations, how might the philosophical approach to the second-person perspective discussed here translate into a science of consciousness—resulting in a body of empirical data and testable hypotheses? Methodologically, how might it differ from first- or third-person perspectives? As we have seen, the most obvious difference is that the intersubjective approach would involve two or more people committedly engaged in the presence of the other(s)—an epistemology of *presence*.[4] It is the difference between an "I–it" relationship (third-person) or "I-me" relationship (first-person) and "I-you" (second-person). In this last case, consciousness is experienced truly as "intersubjective" and transpersonal, that is, transcending the individual Cartesian subject. Loosely, we might say it occurs "somewhere between and enveloping" the participants (recognizing, of course, the use of the spatial "somewhere" and "enveloping" are just metaphors).

The point is that consciousness "shows up" as a co-creativity between or among the participants. The implications range from, in philosophy, prompting us to reconsider our basic ontology (substituting a process-oriented relational ontology of interpenetrating experiences for discrete physical substances) to, in philosophy and science, providing a different way to approach the problem of other minds, or possibly even elucidating the mystery of parapsychological phenomena.

As an epistemology of "presence," second-person intersubjectivity opens the way to a deep exploration of *relationship*—an approach that could take science beyond an epistemology of objects, beyond methodologies of objectivity, measurement and quantification, beyond a preoccupation with mechanisms.

As in first-person methodologies, the emphasis in second-person science would be on engagement rather than measurement, on meaning rather than mechanism. Explanations in terms of mechanism are inappropriate for consciousness and mental phenomena because mechanisms involve exchanges of energy. They can provide explanations only of objective, physical things and processes. Where consciousness is involved, where subjective, interior experience is concerned, connections occur through shared meaning, not via physical mechanisms. Thus, instead of third-person explanations in terms of physical causes and effects, consciousness invites us to look for *understanding* or *insight* in terms of intersubjective, shared participation in the meanings of things and their relationships—and in the meaning of the world as a whole.

Wilber and de Quincey: I-to-I

As I mentioned in chapter 16, when I examined Ken Wilber's writings I found his discussion of intersubjectivity to be weak; and, because it plays such a critical role in Wilber's quadrant model, I will now give my reasons in detail.

This appendix is based on a critique of Wilber's book *Integral Psychology*, which I published in the *Journal of Consciousness Studies* (JCS), and includes my response to Wilber's reaction to the critique posted on my website (www.deepspirit.com). My original JCS paper was "The Promise of Integralism: A Critical Appreciation of Ken Wilber's Integral Psychology," Wilber's retort was "Do Critics Misrepresent My Position?" and my website response was "Critics Do, Critics Don't."

I include these excerpts for a number of reasons: First, Wilber is one of the most popular (and controversial) contemporary writers in the field of consciousness studies and is regarded by many as the foremost theorist and commentator on the growing field of transpersonal psychology. Second, because of his large and dedicated following (mostly, it seems, younger Gen X guys), his views have a significant influence on the development of these fields of study.

Third, as I will show, Wilber's treatment of intersubjectivity is both misleading and contradictory, and this needs to be clarified so that future generations of theorists do not set off on the wrong foot with a distorted notion of the second-person approach to the study of consciousness. And fourth, I have not previously gone into print with my response to Wilber's claim that my critique "misinterpreted" him, and I think it is important to set the record straight.

My original paper is much longer and covers many aspects of Wilber's work, such as "the mind-body problem," "panpsychism," and, perhaps most controversial of all, Wilber's "tone and style," which is often criticized as unnecessarily belligerent. Here, I focus on the issue of intersubjectivity, beginning with my response to him, published on my website:

I hadn't planned on responding to Ken Wilber's lengthy reply ("Do Critics Misrepresent My Position") to my paper ("The Promise of Integralism") but a recent remark by a mutual colleague made me think twice: "Of course, you got Wilber wrong," he said matter-of-factly. On further probing, I discovered that he and other members of a Wilber dialogue group had concluded that my critique must have been "factually wrong" because I had not responded to Wilber's very strong claim that I had "misrepresented" him and his ideas. My silence was interpreted as an acknowledgement of Wilber's slam-dunk retort. And, he said, Wilber had commented something to the effect: "There. That's the end of that," meaning he believed he had put me in my place.

Actually, my silence indicated nothing of the sort. I didn't respond before now for two reasons: One, because I was just too busy with other projects, such as fine-tuning my [then] forthcoming book *Radical Nature*, various teaching commitments, my full-time job as managing editor for *IONS Review*, and a couple of papers and articles I had been commissioned to write for other journals.

Second, I saw no particular merit in continuing a de Quincey-Wilber ping-pong match. My original intent for publishing the JCS critique was to stimulate a dialogue with Wilber on some specific areas of his model that I felt were problematic—especially as developed in his book *Integral Psychology*. It was clear from the tone of his response that dialogue was not something he was interested in. In fact, I felt—along with many others I have spoken with about this—that Wilber's reply had demonstrated a surprising lack of emotional maturity, confirming a point I had made in my paper.

Aside from the emotional tone, I was immediately struck by the degree to which Wilber manifested many of the critical failings he had accused me of—not least of which were the "misrepresentations," "distortions," out-of-context quotes, ad hominems, and plain factual inaccuracies in his "test case" response.

Because of these ostensibly deliberate misrepresentations and factual errors, and because my silence has been taken to be a *mea culpa*, I now feel I should take some time out of my schedule to put the record straight. I don't expect to change Wilber's views, or the views of those devoted

Wilberphiles who rushed to his defense (some of whom even attempted to prevent publication of my original critique). This response is intended for unbiased readers interested in hearing both sides.

A close and discerning reading of Wilber's response along with my original paper would probably make most of this reply redundant. But since I don't expect many people will invest the time to rigorously analyze "what-he-said-I-said" and compare it to what I actually said, I'll do so myself.

In my original critique I wrote that in *Integral Psychology* (IP), Wilber gives a very clear account of his understanding of intersubjectivity:

> You, as subject, will attempt to understand me as *a subject*—as a person, as a self, as a bearer of intentionality and meaning. *You will talk to me, and interpret what I say* [emphasis added]; and I will do the same with you. We are not subjects staring at subjects; we are subjects trying to understand subjects—we are in the intersubjective circle, the dialogical dance.[1]

Then, in the next paragraph: "The *interior* of a holon can *only* be accessed by interpretation." In *Eye of Spirit*, he makes the same point: "The *only* way you and I can get at each other's interiors is by dialogue and interpretation."[2] But then later in IP, he wavers: "The only way you can get at interiors is via introspection and interpretation."[3] Here, Wilber recognizes that interpretation *alone* is insufficient to "get at" interiors.

Wilber leaves us in no doubt what he means by "intersubjectivity": It is a subject-to-subject connection mediated by language and interpretation—and "*only* . . . by interpretation." There is no unmediated, *direct* experience of the other. Wilber's "interpretative circle," he makes clear, is identical to the "hermeneutic circle." But interpretation is a cognitive operation, a manipulation of symbols, or, at best, an extraction of meaning from symbols. In either case, interpretation is always at least one remove from *immediate* experience.

True intersubjectivity, on the other hand, is *direct* subject-to-subject sharing of presence—where both (or more) subjects either mutually *condition* each other's sense of self, or, more strongly, mutually *co-create* each other's sense of self.

As pointed out in this book, we need to make an important distinction between *linguistic* and (two forms of) *experiential* meanings of intersubjectivity (see chapter 15, "*Intersubjectivity-1: We Are the World*"). Let's recap:

Intersubjectivity-1: The *linguistic* meaning. It refers to consensual validation between independent subjects via exchange of signals. This is Cartesian intersubjectivity, and it relies on exchanges of physical signals (e.g., speech or writing). It is *physically mediated* intersubjectivity—and, as such, is remote, indirect, and, therefore, very weak.

Intersubjectivity-2: The *mutual-conditioning* meaning. This refers to mutual engagement and participation between independent subjects that *conditions* their respective experience. It is *psychological intersubjectivity* relying on non-physical *presence* and affects the mental contents of preexisting subjects. It is direct *immediate* mutual apprehension between subjects (although it can also involve intersubjectivity-1, communication via linguistic tokens). This is "medium-strength" intersubjectivity, where two or more subjects mutually alter or condition each other's experience.

Intersubjectivity-3: The *co-creation* meaning. This refers to the mutual co-arising and engagement of interdependent subjects, or "intersubjects," that *creates* their respective experience. It is *ontological intersubjectivity* relying on co-creative non-physical presence and brings distinct subjects into being out of a prior matrix of relationships.

Note the difference between (1) *intersubjective agreement* where my language about the world conforms to yours through exchange of conceptual and linguistic tokens (objective); and (2) *intersubjective participation* or (3) *intersubjective co-creativity* where my *experience* (subjectivity-1) of myself shows up qualitatively different when I engage with you as a reciprocating center of experience.

True intersubjectivity, as I have described it, is unmediated communication or co-creative sharing of presence—it is direct *subject-to-subject*, or "I-to-I," communion. For shorthand, I sometimes refer to it as "I–I."*

Wilber's "intersubjectivity" is not wrong; it's just weak. It's what standard linguistic philosophy, social theory, and philosophy of science refer to as "intersubjectivity" (and is really objectivity or interobjectivity). Yes, two or more subjects come together or share information via language and

---

*I find it interesting that Jamaican Rastafarians, acknowledging the importance of intersubjectivity, back in the 60s and 70s contributed the phrase "I and I" to our culture. I have always liked that perspective.

therefore come to know something about each other. And, in *this* sense, there is a subject-to-subject communication. But, as I point out and as Wilber emphasizes, such communication is mediated via exchanges of linguistic tokens, which are *exteriors*. In this kind of "intersubjectivity" *alone* there is no direct *interior-to-interior* connection or sharing. And unmediated *interior-to-interior* connection or sharing is true *inter*-subjectivity.

Actually, in reality, there is direct interior-to-interior engagement even when contact is made via language—in fact, that's the *only* way people can share meaning and understand each other. But the point is the actual sharing of meaning is not accomplished by linguistic exchanges, but by the accompanying *interior-to-interior participatory presence*—by true intersubjectivity. As we know from evidence for telepathy, shared meaning doesn't even require language (or any exchange of physical signals).

Wilber does emphasize that a central function of the Lower Left (LL) "intersubjective" cultural quadrant is *meaning*—and he would unhesitatingly agree that meaning cannot be reduced to physical scratches on paper or digital blips on a screen (in fact, he sides with first-person subjectivists in criticizing philosophers such as Daniel Dennett and other cognitivists and eliminativists for reducing semantics to syntax). But the point is, according to Wilber's model, for meaning to be *communicated* or shared, it can do so "only" by dialogue and interpretation, by "talk"—that is, by exchange of linguistic tokens, physical signals. No room here for silent engaged presence (see chapter 14). No room for shared feeling. No room for telepathic communion. No room, in other words, for true intersubjectivity where one subject is actually shaped or changed by literally participating in, and incorporating, something of the being of another subject (intersubjectivity-2), and certainly no room for one or more subjects dynamically, mutually creating each other's "node" or nexus of subjectivity within the (universal) matrix of the ground of being of intersubjective relationships (intersubjectivity-3).

Wilber is clearly aware that LR connections (networks of communication via exterior signals) cannot, *by themselves,* account for intersubjectivity (LL phenomena)—yet almost all his references to intersubjectivity are couched in terms of communities engaged in linguistic exchange.[4] As anyone familiar with his work would suspect: Wilber knows better. He knows that LL signifiers (meaning or semantics) cannot be reduced to exchanges of LR signifieds (mechanism or syntax). But he doesn't talk or write that way most of the time.

My proposal for including true intersubjectivity (that is, non-physically-mediated meaning) does not preclude physical correlates of such shared meaning (e.g., changes in brain states or marks on paper or dots on screen or spoken words). Like Wilber, I agree that every interior has (*must have*) a corresponding exterior. My concern, my objection, is that when he confines intersubjectivity to *only* dialogue or talk and interpretation he leaves no room for intersubjective *interiority*. I'm puzzled why Wilber doesn't see this, and shift his emphasis from language to *presence* (or *interiority*) when talking about intersubjectivity.

But there's another, more serious, problem here: If the defense of Wilber's position on intersubjectivity is based on the fact that as a whole his philosophy is "nondual" then, actually, the defense evaporates.* For in that case, the notion that all beings are immediately co-present in Spirit—that intersubjectivity arises from direct and immediate contact of all interiors with Spirit—applies to *all four quadrants* (for, ultimately, in Wilber's scheme, even all exteriors are Spirit). There would be nothing special about LL. In what way would LL intersubjectivity differ from "intersubjectivity" in any of the other quadrants? Wilber's answer: through cultural exchanges of meaning via linguistic tokens. And so we're back to the original problem. Thus, it seems, by taking the "One Taste" perspective (where *everything* is intersubjective), Wilber is forced to single out a particular type of "intersubjectivity," i.e., exchange of linguistic tokens.

Bottom line: This is not an incidental or "nit-picking" critique. Basically, to spell it out: *One quarter of Wilber's four quadrants is left void or vacant.* His LL is not what he claims it to be, i.e., the locus of intersubjectivity.

It was precisely the lacuna of true intersubjectivity in consciousness studies and philosophy of mind that prompted me to present a paper at the Tucson III conference "Toward a Science of Consciousness," in 1998, calling for comprehensive first-, *second-*, and third-person perspectives in investigating consciousness. It seemed to me to be such a glaring oversight that I wondered if I was somehow blind or mistaken: Had no-one in philosophy of mind really seriously considered the second-person perspective? So, as part of a reality check, I sent an early draft of my paper to a number of theorists in consciousness studies, and Wilber was among them. He wrote back affirming my perception, pointing out that except for his own

---

*This defense has, in fact, been made by some of Wilber's "disciples."

work (meaning his LL quadrant), few contemporary consciousness theorists besides me were taking intersubjectivity seriously. I was pleased to see Wilber subsequently emphasize what I was calling for: a comprehensive first-, second-, and third- person approach to consciousness studies (which he now calls the "1-2-3 of consciousness studies."[5]

In the four quadrants model, Wilber is weakest in his treatment of LL intersubjectivity and second-person perspective, and—not incidentally, I think—he wants to downplay the ontological and epistemological significance of feeling, so central to a more comprehensive and deep understanding of intersubjectivity.

In other words, it is the *felt relational* component of Wilber's theoretical psycho-philosophical work that is most conspicuously missing. This criticism in one form or another, with varying degrees of emotionality, has been leveled at Wilber from many quarters (e.g., feminists, eco-systems theorists, spiritual practitioners) for whom relation is primary. And, of course, in typical Wilber style, he has responded forcefully to their critiques.

In the "I-We-It" stakes, Wilber is strongest on the I and It. His writings lack a sense of felt bodily meaning and relationship. And this has tended to alienate him from those for whom "We" is primary. Wilber has a tendency to reduce "We" (i.e., "I–you" or "I–I") to the terms of "I–It"—*even while proclaiming the very opposite.*

Even though I pointed out what I take to be a deficiency in Wilber's treatment of intersubjectivity, I had hoped he would see me as an ally in the project to put the second-person perspective on the radar screen in consciousness studies and philosophy of mind. I think there is room in his four quadrants for true intersubjectivity, and I was just trying to clarify what it is. Colleagues who know me well know that I've been passionate about this issue for many years, and I have tried to draw attention to it in my own work. (This book is one more attempt.)

That's the essence of what I wrote in JCS. Now here's Wilber's retort, and my response.

CRITICS DO, CRITICS DON'T

Wilber responded in "Do Critics Misrepresent My Position?":[6] "de Quincey's major criticism, and the one he spends the most time on, is that I identify intersubjectivity solely and exclusively with verbal linguistic exchanges. This is pretty much the opposite of my view."

I'm glad to hear him say this. Given his emphasis on the ultimate nature of nondual Spirit, this is what I would have expected from Ken Wilber. I was very surprised, therefore, to come across, again and again, his claim that intersubjectivity (I'll use "I–I" as shorthand) takes place only via exchanges of linguistic tokens or signals. I quoted Wilber's words exactly as he wrote them . . . without any distortion or misrepresentation. To repeat, he said: "You, as subject, will attempt to understand me as *a subject*—as a person, as a self, as a bearer of intentionality and meaning. *You will talk to me, and interpret what I say.*"[7] (Emphasis added.)

In *Eye of Spirit*, he makes the same point: "The *only* way you and I can get at each other's interiors is by dialogue and interpretation."[8] In *Sex Ecology, Spirituality*, he is even more emphatic: "Interiors must be *interpreted*. If I want to know what your brain looks like *from within*, what its actual lived *interior* is like (in other words, your *mind*), then I *must talk to you*. There is absolutely no other way. . . . And as we talk, I will have to *interpret* what you say."[9] His position couldn't be more clear or explicit. Then, missing the subtle reduction he has just expressed, he goes on to say, in contradiction: "But you can only study interiors empathically, as a feel from within, and that means interpretations."[10]

If, indeed, as Wilber complains, my critique of his version of intersubjectivity focuses on a partial view and misrepresents his total view, then he must take responsibility for emphasizing, repeatedly, this self-misrepresentation. The plain fact is that in many places Wilber has emphasized merely a partial aspect of I–I (and even emphatically stated that talking is the "only" way), and this can easily mislead readers into thinking that, for Wilber, "talking" and "interpretation" are the main aspects of I–I.

Wilber objected that I gave "two examples" of his very weak description of I–I, "both taken out of context," that fly in the face of hundreds of examples to the contrary (and he offers a quote from *A Brief History of Everything*: "So there is intersubjectivity woven into the very fabric of the Kosmos at all levels." Why, then, does he say (and I give not two, but *seventeen* examples from *Integral Psychology* alone) over and over that intersubjectivity is a matter of "talking" and "interpretation"—clearly meaning linguistic exchanges, and *these* are not woven into the cosmic (or Kosmic) fabric at all levels?

And what does he mean by "taken out of context"? Since I refer readers to exact pages in *Integral Psychology* where he makes this claim, it is clear I'm encouraging them to see the context for themselves. Obviously, in a review (even a lengthy one) there isn't enough room to quote whole chunks of text to *reproduce* the original context. That would be an absurd expectation. In standard academic work, it is sufficient to note the context by (1) accurately quoting the author's own words without selective bias or distortion, and (2) by indicating the context in the original work. That is what I did. Unfortunately, it is not what Wilber did in his response: "Never do I say, at any point, that in the entire Kosmos this is the ONLY type of intersubjectivity. . . . I *never* say there is only linguistic intersubjectivity . . . ."[11]

Well, don't just take my word for it—read Wilber's own words and see what you think: "The interior of a holon can *only* be accessed by interpretation" or "the *only* way you and I can get at each other's interiors is by dialogue and interpretation," and, the emphatic "interiors must be *interpreted*" and "I *must talk to you*" (italics added). True, he doesn't say verbatim "this is the only type of intersubjectivity in the entire Kosmos" (nor do I say that he does). But he does come very close when he asserts: "The *interior* of a holon can *only* be accessed by interpretation" (italics added).

If Wilber meant specifically human holons when using "only"—and not the entire Kosmos—it doesn't affect my critique. First, the position that the interiors of human holons can be accessed "only" by linguistic exchanges would be false, in any case. The specifically human kind of I–I that each of us encounters every day (or human-animal I–I) involves what I have called non-linguistic "engaged presence." We do not experience each other "*only*" through "dialogue and interpretation," as Wilber states over and over. Second, what is essentially true of human interiors is essentially true of interiors anywhere in the Kosmos. Engaged presence is the essence of I–I between *any* holons.

In his defense, Wilber offers this clarification: "When I talk about having 'only' linguistic interpretation, I mean that, as far as the linguistic signifiers themselves go, we must add interpretation . . . ."[12] This is good. I'm glad to hear him be explicit about this (even though it is hardly news that words or symbols make sense to us only when we interpret them). But nowhere in *Integral Psychology* or *A Theory of Everything* does he make this clear—which is what I was criticizing. This "weak" form of I–I is what dominates Wilber's discussion of the phenomenon in both of these books (also in *Eye of Spirit* and *Sex, Ecology, Spirituality*). The point of my critique was to draw attention to the fact that this is just one—the weakest—of three different kinds of I–I.

Given this, Wilber is clearly being disingenuous when he says: "That I maintain there is only linguistic intersubjectivity is something de Quincey himself adds to my work." This is blatantly false (see the seventeen examples

I cite from *Integral Psychology*). He then attempts a typical Wilber wriggle: "I define interpretation as a 'sympathetic resonance from within.'"[13] I like that definition. But it doesn't appear in *Integral Psychology*.

He goes on: "And yet de Quincey himself gives my primary definition of intersubjectivity by correctly using the following quote from me: 'Subjective experiences *arise in the space created by intersubjectivity.*'" Yes, I do quote this to underscore how contradictory it is for Wilber to repeatedly emphasize the linguistic version as the "only" form of I–I. As I said in my JCS paper, I know that Wilber knows better and I cite an example to support that claim. I then critique him for not acknowledging this other, more primary, form of I–I in *Integral Psychology*.

Wilber is here indulging in what he claims his critics do: He is lifting my reference to his "subjective experiences" quote out of context. The point of my JCS critique of I–I, let me emphatically repeat, was *to draw attention to the very limited meaning Wilber ascribes to I–I in* Integral Psychology—and that he should, and apparently does, know better. Hence the "primary definition" quoted above.

MORE TYPES OF INTERSUBJECTIVITY?

Wilber accuses me of "focusing on a specific example"—remember, I cite seventeen examples—"about one type of interpretation." As I've pointed out, he does not make it clear in *Integral Psychology* that he acknowledges more than one type of I–I in his total model. In fact, I believe *he began to talk about different types of I–I only after seeing my critique where I offered three distinct types.*

He says: "Moreover, I add at least two more types of intersubjectivity not dealt with by de Quincey." He then goes on to describe his I–I #4: "The agency of all holons opens directly, immediately, onto Spirit itself, and thus all holons share a deep, non-mediated, non-local, profound intersubjectivity due to the fact that all holons immediately touch each other via the Spirit that each of them fully is."[14]

This is a wonderful *restatement* of what I have identified as I–I #3—"(the *co-creativity,* strong-experiential meaning): mutual co-arising and engagement of interdependent subjects, or 'intersubjects,' that *creates* their respective experience. It is *ontological intersubjectivity* relying on co-creative non-physical presence and brings distinct subjects into being out of a prior matrix of relationships." (The *interiority* of all participants in I–I #3 is the "common Self" that Schopenhauer rightly noted must exist for *any* form of I–I to exist in the first place.)

And if Wilber's I–I #4 is not merely a restatement of my I–I #3, then it is not any form of I–I at all—not a fourth variation of I–I, as he claims. If there is only *one* Spirit then there is only one, non-dual, pure subjectivity (as interiority), so there is no possibility of any "*inter*-subjectivity" between distinct "centers" of I–I.

At one point, Wilber turns for assistance to one of his acolytes who points out: "Wilber's model, as it relates to intersubjectivity, is often buried in footnotes and/or is implicit . . . ."[15] Well, this is a limp defense because nothing like I–I #4 is "buried" in any footnotes. And if it is only "implicit" in *Integral Psychology*, then my critique stands, and is in fact supported by the backfiring of his "defense." Bottom line: His repeated and explicit position in *Integral Psychology* is the very narrow and weak meaning of I–I.

Wilber then uses a surprising claim in his defense, quoting one of his defenders: "de Quincey only cites one book (out of 18) to support this claim [that I–I is not a central concern for Wilber]—although that one book [*Integral Psychology*], surprisingly, contains passages which speak to all five dimensions." Surprising indeed. If there is any passage in *Integral Psychology* that "speaks to" all of Wilber's purported "five dimensions" of I–I, I would certainly like to be directed to it. I have asked Wilber and his followers to identify any such passage, but so far my requests have been met with an unsurprising silence. If such passages are unequivocally there, I would, of course, withdraw the part of my critique, based on *Integral Psychology*, that suggests Wilber's Lower Left quadrant is effectively vacant thereby leaving his complex theoretical edifice for "a theory of everything" precariously balanced on three, not four, quadrants.

That was the main thrust of my critique. And if it has served to alert Wilber (and his readers) to the very narrow meaning of I–I he has emphasized most, and if it has encouraged Wilber (and others) to be more explicit and careful about expressing his full position on I–I, then our interchange has been worthwhile. It does seem that more people are now paying attention to the significance of intersubjectivity in the overall understanding of consciousness. And that is a good thing. For many years, it has been my hope and intention to put intersubjectivity on the consciousness studies map.

Appendix 4

Integrating Worldviews

In *Radical Nature*, I explored the various worldviews or ontologies that have attempted to solve the perennial "hard problem" of how mind and body, consciousness and the physical world, are related. I concluded that the worldview of panpsychism provides our best shot at solving this mind-body problem, which Schopenhauer called the "world knot." I also mentioned that of all the ontologies, panpsychism offers a way to honor and integrate the fundamental insights of the other three.

Because of the epistemological implications of panpsychism, I'd like to now take another look at the major ontologies and see how they might cohere if we view them through the lens of Alfred North Whitehead's panpsychist process philosophy. (You may view this as a kind of "Cliff Notes" to *Radical Nature*.)

Recall that the central problem with dualism is the thorny issue of mind-body interaction. How could two such utterly different substances ever interact? What would be the nature of their point of contact—physical or mental, or both? If the contact point is either physical or mental, then that leaves unexplained how the other half could make contact. If the contact point is both physical and mental, then the original problem remains: How, *within that point,* could two utterly different substances interact? Pushing the problem back and reducing its size, even to a point, does not solve the *ontological* problem.

The problem with materialism is that it begins with the assumption that *every actuality* is physical, made up *entirely* of some form of matter-energy. Given that consciousness is an undeniable actuality (notwithstanding the intellectual contortions of so-called eliminative materialists), and that its fundamental characteristic is interiority or subjectivity, how then do we account for it? How could subjective consciousness ever *emerge* from wholly objective, insentient, non-mental matter-energy?

The problem with idealism is two-pronged: Either matter is illusory *(maya)*, or it *emanates* from pure consciousness or spirit. The first option, though irrefutable logically or empirically, is pragmatically problematic and encounters a dramatically obvious performative contradiction: *We just don't live as though matter is an illusion*—resulting in a major inconsistency between our stated belief in the illusion of matter, and our actual practice. And for very good reasons: If we didn't treat matter as though it were real, we wouldn't survive very long. The second option states that matter *emanates* from pure spirit. But how? This position encounters the reverse of the problem facing materialists. How could *pure* spirit—unadulterated with even the slightest trace of physicality—ever produce something so ontologically different as *real* matter?

These problems remain unsolvable, it seems, as long as we think of mind and matter as substances—that is, independent and self-subsisting realities needing nothing but themselves to exist. If we switch from substance-thinking to *process*-thinking, everything shifts.

Whitehead's panpsychism is rooted in the metaphysical assumption that the fundamental units of reality are "moments of experience." Every individual actuality—whether man, mouse, or molecule, woman, worm, or light wave—is experiential, possessing interiority or feeling. Mind or consciousness, in other words, goes all the way down to quanta or quarks or whatever might lie beyond. And this is necessarily so because the ultimate nature of every actual entity (moment of experience) is eventlike, a process. And every event or process exists for at least a minimal duration. Anything that endures is necessarily spread out over time so that past is distinguishable from present, and both of these from future. But only an experiencing entity could *distinguish* the moment "now" that separates past from future. If there were no center of experience, what would identify the moment of now, and how?

Furthermore, besides being experiential, all events are constituted by internal relations. *Nothing* exists as wholly itself, independent of everything else, for a timeless instant. That is to say, if we could reduce time to zero, no actual entity would remain in existence. To exist means to endure, and to endure means that whatever exists is "smeared out" over time. The past, in other words, pours into the present and *constitutes* it. Each actual entity existing now is constituted by past actualities.

The apparent contradiction between materialism and idealism is resolved by recognizing the fundamentality of process, of time: This moment's unit experience is completed as soon as its brief duration is over. At that "instant" it is no longer "now" and becomes part of the past. It ceases being an experiencing subject and becomes an object experienced by the subsequent moment of experience—the subject occupying the next "now."

Process, therefore, involves an alternation or spiral of phases—from experiencing subject (the unifying agent of past objective moments) to a completed subject-as-object (physical), which in turn becomes "raw material" for the next moment of experience (mental). The slogan "now subject, then object" sums up the panpsychist solution to the mind-body problem—or alternatively: "past matter, present mind."[1]

Panpsychism, thus, shares with dualism the insight that mind and body are distinct (but as phases in a continuous process, not as separate and discrete substances). And it shares with materialism the insight that physical, objective reality gives rise to mind. But it does so by redefining the nature of "physical." Again, no longer does physical refer to a kind of substance, but to a phase in a process. "Physical" equates with "objective," whatever is past—completed moments of experience. No sooner does a moment of experience come into being than it completes itself and becomes an *expired experience*—an object. Such objects, streaming in from the past—or, more accurately, scooped up or prehended by the present subject—actually constitute the present subject. But not entirely—and that's where idealism comes in.

Idealism is typically understood to mean a worldview that denies the reality of matter independent of mind. And to this extent, panpsychism accords with idealism: No "physical pole" of a moment of experience exists independently of a "mental pole." The reverse is equally true (which seems to support materialism). However, since the common factor in both poles is *experience,* idealism appears to win out.

Whitehead is emphatic that the "physical pole" (matter) is just as real as the "mental pole" (mind). His philosophy is a detailed, rational, and *empirical*—in the broadest sense of being based on experiential data—working out of what we could call "idealist realism." It is idealism, as already suggested, because its ultimate ontology is experiential—moments of experience—and it is realism because these ultimate units are the paradigm actualities.

Panpsychism, thus, achieves the impressive function of providing a bridge or tunnel between the apparently opposing ontologies of materialism and idealism—while acknowledging, along with dualism, a mind-body distinction (without the ontological split of dualism). It does so by showing that "matter" (physical actuality) is fundamentally real, as materialists insist, but that this matter/energy is essentially constituted by experiential occasions, as idealists insist.

As a philosophy, panpsychism honors reason as an effective epistemology and honors feeling as fundamental to both epistemology and ontology. Not only is primitive feeling—what Whitehead calls "prehension"—at the root of all knowledge, it is also what the world of actual entities is made of—or, rather, what the world is *doing*.

But is this truth or wisdom? If this understanding of the world as a network or matrix of feelings remains in the abstract language of concepts, then at best it can point the way toward truth, while falling short of wisdom. However, if such rational analysis is grounded in and complemented by embodied feelings and intuitive insight—where we actually *feel* the process relationship between present and past, between subject and object, between mind and matter, between self and other—then the philosophy of panpsychism, now coupled with intersubjectivity, can put us on the road toward wisdom and not merely truth.

Such an expanded philosophy of mind will require a willingness to engage in different ways of knowing consciousness—through first-person meditation and contemplation, through second-person relationship and communion, and through third-person objective correlations between body and mind.

The Philosopher's Stone

"It just doesn't feel right," she protested, unhappy at the suggestion that perhaps rocks don't have consciousness. She looked genuinely troubled, as I held up the stone.

"My job as a philosophy teacher is to get students to 'think outside the box,' to become more conscious of *how* they think. This is not supposed to be an exercise in *what* to think, it is not about finding 'right' ideas." I rubbed the rounded stone between my hands, feeling the paradox of its cool warmth.

"Donna," I said, "I'm not asking you to change any particular belief about rocks. If you think rocks or stones are conscious, that's fine." Though silently I wondered why it seemed to matter so much to her that lumps of granite pulsed with what she called "vibrations." In my experience, rocks—immobile, inert, unresponsive, hard, and cold—are the very epitome of something that's thoroughly *non*-conscious. Of course, I could be wrong. But how could we ever tell for sure?

"The issue isn't whether rocks really do or do not have consciousness," I went on, unconsciously stroking the stone against my chin, searching for the best words. "There really isn't any decisive way to know. There's no conclusive test for consciousness." I hesitated, knowing there's no kind of test at all. "Whether or not rocks, or anything else, actually have consciousness is a *scientific* question, and as things stand science cannot even begin to answer this."

"But scientists would laugh at the idea of rock-consciousness," another student blurted out as a question, "wouldn't they?"

"Yes, I do believe most of them would," I agreed, and went on to explain how that's a good example of a metaphysical prejudice masquerading as scientific knowledge. "Without having the faintest idea how to test such a belief, most scientists I know would insist that the idea of rock-consciousness is absurd."

"It's like 'believe first, ask questions later,'" the student mumbled to her neighbor.

"That's not science, it's *scientism*," I offered, still agreeing. "It's bad science. It's confusing the *how* with the *what*—the process of thinking with the contents of thinking."

I could see that this last statement drew blank looks, so I tried to explain.

"You've just identified a bias common in 'scientific' thinking about rocks. And this serves as a good example of where I'd like you to focus your own awareness." A rustle echoed around the room as students shifted in their seats.

"Notice how these scientists (whoever they are) engage in a form of thinking we might call 'jumping to conclusions.' They believe that only creatures with brains could have consciousness, and since rocks don't have brains, therefore rocks couldn't have consciousness. That kind of thinking is called a syllogism. And it's quite valid as stated. Yes, *if* it's true that only brains have consciousness, then the conclusion logically follows: Rocks don't have consciousness. But that's a *philosophical* conclusion, not a scientific one. Science works by testing the 'ifs' using experiments that yield tangible evidence. *And there's no tangible evidence for consciousness*—not in rocks, nor in human beings, either, for that matter.

"Even philosophically the conclusion hinges on the truth or accuracy of the initial premise: 'Only creatures with brains have consciousness.' Is that really true? The second premise, 'rocks don't have brains' is not a problem. Plenty of people, including scientists, have split open rocks and nobody has ever seen a brain inside.

"But for the conclusion 'rocks can't be conscious' to be true *both* premises would have to be true. And we simply do not know whether the first premise 'only brains have consciousness' is true. To believe so in advance of testing the hypothesis is scientism, not science."

Looking at the sea of faces, I could see I'd completely lost them by now. How could I make the point more clearly?

"What I'm trying to get at here is that science is about discovering what the *actual* world is really like, whereas philosophy is about exploring *possible* worlds. Science is interested in whether brains actually produce consciousness (and whether rocks really, actually, do have experiences);

philosophy is interested in, for example, whether it's possible that consciousness could exist without brains, or if it's possible that rocks could exist with or without consciousness."

I was still struggling. So I turned to Donna again.

"When I asked you to think of something that didn't have consciousness I suggested a rock might be a good example. But you didn't agree because you felt uncomfortable. It didn't feel right, you said. You may indeed be correct: Perhaps rocks do have consciousness. But I'd like you now to be open to the *possibility* that either you may be mistaken, or that in some other world it's possible that rocks don't have consciousness. You don't even have to give up your belief; I'd just like you to entertain the possibility. Can you do that?"

She squirmed a little in her chair and, after a long silence, her face strained from some internal struggle, she said "No. I just don't believe it's possible."

"Why wouldn't it be possible?" I asked, trying to hide a growing impatience.

"Because it just doesn't feel right," she said. We'd come full circle.

I searched frantically for a new tack. The clock was hungrily devouring the minutes, as the hands inched their way toward 9:45.

"Maybe it doesn't 'feel right' to scientists to consider the possibility of rocks having consciousness. You would feel one thing, they'd feel the exact opposite. Who'd be right? How would we decide?"

Donna thought for a moment: "Well maybe there's no 'right,'" she came back. "Maybe we'd both be right in our own way."

I'd lost.

But I couldn't let it alone. "How could the same thing—our rock—both *have* consciousness and *not have* consciousness at the same time? That's a contradiction. It doesn't make sense. It's incoherent."

My frustration was beginning to show now, as the pitch of my voice climbed an octave. But her *coup de grace* was about to come:

"According to your logic, maybe. That's 'either/or' thinking. In my way of thinking it's 'both/and.'"

At that point I finally gave up. I realized the truth staring me in the face.

"Then we can't communicate," I said. "We can't understand each other. If you are talking from a world where you believe both/and logic applies to contradictory statements then I have no way of making rational sense of what you say. In my world, some statements do require understanding in either/or terms. The same thing (a rock) cannot be both in one state (conscious) and its exact opposite (non-conscious) *at the same time.* All meaning breaks down for me at that point."

Capitalizing on her winning hand, she threw out: "Only if you are looking for meaning through reason and logic."

Bingo. That's it. Maybe I had an opening after all.

"That's precisely what I am looking for," I said with a sense of desperation tinged with a flicker of hope. "We are communicating through language which is the expression of concepts. And for concepts to hang together coherently—to make sense—we have to honor the rules of rationality and logic. I'm looking for *conceptual* coherence. I'm not saying that whatever fits together rationally is necessarily true in the actual world (after all, there's no reason whatsoever that reality should fit our concepts). I'm saying that for me to understand what you *say* about the world I need to hear ideas that fit together coherently. And contradictory statements cancel each other out, they do not fit."

Was I finally getting a foothold? The ticking of the clock picked its way through the silence as I waited for her response.

"Well, if you want me to just *think* that it's possible for a rock to be non-conscious, okay. I can do that. But it still doesn't feel right, and I don't believe it's true."

I was back in the driver's seat. "That's all I wanted you to do all along. Engage in a thought experiment. That's what philosophy is. Now you're beginning to think like a philosopher."

I addressed the room: "So we can agree it's *possible,* either way, that rocks do or do not have consciousness. Philosophers usually take the position that rocks don't have consciousness and use them as paradigm examples of things that are wholly non-conscious. Whether rocks *actually* are or are not conscious is an open question *scientifically* . . . and will remain so as long as science relies on a methodology of objectivity and measurement. There's simply no such thing as a 'consciousness meter.'"

■

After class, when the last student had left, I sat there with the stone between my hands, resting it on my lap. I fingered its smooth curves, emptying my mind of all the day's thoughts, absentmindedly concentrating on the heft and solidity of the rock. Three or four billion years ago, this fragment of planet had been spewed out by some fire-breathing volcano. It cooled and found its place among the Earth's earliest inhabitants. Some rocks got digested and transformed by primitive bacteria and entered the steam of living systems. Others, like this one, remained as they had been, for millions—for billions—of years. There was something very special about such an ancient, almost eternal, object. If only I could see the eons of changes it had weathered, recorded somehow in its elements. I closed my eyes and held the stone lightly, feeling for its almost imperceptible grooves.

For a moment, fleetingly, I could have sworn it carried a silent message . . . .

Notes

Chapter 2. Consciousness: Truth or Wisdom?

1. E. Richard Sorenson, "Preconquest Consciousness" in *Tribal Epistemologies,* ed. Helmut Wautischer (Aldershot, UK: Ashgate, 1998), 79–115.
2. Sorenson, "Preconquest," 97.
3. Sorenson, "Preconquest," 96.
4. Sorenson, "Preconquest," 82–83.
5. Sorenson, "Preconquest," 98.
6. Sorenson, "Preconquest," 99–100.
7. Christian de Quincey, *Radical Nature: Rediscovering the Soul of Matter* (Montpelier, VT: Invisible Cities Press, 2002), 103.
8. de Quincey, *Radical Nature,* 104.
9. See David Abram's excellent book, *The Spell of the Sensuous: Perception and Language in a More than Human World* (New York, NY: Vintage Press, 1997).
10. Abram's *The Spell of the Sensuous.*
11. See de Quincey *Radical Nature* for a detailed account of Whitehead's philosophy. For original sources, see Alfred North Whitehead's *Process and Reality, Science and the Modern World,* and *Adventures of Ideas.*
12. Christian de Quincey, "Past Matter, Present Mind: A Convergence of Worldviews," *Journal of Consciousness Studies* 6 (1): 91–106. (Essex, England: Imprint Academic, 1999).

Chapter 3. Evolution: Up in Arms about Being Put Down

1. Jean Liedloff, *The Continuum Concept: In Search of Happiness Lost* (Boston, MA: Addison Wesley, 1986).
2. I wrote a book on the topic a few years ago, *Aftershocks: Primal Wounding, Creative Healing* (unpublished).
3. Liedloff, *Continuum,* 22 (emphasis in original).
4. Liedloff, *Continuum,* 36.
5. Liedloff, *Continuum,* 43, 104–5.
6. Liedloff, *Continuum,* 109–10 (emphasis in original).

Chapter 4. Paradigms: Intention Creating Reality

1. John Hart Young, a doctoral psychology student at the California Institute for Human Science (http://www.cihs.edu) who had read an earlier draft of this chapter contacted me to report on his research into this myth. Here's what he wrote to me:

THE MYTH OF PARADIGM BLINDNESS

I have reviewed Chapter 10 from Darwin's *Voyage of the Beagle* about Tierra del Fuego, and could not find any words about the purported perceptual anomaly that you cautiously—and rightly—characterize as probably "apocryphal." In fact, quite to the contrary, Darwin mentions the unusual acuity of Fuegian eyesight as compared to the Europeans'.

I wish I could locate a genuine source for this myth, but it just isn't there. I searched though the historical records suggested to me by scholars in the field, and found nothing to corroborate it. At this point, in my opinion, there is *no factual historical evidence* from the colonial or tribal records for this perceptual anomaly having occurred at Tierra del Fuego *or anywhere else.* The amazing thing about this myth is why people have a need to believe and repeat it. I have come to believe that this absurd and subtly ethnocentric piece of social fiction is in fact a racist narrative device on the part of the dominant culture to mystify, justify, rationalize and obfuscate its genocidal roots in the New World. Why is it so appealing?

The most dismaying aspect of this highly contagious social meme is that it is being picked up like an infection by popular culture partly because it is being reinforced by some very smart and influential scientists and thinkers. After receiving the opinions of some leading Native American studies departments, and my own efforts to find the facts, I contacted Dr. Candace Pert, who is featured in *What the Bleep Do We Know?*, and executives of the movie, and asked them for the source of what I consider to be an outrageous claim, but they refused to answer my questions.

I have heard that this social myth originates from a letter written by a priest who sailed with Magellan. Apocryphal or not, this sort of not-being-able-to-see illustrates the intriguing idea that groups of people may be subject to a sort of *mass hysterical "paradigm blindness."* Certainly other events in modern history demonstrate similar "blindness." Denials of the holocaust or global warming are two examples that come to mind. Governments, religions, economic cartels and their media all seem to successfully hypnotize the general public into paradigm compliance by their skilful and pervasive use of agenda setting and social derision toward valid ideas and information that seriously challenge prevailing opinion.

Psychologically, the phenomenon might be called a *cultural conversion disorder* or *societal somataform condition* arising from the invasion of inherently foreign or threatening material that has no logical correlate within the mental and emotional constructs that define the collective perception of the universe. Hypothetically, this intruding information attacks the ruling paradigm with such symbolic and literal force that denial overwhelms the population rendering them blind to the offending stimulus. *Cognitive dissonance* (Festinger) becomes so intense that it produces a *consensus trance* (Tart) supporting that blindness. Part of me wishes that these memes about perceptual anomalies were true so that there would be an explanation or at least a mitigating factor for why the world participates so avidly in its own destruction by ignoring the essential sentience of matter.

I should add the caveat that I am not a historian and have not made a completely exhaustive search of all possible colonial and tribal sources to determine absolutely that the claim of an indigenous people's perceptual anomaly is fallacious. But based on my limited research and the opinions of consulting historical scholars I have come to that opinion.

2. Joseph Chilton Pearce, *The Biology of Transcendence: A Blueprint of the Human Spirit* (Rochester, VT: Park Street Press, 2002).

3. Christian de Quincey, *Radical Nature: Rediscovering the Soul of Matter* (Montpelier, VT: Invisible Cities Press, 2002).

4. Max Ehrmann, *Desiderata* (New York, NY: Brook House, 1972, originally written in 1927).

Chapter 5. Transformation: Experience Beyond Belief

1. This topic will be developed further in *Radical Science: Exploring the Frontiers of Consciousness,* volume three of my "Radical Consciousness" trilogy.

Chapter 6. Meanings: Clarifying Consciousness

1. Nicholas Humphrey, *A History of the Mind: Evolution and the Birth of Consciousness* (1992), 37.

I am indebted to Nick Humphrey for the metaphor of the "slippery fish" of consciousness. In this excellent, beautifully written, book he says: "There are several ways to catch a fish (if not a monster). You can drag a net across the river, and pull in everything there is: but this way you get the weeds, the frogs, and old boots too. You can put a worm on a hook, and cast it into a likely looking pool; but this way you risk choosing the wrong pool or a day when the fish are just not feeding. Or (so an old Scotsman told me) you can tickle it: you walk stealthily along the riverbank until you see your fish hanging in the water just upstream; you lean down from the bank and lower your fingers ever so slowly under the fish's belly; you stroke it; and then (so he said) the fish just lets you lift it out.

"I believe the way to catch consciousness will be to tickle it. That is to say we should discover where it is lying, approach it slowly, and then charm it into our hands." See also *Radical Nature*, 311.

2. Güven Güzeldere, "Consciousness: What It Is & How to Study It." *Journal of Consciousness Studies* 2 (1) (1995), 30.

3. Thomas Natsoulas, "Basic Problems of Consciousness" *Journal of Personality and Social Psychology* 41 (1981), 132–78; and "Concepts of Consciousness" *Journal of Mind and Behavior* 4 (1983), 13–59.

4. David Ray Griffin, "Introduction: The Reenchantment of Science" in *The Reenchantment of Science: Postmodern Proposals,* ed. D. R. Griffin (1988). See also de Quincey, *Radical Nature.*

5. David Levin and George Solomon, "The Discursive Formation of the Body in the History of Medicine," *The Journal of Medicine and Philosophy* 15 (1990), 515–37.

Chapter 7. Synchronicity-1: Beyond Energy

1. Carl Gustav Jung. *Synchronicity: An Acausal Connecting Principle* (1973), 25.

2. See, for example, Willis Harman, *A Re-examination of the Metaphysical Foundations of Modern Science* (1991); Charles Laughlin, *Scientific*

Explanation and the Lifeworld: A Biogenetic Structural Theory of Meaning and Causation (1992); Alastair Taylor and Angus Taylor, *Science and Causality: A Historical Perspective* (1993); and Willis Harman and Christian de Quincey, *The Scientific Exploration of Consciousness: Toward an Adequate Epistemology* (1994).

Chapter 8. Synchronicity-2: Reality without a Cause

1. Richard Tarnas, *The Passion of the Western Mind: Understanding the Ideas That Have Shaped Our World View* (1991).
2. de Quincey, *Radical Nature*, 215–238.
3. Arthur Koestler wrote about holons in a number of books, including *Janus: A Summing Up* (1979); *The Ghost in the Machine* (1967); and with J. R. Smythies, *Beyond Reductionism* (1969).

Chapter 9. Knowing-1: Shafts of Wisdom

1. Alfred North Whitehead, "Mathematics and the Good" in *The Philosophy of Alfred North Whitehead.* (ed. P. A. Schilpp), (1941), 270.
2. R. G. H. Siu's *Tao of Science* (1957) and Ken Wilber's *Eye to Eye* (1983) are two of the best and most accessible comparative critiques of science and mysticism.

Chapter 10. Knowing-2: Radical Science

1. Willis Harman and Christian de Quincey, *The Scientific Exploration of Consciousness: Toward an Adequate Epistemology* (1994).

Chapter 11. Knowing-3: Beyond Intuition

1. R. G. H. Siu (1957) *Tao of Science*, 79.

Chapter 12. Grounding: Embodied Meaning

1. David Levin and George Solomon, "The Discursive Formation of the Body in the History of Medicine," *The Journal of Medicine and Philosophy* 15 (1990), 515–37.
2. Levin and Solomon, "Discursive Formation."
3. de Quincey, *Radical Nature*, 263.

Chapter 13. Dialogue: Consciousness and Cosmology

1. See de Quincey, *Radical Nature*, for a detailed discussion of the need to include the "storyteller" in our cosmologies 19–21, 40–42.
2. Renée Weber, "Reflections on David Bohm's Holomovement: A Physicist's Model of Cosmos and Consciousness," in *The Metaphors of Consciousness*, ed. Ron Valle and Rolf von Eckartsberg (1981). I am indebted to Weber for many of the insights in this "thumbnail" sketch of David Bohm's lifework.

Chapter 14. Participation: Engaging Presence

1. For a scholarly non-Western view, see Ha'iri Yazdi, *The Principles of Epistemology in Islamic Philosophy: Knowledge by Presence* (1992).
2. Piet Hut and Roger Shepard. "Turning the Hard Problem Upside Down and Sideways" *Journal of Consciousness Studies* 3(4), 1996, 313–29.
3. I thank my friend and colleague Peter Russell for this observation, for our many

dialogues on consciousness, and for his generous feedback on an earlier draft of this chapter.

Chapter 15. Intersubjectivity-1: We Are the World

1. See Whitehead's *Process and Reality* (1979) and Joanna Macy's *Mutual Causality in Buddhism and General Systems Theory: The Dharma of Natural Systems* (1991).

Chapter 16. Intersubjectivity-2: Steps Along the Way

1. Scholars in the third-person, materialist-objectivist or positivist tradition, who view the mind as a product of brain events, include linguist Noam Chomsky (1971), philosophers Daniel Dennett (1991), John Searle (1992 and 2004), Paul Churchland (1993), Patricia Churchland (1989), and, perhaps the most influential philosopher of the twentieth century, Ludwig Wittgenstein (1958).

2. Continental European scholars in the first-person, introspective or contemplative tradition, who view mind as a topic for private, subjective inquiry, include Edmund Husserl (1931), Maurice Merleau-Ponty (1995), and Martin Heidegger (1978). And, of course, scholars and practitioners from the world's meditative traditions, such as Buddhism, emphasize the necessity for first-person exploration of consciousness. Insight into the nature and dynamics of the mind, they teach, requires practices leading to direct experience beyond all knowledge of brain events, and even beyond conceptual thought.

3. See George Steiner's *Heidegger* (1978), 53.

4. See Hameroff, Kaszniak, and Scott (1996) and de Quincey (1997).

5. See Husserl (1931), Mensch (1988), Sartre (1960 and 1969), and Binswanger (1963). On Sartre's view of consciousness as a prereflective experience of *presence*, see Aboulafia (1986), 37.

6. See Binswanger's *Dream and Existence* (1986), 100.

7. Binswanger quoted in Roger Frie's *Subjectivity and Intersubjectivity in Modern Philosophy and Psychoanalysis* (1997).

8. See Baxter and Montgomery, *Relating: Dialogues & Dialectics* (1996), 25.

9. See Edmund Arens, *The Logic of Pragmatic Thinking* (1994).

10. Joseph Prabhu, professor of philosophy and religion at California State University drew my attention to the "dialogue philosophers," particularly Rozenzweig and Rosenstock-Huessy, and to the relevance of Dewey's and Taylor's discussions of the social context for self. See also George Herbert Mead (1967); Carl Rogers (1951); R. D. Laing (1981); Stolorow and Atwood, (1992); Stolorow, Atwood, and Brandchaft (1994); Jürgen Habermas (1984 and 1992); Mikhail Bakhtin (1981); Valentin N. Voloshinov (1996); Holquist (1990); Leslie Baxter and Barbara Montgomery (1996); Arens (1994); Francis Jacques (1991); Emile Benveniste (1973); Emmanuel Levinas (1969 and 1981); Max Velmans (1992 and 1993); Ken Wilber (1995); Stephane Mosès (1992); John Dewey (1949); and Charles Taylor (1989).

11. For an excellent discussion of the philosophical challenges posed by subjectivity, see Thomas Nagel's landmark paper "What Is It Like to Be a Bat?" in *Mortal Questions* (1992), and *The View from Nowhere* (1989).

12. John Locke, *An Essay concerning Human Understanding* (1948, originally published 1690).

13. See William Mark Hohengarten's introductory commentary in Jürgen Habermas, *Postmetaphysical Thinking* (1992).

14. See Robert Forman's *The Problem of Pure Consciousness: Mysticism and Philosophy* (1990).

15. See Jacob Needleman and Christian de Quincey, "Questions of the Heart: Inner Empiricism as a Way to a Science of Consciousness," in *Noetic Sciences Review* 26 (1993), 4–9.

16. Johann Gottlieb Fichte, *The Science of Ethics*, trans. A. E. Kroeger (1907).

17. See Dewey (1949), and Heidegger (1978).

18. See Søren Kierkegaard, *Either/Or* (1987), and Habermas, *Postmetaphysical Thinking*.

19. Kierkegaard, *Either/Or*.

20. See Habermas, *Postmetaphysical Thinking*, 163.

21. George Herbert Mead, *Mind, Self & Society: From the Standpoint of a Social Behaviorist* (1967).

22. Voloshinov, *Marxism and the Philosophy of Language* (1996).

23. Mead, *Mind, Self & Society*, 140.

24. Hohengarten, *Postmetaphysical Thinking*, (xvi).

25. Mead, *Mind, Self & Society*, 175.

26. Hohengarten, *Postmetaphysical Thinking*, xvi–xvii.

27. Quoted by Gabriel Marcel, "I and Thou" in *The Philosophy of Martin Buber*, eds. P. A. Schilpp and M. Friedman (1967), 42.

28. Martin Buber, *I and Thou* (1970), *The Knowledge of Man* (1965), and *Between Man and Man* (1961).

29. Buber, *I and Thou*, 89.

30. Gabriel Marcel, "I and Thou," in *The Philosophy of Martin Buber*, eds. P. A. Schilpp and M. Friedman (1967).

31. Charles Hartshorne, *Beyond Humanism: Essays in the Philosophy of Nature* (1968).

32. William James, *Essays in Radical Empiricism* (1912) and "Radical Empiricism," in *The Writings of William James: A Comprehensive Edition*, ed. John McDermott (1977).

33. Philip Wheelwright, "Buber's Philosophical Anthropology," in *The Philosophy of Martin Buber*, eds. P. A. Schilpp and M. Friedman (1967), 75.

34. Francis Jacques, *Difference and Subjectivity: Dialogue and Personal Identity*, trans. Andrew Rothwell (1991), xii.

35. Jacques, *Difference and Subjectivity*, xv.

36. Jacques, *Difference and Subjectivity*, xv.

37. Jürgen Habermas, *Postmetaphysical Thinking* (1992), 186.

38. Jacques Derrida, *Of Grammatology* (1967); Michel Foucault, *The Order of Things: An Archaeology of the Human Sciences* (1970).

39. Habermas, *Postmetaphysical Thinking*, 170.

40. Ken Wilber, *Integral Psychology: Consciousness, Spirit, Psychology, Therapy* (2000), 119.

Chapter 17. Origins: Evolution of Consciousness

1. See Thomas Natsoulas, "Concepts of Consciousness" *Journal of Mind and Behavior* 4 (1983), 13–59; and H. T. Hunt, *On the Nature of Consciousness* (1995).

2. Hunt, *Nature of Consciousness*.

3. Güven Güzeldere, "Consciousness: What It Is & How to Study It," *Journal of Consciousness Studies* 2(1) (1995), 30–51.
4. See, for example, Ken Wilber, *Sex, Ecology, Spirituality* (1995).
5. See Richard Tarnas, *The Passion of the Western Mind* (1991); and R. B. Onians, *The Origins of European Thought about the Body, the Mind, the Soul, the World, Time, and Fate* (1994).
6. Julian Jaynes, *The Origins of Consciousness in the Breakdown of the Bicameral Mind* (1976); John Hurrell Crook, *The Evolution of Human Consciousness* (1980); and de Quincey, "Transformation of Western Consciousness" (unpublished manuscript).
7. David Albert, *Quantum Mechanics and Experience* (1992).
8. Dean Radin, *The Conscious Universe: The Scientific Truth of Psychic Phenomena* (1997).
9. David Korten, *When Corporations Ruled the World* (1995).
10. Theodore Roszak, *The Voice of the Earth* (1992).
11. Duane Elgin, *The Awakening Earth* (1993); Peter Russell, *The Global Brain Awakens* (1995).
12. Joanna Macy, *Mutual Causality in Buddhism and General Systems Theory* (1991).
13. Thomas Nagel, "What Is It Like to Be a Bat?," in *Mortal Questions* (1992).

Chapter 18. Radical Knowing: The Four Gifts

1. Jeremy Narby, *The Cosmic Serpent: DNA and the Origins of Knowledge* (1998).
2. Arthur M. Young, *The Reflexive Universe: Evolution of Consciousness* (1999).
3. Narby, *The Cosmic Serpent*.
4. Young, *The Reflexive Universe*.
5. Narby, *The Cosmic Serpent*, 88.
6. Narby, *The Cosmic Serpent*, 117.
7. Narby, *The Cosmic Serpent*, 124.
8. Arthur Waley, trans., *Tao Te Ching*, (1958), chapter 48.
9. Matthew Purdon, private communication, 2004.

Epilogue: Cosmos and Communion

1. Christopher Bache, *Dark Night, Early Dawn: Steps to a Deep Ecology of Mind* (2000), 5–6.
2. Linda Weilgart, "When Sound Is Dangerous," *The Christian Science Monitor,* Saturday, March 31, 2001. Linda Weilgart, Ph.D., is a research associate at Dalhousie University, in Halifax, Nova Scotia. She is a leading expert in sperm whale acoustic communication. Reprinted with permission from *The Christian Science Publishing Society.*
3. Charles Tart, *Transpersonal Psychologies: Perspectives on the Mind from Seven Great Spiritual Traditions* (1992).

Appendix 1. What Jung Meant by "Synchronicity"

1. Carl Gustav Jung, *Synchronicity: An Acausal Connecting Principle* (1973).
2. Jung, *Synchronicity*, 25.
3. Ibid.
4. Jung, *Synchronicity*, 28–29.
5. Jung, *Synchronicity*, 29.
6. Jung, *Synchronicity*, 30.

7. Ibid.
8. Jung, *Synchronicity,* 31.
9. Ibid.
10. Jung, *Synchronicity,* 69.
11. Jung, *Synchronicity,* footnote, 85–86.
12. Jung, *Synchronicity,* 89.
13. Jung, *Synchronicity,* 89-90.
14. Jung, *Synchronicity,* 95.
15. Jung, *Synchronicity,* 98.
16. Jung, *Synchronicity,* 100.
17. Ibid.
18. Jung, *Synchronicity,* 102.
19. Jung, *Synchronicity,* 110.
20. Jung, *Synchronicity,* 115.
21. Ibid.
22. Ibid.

Appendix 2. Subjectivity and Intersubjectivity

1. See Max Velman's *Understanding Consciousness* (2000).
2. Glenna Gerard and Linda Teurfs, *The Art and Practice of Dialogue* (12-tape audio course) (The Dialogue Group, 1994).
3. David Bohm, *On Dialogue* (1996), 24.
4. Ha'iri Yazdi, *The Principles of Epistemology in Islamic Philosophy: Knowledge by Presence* (1992).

Appendix 3. Wilber and de Quincey: I-to-I

1. Wilber, *Integral Psychology, Consciousness, Spirit, Psychology, Therapy* (2000), 161.
2. Wilber, *The Eye of Spirit: An Integral Vision for a World Gone Slightly Mad* (2001), 14.
3. Wilber, *Integral Psychology,* 172–173.
4. See, for example, Wilber, *Integral Psychology,* 73; 77; 114; 119; 122; 145; 161; 183; 186; 192; 254; 255; 278; 283; 284; 286; 288.
5. Ken Wilber, *One Taste: The Journals of Ken Wilber. Collected Works,* vol. 8 (2000).
6. Wilber published his response "Do Critics Misrepresent My Position?" on his section of his publisher's website: www.wilber.shambhala.com.
7. Wilber, *Integral Psychology,* 161.
8. Wilber, *The Eye of Spirit,* 14.
9. Wilber, *Sex, Ecology, Spirituality,* 134.
10. Ibid.
11. Wilber, "Do Critics Misrepresent My Position?"
12. Ibid.
13. Ibid.
14. Ibid.
15. Ibid.

Appendix 4. Integrating Worldviews

1. See de Quincey, *Radical Nature,* chap. 9 (2002).

Bibliography

Aboulafia, Mitchell. *The Mediating Self: Mead, Sartre, and Self-Determination.* New Haven, CT: Yale University Press, 1986.

Abram, David. *The Spell of the Sensuous: Perception and Language in a More Than Human World.* New York, NY: Vintage Press, 1997.

Albert, David, Z. *Quantum Mechanics and Experience.* Cambridge, MA: Harvard University Press, 1992.

Arens, Edmund. *The Logic of Pragmatic Thinking: From Peirce to Habermas.* Translated by David Smith. Amherst, NY: Prometheus Books, 1994.

Bache, Christopher. *Dark Night, Early Dawn: Steps to a Deep Ecology of Mind.* New York, NY: State University of New York Press, 2000.

Bakhtin, Mikhail. *The Dialogic Imagination: Four Essays by M. M. Bakhtin.* Translated by M. Holquist. Austin, TX: University of Texas Press, 1981.

Baxter, Leslie A., and Barbara M. Montgomery. *Relating: Dialogues & Dialectics.* New York, NY: The Guildford Press, 1996.

Benveniste, Emile. *Problems in General Linguistics.* Miami, FL: University of Miami Press, 1973.

Binswanger, Ludwig. *Being-in-the-World: Selected Papers of Ludwig Binswanger.* Translated with introduction by Jacob Needleman. New York: Harper & Row, 1963.

———. *Dream and Existence: Michel Foucault & Ludwig Binswanger.* Edited by Keith Hoeller. Seattle, WA: *Review of Existential Psychology & Psychiatry,* 1986 (originally published in Binswanger, 1963).

Bohm, David. *On Dialogue.* Edited by Lee Nichol. London, UK: Routledge, 1996.

———. *Unfolding Meaning: A Weekend of Dialogue.* London, UK: Routledge, 1985.

Bowie, Andrew. *Schelling and Modern European Philosophy: An Introduction.* London, UK: Routledge, 1993.

Buber, Martin. *I and Thou.* Translated by Walter Kaufmann. New York, NY: Charles Scribner's Sons, 1970.

———. *The Knowledge of Man: Selected Essays.* Edited by Maurice Friedman. New York, NY: Harper & Row, 1965.

———. *The Philosophy of Martin Buber.* Edited by P. A. Schilpp & M. Friedman. La Salle, IL: Open Court, 1967.

———. *Between Man and Man.* Translated by R. G. Smith. London, UK: Collins/Fontana, 1961.

Chomsky, Noam. *Language and Mind: Problems of Knowledge and Freedom.* New York, NY: Pantheon Books, 1971.

Churchland, Patricia. *Neurophilosophy: Toward a Unified Science of the Mind-Brain.* Cambridge, MA: Bradford Books, 1989.

Churchland, Paul. *Matter and Consciousness*. Cambridge, MA: MIT Press, 1993.

Crook, John Hurrell. *The Evolution of Human Consciousness*. Oxford, UK: Clarendon Press, 1980.

de Quincey, Christian. *Radical Nature: Rediscovering the Soul of Matter*. Montpelier, VT: Invisible Cities Press, 2002.

———. "The Promise of Integralism: A Critical Appreciation of Ken Wilber's Integral Psychology," *Journal of Consciousness Studies* 7 (11/12). Essex UK: Imprint Academic, 2000.

———. "Past Matter, Present Mind: A Convergence of Worldviews," *Journal of Consciousness Studies*, 6 (1): 91–106. Essex, UK: Imprint Academic, 1999.

———. "Consciousness: The Final Frontier?" *IONS Review* 42. Sausalito, CA: Institute of Noetic Sciences, 1997.

Dennett, Daniel. *Consciousness Explained*. Boston, MA: Little, Brown & Co., 1991.

Derrida, Jacques. *Of Grammatology*. Translated by G. C. Spivak. Baltimore, MD: John Hopkins University Press, 1967.

Dewey, John. *Experience and Nature*. New York, NY: Macmillan, 1949.

Ehrmann, Max. *Desiderata*. Brook House, New York, NY, 1972.

Eisenstadt, S. N. (ed.). *On Intersubjectivity and Cultural Creativity*. Chicago, IL: The University of Chicago Press, 1992.

Elgin, Duane. *The Awakening Earth: Exploring the Evolution of Human Culture and Consciousness*. New York, NY: William Morrow, 1993.

Fichte, Johann Gottlieb. *The Science of Ethics*. Translated by A. E. Kroeger. London, UK: Kegan Paul, Tranch, Trübner & Co., 1907.

Forman, Robert (ed.). *The Problem of Pure Consciousness: Mysticism and Philosophy*. New York, NY: Oxford University Press, 1990.

Foucault, Michel. *The Order of Things: An Archaeology of the Human Sciences*. Translated by Alan Sheridan. New York, NY: Pantheon, 1970.

Frie, Roger. *Subjectivity and Intersubjectivity in Modern Philosophy and Psychoanalysis: A Study of Sartre, Binswanger, Lacan, and Habermas*. Lanham, MD: Rowman & Littlefield, 1997.

Gerard, Glenna, and Linda Teurfs. *The Art and Practice of Dialogue*. (12-tape audio course.) Laguna Hills, CA: The Dialogue Group, 1994.

Griffin, David Ray. "Introduction: The Reenchantment of Science." In *The Reenchantment of Science: Postmodern Proposals*. Edited by D. R. Griffin Albany, NY: State University of New York Press, 1988.

Grof, Stanislav. *Beyond the Brain: Birth, Death and Transcendence in Psychotherapy*. Albany, NY: State University of New York Press, 1985.

Güzeldere, Güven. "Consciousness: What It Is & How to Study It." *Journal of Consciousness Studies* 2(1). Essex, UK: Imprint Academic, 1995.

Habermas, Jürgen. *The Theory of Communicative Action*. Vol. 1. London, UK: Heinemann; Vol. 2. Cambridge, MA: Polity, 1984/87.

———. *Postmetaphysical Thinking*. Cambridge, MA: MIT Press, 1992.

Ha'iri Yazdi, M. *The Principles of Epistemology in Islamic Philosophy: Knowledge by Presence*. Albany, NY: State University of New York Press, 1992.

Halliday, Eugene. *Reflexive Self-Consciousness*. Volume 2 in *The Collected Works of Eugene Halliday*. Edited by D. Mahlowe. Parklands, Cheshire, UK: The Melchisedec Press, 1989.

———. *Contributions from a Potential Corpse*. Volume 4 in *The Collected Works of Eugene Halliday*. Edited by D. Mahlowe. Parklands, Cheshire, UK: The Melchisedec Press, 1990.

Hameroff, S. Kaszniak, A. and A. Scott. *Toward a Science of Consciousness: The First Tucson Discussions and Debates.* Cambridge, MA: MIT Press, 1996.

Harman, Willis, and Christian de Quincey. *The Scientific Exploration of Consciousness: Toward an Adequate Epistemology.* Sausalito, CA: Institute of Noetic Sciences, 1994.

Hartshorne, Charles. *Beyond Humanism: Essays in the Philosophy of Nature.* Lincoln, NE: University of Nebraska Press, 1968.

Heidegger, Martin. *Introduction to Metaphysics.* New Haven, CT: Yale University Press, 2000.

———. *Being and Time.* Translated by John Macquarrie and Edward Robinson. Oxford, UK: Basil Blackwell, 1978.

Holquist, Michael. *Dialogism: Bakhtin and His World.* New York, NY: Routledge, 1990.

Humphrey, Nicholas. *A History of the Mind: Evolution and the Birth of Consciousness.* New York, NY: Simon & Schuster, 1992.

Hunt, H. T. *On the Nature of Consciousness: Cognitive, Phenomenological, and Transpersonal Perspectives.* New Haven, CT: Yale University Press, 1995.

Husserl, Edmund. *Ideas: Toward a Pure Phenomenology.* Translated by W. R. B. Gibson. New York, NY: Macmillan, 1931.

Hut, Piet, and Roger Shepard. "Turning the Hard Problem Upside Down and Sideways." *Journal of Consciousness Studies* 3 (4) Essex, UK: Imprint Academic, 1996.

Jackson, Michael. *Minima Ethnographica: Intersubjectivity and the Anthropological Project.* Chicago, IL: Chicago University Press, 1998.

Jacques, Francis. *Difference and Subjectivity: Dialogue and Personal Identity.* Translated by Andrew Rothwell. New Haven, CT: Yale University Press, 1991.

James, William. "Radical Empiricism." In *The Writings of William James: A Comprehensive Edition.* Edited by John McDermott. Chicago, IL: University of Chicago Press, 1977.

———. *Essays in Radical Empiricism.* London, UK: Longmans, Green & Co., 1912.

———. *A Pluralistic Universe.* London, UK: Longmans, Green, & Co., 1909.

Jaynes, Julian. *The Origins of Consciousness in the Breakdown of the Bicameral Mind.* Boston, MA: Houghton Mifflin, 1976.

Joas, Hans. *G. H. Mead: A Contemporary Re-examination of his Thought.* Translated by Raymond Meyer. Cambridge, MA: MIT Press, 1985.

Jung, Carl Gustav. *Synchronicity: An Acausal Connecting Principle.* Princeton, NJ: Princeton University Press, 1973.

Kant, Immanuel. *Critique of Pure Reason.* Translated by N. K. Smith. New York, NY: St. Martin's Press, 1977 (original work published 1781).

Kierkegaard, Søren. *Either/Or.* Translated by Hong & Hong. 2 vols. Princeton, NJ: Princeton University Press, 1987.

Koestler, Arthur. *Janus: A Summing Up.* New York, NY: Vintage, 1979.

———. *Beyond Reductionism: New Perspectives in the Life Sciences. The Alpabach Symposium 1968.* London, UK: Hutchinson, 1969.

———. *The Ghost in the Machine.* London, UK: Hutchinson, 1967.

Korten, David. *When Corporations Ruled the World.* San Francisco, CA: Berrett-Koehler, 1995.

Laing, R. D. *Self and Other.* London, UK: Penguin, 1981.

Levin, David, and George Solomon. "The Discursive Formation of the Body in the History of Medicine." *The Journal of Medicine and Philosophy.* 15. Philadelphia, PA: Taylor & Francis, 1990.

Levinas, E. *Totality and Infinity*. Translated by A. Lingis. Pittsburgh, PA: Duquesne, 1969.

———. *Otherwise Than Being or Beyond Essence*. Translated by A. Lingis. The Hague, NL: Nijhoff, 1981.

Liedloff, Jean. *The Continuum Concept: In Search of Happiness Lost*. Boston, MA: Addison Wesley, 1986.

Locke, John. *An Essay Concerning Human Understanding*. London, UK: J. M. Dent & Sons, 1948 (originally published 1690).

Macy, Joanna. *Mutual Causality in Buddhism and General Systems Theory: The Dharma of Natural Systems*. Albany, NY: State University of New York Press, 1991.

Marcel, Gabriel. "I and Thou." In *The Philosophy of Martin Buber*. Edited by P. A. Schilpp and M. Friedman. La Salle, IL: Open Court, 1967.

Mead, George, Herbert. *Mind, Self, & Society: From the Standpoint of a Social Behaviorist*. Chicago, IL: University of Chicago Press, 1967.

Mensch, J. R. *Intersubjectivity and Transcendental Idealism*. Albany, NY: State University of New York Press, 1988.

Merleau-Ponty, Maurice. *Phenomenology of Perception*. Translated by Colin Smith. London, UK: Routledge, 1995.

Mitchell, Stephen (trans.). *Tao Te Ching*. New York, NY: Perennial, 1992.

Mosès, Stephane. *System and Revelation: The Philosophy of Franz Rosenzweig*. Translated by Catherine Tihanyi. Detroit, MI: Wayne State University Press, 1992.

Nagel, Thomas. "What Is It Like to Be a Bat? *Mortal Questions*. Cambridge, UK: Cambridge University Press, 1992.

———. *The View from Nowhere*. New York, NY: Oxford University Press, 1989.

Narby, Jeremy. *The Cosmic Serpent: DNA and the Origins of Knowledge*. New York, NY: Tarcher/Putnam, 1998.

Natsoulas, Thomas. "Basic Problems of Consciousness." *Journal of Personality and Social Psychology*. 41. Washington, DC: APA Journals.

———. "Concepts of Consciousness." *Journal of Mind and Behavior* 4. New York, NY: The Institute of Mind and Behavior, 1983.

Needleman, Jacob, and Christian de Quincey. "Questions of the Heart: Inner Empiricism as a Way to a Science of Consciousness." In *Noetic Sciences Review*, (Summer, 26) 1993, 4–9.

Neuhouser, Frederick. *Fichte's Theory of Subjectivity*. Cambridge, MA: Cambridge University Press, 1990.

Onians, R. B. *The Origins of European Thought about the Body, the Mind, the Soul, the World, Time, and Fate*. Cambridge, UK: Cambridge University Press, 1994.

Pearce, Joseph Chilton. *The Biology of Transcendence: A Blueprint of the Human Spirit*. Rochester, VT: Park Street Press, 2002.

Radin, Dean. *The Conscious Universe: The Scientific Truth of Psychic Phenomena*. San Francisco, CA: HarperSanFrancisco, 1997.

Rogers, Carl. *Client-Centered Therapy*. Boston, MA: Houghton Mifflin, 1951.

Roszak, Theodore. *The Voice of the Earth*. New York, NY: Simon & Schuster, 1992.

Russell, Peter. *From Science to God: A Physicist's Journey into the Mystery of Consciousness*. San Rafael, CA: New World Library, 2003.

———. *The Global Brain Awakens: Our Next Evolutionary Leap*. Palo Alto, CA: Global Brain Inc., 1995.

Sartre, Jean-Paul. *Being and Nothingness*. Translated by H. E. Barnes. London, UK: Methuen, 1969.

————. *The Transcendence of the Ego: An Existentialist Theory of Consciousness.* New York, NY: Hill & Wang, 1960.

Schilpp, Paul A. (ed.). *The Philosophy of Alfred North Whitehead.* Evanston, IL: Northwestern University Press, 1941.

Schilpp, Paul A. and Friedman, M. (eds.). *The Philosophy of Martin Buber.* La Salle, IL: Open Court, 1967.

Searle, John. *Mind: A Brief Introduction.* New York, NY: Oxford University Press, 2004.

————. *The Rediscovery of the Mind.* Cambridge, MA: MIT Press, 1992.

Siu, R. G. H. *The Tao of Science: An Essay on Western Knowledge and Eastern Wisdom.* Cambridge, MA: MIT Press, 1957.

Sorenson, E. Richard. "Preconquest Consciousness." In *Tribal Epistemologies,* edited by Helmut Wautischer, Aldershot, UK: Ashgate, 1998. 79–115.

Steiner, George. *Heidegger.* London, UK: Fontana, 1978.

Stolorow, R. D., and G. E. Atwood. *Contexts of Being: The Intersubjective Foundations of Psychological Life.* Hillsdale, NJ: The Analytic Press, Psychoanalytic Inquiry Book Series, 1992.

Stolorow, R. D., G. E. Atwood, and B. Brandchaft, B. (eds.). *The Intersubjective Perspective.* Northvale, NJ: Jason Aranson, 1994.

Strasser, Stephen. *Phenomenology of Feeling: An Essay on the Phenomena of the Heart.* Pittsburgh, PA: Duquesne University Press, 1997.

Tarnas, Richard. *The Passion of the Western Mind: Understanding the Ideas That Have Shaped Our World View.* New York, NY: Harmony Books, 1991.

Tart, Charles. *Transpersonal Psychologies: Perspectives on the Mind from Seven Great Spiritual Traditions.* New York, NY: HarperCollins, 1992.

Taylor, Charles. *Sources of the Self: The Making of the Modern Identity.* Cambridge, MA: Harvard University Press, 1989.

Theunissen, Michael. *The Other: Studies in the Social Ontology of Husserl, Heidegger, Sartre, and Buber.* Translated by Christopher Macann. Cambridge, MA: MIT Press, 1984.

Valle, Ron, and Rolf von Eckartsberg (eds.). *The Metaphors of Consciousness.* New York, NY: Plenum Press, 1981.

Velmans, Max. *Understanding Consciousness.* London, UK: Routledge, 2000.

————. "A Reflexive Science of Consciousness." In *Experimental and Theoretical Studies of Consciousness.* New York, NY: John Wiley & Sons, 1993.

Voloshinov, Valentin, N. *Marxism and the Philosophy of Language.* Translated by Ladislav Matejka and I. R. Titunik. Cambridge, MA: Harvard University Press, 1996.

Waley, Arthur. *The Way and its Power: Lao Tzu's Tao Te Ching and its Place in Chinese Thought.* New York, NY: Grove Press, 1958.

Weber, Renée. "Reflections on David Bohm's Holomovement: A Physicist's Model of Cosmos and Consciousness." In Ron Valle and Rolf von Eckartsberg, eds. *The Metaphors of Consciousness.* New York, NY: Plenum Press, 1981.

Weiss, Paul. *You, I and the Others.* Carbondale, IL: Southern Illinois University Press, 1980.

Wheelwright, Philip. "Buber's Philosophical Anthropology." In *The Philosophy of Martin Buber,* edited by P. A. Schilpp and M. Friedman. La Salle, IL: Open Court, 1967.

Whitehead, Alfred North. *Adventures of Ideas.* New York, NY: Macmillan, 1933.

————. *Process and Reality: An Essay in Cosmology.* (Corrected edition). Edited by D. R. Griffin and D. W. Sherburne. New York, NY: The Free Press, 1979 (original work published 1929).

————. *Science and the Modern World.* Glasgow, UK: Fontana, 1975 (original work published 1925).

————. *Science and the Modern World.* New York, NY: Free Press, 1967 (original work published 1925).

Wilber, Ken. *Integral Psychology: Consciousness, Spirit, Psychology, Therapy.* Boston, MA: Shambhala, 2000.

————. *A Theory of Everything: An Integral Vision for Business, Politics, Science, and Spirituality.* Boston, MA: Shambhala, 2000.

————. *One Taste: The Journals of Ken Wilber. Collected Works.* Vol. 8, Boston, MA: Shambhala, 2000.

————. *Collected Works.* 8 vols. Boston, MA: Shambhala, 1999–2000.

————. *The Eye of Spirit: An Integral Vision for a World Gone Slightly Mad.* Boston, MA: Shambhala, 1997.

————. *A Brief History of Everything. Collected Works.* Vol. 7, Boston, MA: Shambhala, 1996.

————. *Sex, Ecology, Spirituality: The Spirit of Evolution.* Boston, MA: Shambhala, 1995.

————. *Eye to Eye: The Quest for the New Paradigm.* Boston, MA: Shambhala, 1983.

Wittgenstein, Ludwig. *Tractatus Logico Philosophicus.* London, UK: Routledge, 2001.

————. *Philosophical Investigations.* Translated by G. E. M. Anscombe. London, UK: Basil Blackwell, 1958.

Young, Arthur M. *The Reflexive Universe: Evolution of Consciousness.* Cambria, CA: Anodos, 1999.

Index